THE QUEST FOR EXCELLENCE

STERLING W. SILL

THE QUEST FOR
EXCELLENCE

by

STERLING W. SILL

BOOKCRAFT
Salt Lake City, Utah

FIRST PRINTING, 1967

LITHOGRAPHED BY
PUBLISHERS PRESS

SALT LAKE CITY, UTAH
UNITED STATES OF AMERICA

Foreword

AMONG THE UNUSUAL FEATURES OF THE SOCIETY OF OUR DAY ARE its contrasts and paradoxes. We look down from great heights of scientific accomplishment, and hear people speculating about whether or not we are losing that idealism and hardiness of spirit that made our nation and its people great. In the most enlightened age of the world we are mounting our biggest crime waves and setting up our most impressive records of divorce. While church membership is going up, church attendance is going down. Someone has said that we want the front seat in the bus and the back seat in the church. We want the benefits without paying the price. To cap it all off, we are having some unheard of problems with juvenile, adult, and occupational delinquency.

Sometime ago, Charles Brower of New York made an interesting commentary on our day before the National Sales Executive Club. He pointed out that while we are living in the greatest of all the ages so far as wonders, enlightenment, and blessings are concerned, yet we are also experiencing a high tide in mediocrity. He called our day the era of the great "goof off," the age of the "half-done job." He said that from coast to coast our people have been enjoying a stampede away from responsibility. Our land is populated with laundry men who won't iron shirts, and waiters who won't serve, and carpenters who will "come around someday, maybe"; executives whose minds are on the golf courses, and teachers who demand a single salary schedule so that achievement cannot be rewarded nor poor work punished.

We have students who take cinch courses because the hard ones make them think. Many who go to college couldn't care less about higher education, and yet being in school just seems to them to be "the thing to do." Frequently we act wisely only after all other alternatives have been exhausted. The presence of these inconsistencies creates problems which, if honestly faced, would be grounds for genuine concern. We have taken such delight in our new leisure and in doing as we please that we have brought a crisis upon ourselves. There is a necessary sense of importance about life that cannot coexist with the inferiority that many of our lives produce.

Thomas Huxley once said that the most severe shock that the human system can sustain is a sense of uselessness, and we need some kind of civil service act to establish in us an improved system of producing individual merit. We also need a faster-moving sense of urgency in accomplishment, as life itself is very fleeting. In our normal expectancy of three-score years and ten, we have 25,550 days made up of 613,200 hours. Because there isn't time for everything, we must specialize and concentrate if we expect to finish successfully and on time. How can we spare time for shoddy work when there is not enough time for many of the best things?

Some football teams have an interesting success rule that no player ever *walks* onto the football field. It seems to be helpful to the spirit of victory when every player charges onto the playing grounds in full power. And it is the same with life. If we plan an important destination, we should take the most direct route and then go forward with sufficient speed. Life itself is a kind of struggle for survival that requires that we not only get into the battle ourselves, but we must also get enough of the battle into us to bring about a victory.

Goethe once said that every man has only enough strength to complete those assignments of which he is fully convinced of their importance. And our own performance can help us build that conviction and show ourselves that we have the power to accomplish. In the golden age of Greece, Pericles said that before anyone should be appointed to fill a big office, he should have filled a number of little offices well. We need the ability to get our own ships into port, so to speak, in both big and little things.

When the British government was thinking of sending a military expedition to Burma to capture Rangoon, the cabinet summoned the Duke of Wellington and asked him who he thought was the most able general to head such an undertaking. The Duke said, "Send Lord Combermere." In protest, one official said, "But we have always understood that your Grace thought Lord Combermere a fool." The Duke's vigorous response was right to the point as he said, "He is a fool, and a big fool, but he can take Rangoon!" We must be on constant guard against our foolishness, but we also need the ability to take Rangoon.

The other day, I heard a doctor advising a patient to take some medical inoculations that he referred to as "booster shots." The patient had already been immunized against this disease, but because of the subsequent lapse of time, the doctor thought that perhaps the safety margin of the vaccine may be wearing a little too thin and its power may now be too weak to withstand the onslaught that some new attack of that disease might make. Therefore, the doctor gave some additional shots of antitoxin to bolster up the strength of those forces of resistance that were already on the job.

We are familiar with the application of this important idea in many fields. In the area of missiles, we have some boosters that give extra power to the rocket after the force of the original thrust has been spent. Water systems have auxiliary pumps to boost the prevailing pressure in the lines. There are boosters in electricity in radio and in television. There are ways of substantially boosting the horsepower in automobiles. But it seems that the most important booster devices are applied to human beings, where they are used to build up enthusiasms, ambitions, faith, and every other worthwhile thing.

Coach Knute Rockne of Notre Dame was famous for the booster shots he used to give his football players between the halves of a football game. Sometimes when their fighting spirit needed some reinforcements, their courage needed greater strength, or their will-to-win lacked vitalization, he used to give them some booster inoculations in the form of pep talks. A pep talk is a talk filled with pep, and the word pep is an abbreviation of the word pepper. A player with pep is a player with high spirits who is filled with initiative, animated with energy, and supported with power. Through this boosting device of the personality, the coach could inject his own enthusiasm and spirit into the players to help win a victory for the school.

Of course, God is the Creator of this science of stimulating people. It was for this purpose that he promised that he would pour out his spirit upon all flesh. The Lord said to Jeremiah, "I will put my law in their inward parts, and write it in their hearts." (Jer. 31:33.) The third member of the Godhead is that great personage called the Holy Ghost, or the Holy Spirit, whose function is to inspire us and give us direction. There are a great number of ways that the Spirit of the Lord benefits us.

The word enthusiasm itself comes from words meaning "God in us." It refers to a kind of divine fervor. It represents a kind of divine boosting operation that increases the spirit of understanding, the spirit of faith, the spirit of prophecy, and the spirit of Godliness.

Jesus himself motivated many people to live better lives by speaking of such everyday things as the sower planting his wheat, the good Samaritan, and the Prodigal Son, and the pearl of great price. These all represented experiences with which the people were familiar, and they were lifted up by them. God has also given us some divine gifts to help us put our inspirations into activity and win life's victories. Of course, He expects us to add to their strength by using them. In writing to Timothy, the Apostle Paul said, "Neglect not the gift that is in thee." "Wherefore I put thee in remembrance that thou stir up the gift of God, which is in thee by the putting on of my hands." (II Tim. 1:6.) What Paul had in mind was for Timothy to give these divine powers within him a boost by exercising them.

Even in the creation of the earth, God set the pattern for our own stimulation. After each six days of labor the Lord provided one day for worship, rest, and spiritual revitalization. And our faith, our courage, and our works are usually in need of some boosting after a lapse of six days. To solve this important need, places of worship have been provided where our minds and our hearts and our spirits can be lifted up to make us better. We talk a great deal about our right to receive inspiration from God; and what a thrilling thought it is that if we effectively order our lives, we may entitle ourselves to receive guidance and direction from the source of all intelligence and power. But what we don't always understand is our right to also uplift and motivate ourselves and each other.

There is a sacred song that says, "I walked today where Jesus walked," and wouldn't it be a thrilling experience if we could go and stand on that very spot of ground where Jesus stood while we tried to absorb the spirit of his life; or suppose that we could go on into the Garden of Gethsemane and kneel on that place where under the burden of our sins he sweat great drops of blood at every pore. And while that may not be possible for some of us, yet there is something that is possible and that is much more important; that is, that we can think today what Jesus thought. We can memorize his sentences and rerun his ideals and ambitions through our hearts so as to give a boost to our lives.

Getting ourselves properly motivated is all in our own interest, inasmuch as no righteous effort is ever lost, it is always a very profitable operation. Certainly it is a mistake to think of our dedication as a sacrifice. There is exhilaration in intense effort applied toward a meaningful end that gives our lives these greatest values of excellence. We are not all equal in our native gifts, but we can make up for many of our deficiencies by our motivations. The following discussions are each centered in some important principle involving our eternal success, and it is hoped that we may want to think about one of them each week with the expectation of getting their principles into our faith and activities so that they may give us an upward boost toward our eternal success and happiness.

Contents

The Quest for Excellence

A NUMBER OF YEARS AGO, THE CHESAPEAKE AND POTOMAC TELE-
phone Companies ran a series of ads under the general title
"The Quest for Excellence." Because of what appears to be a low-
ering of standards in so many areas of present-day activity, it was
thought that these four ordinary words might also serve as the
heading under which some of the values in our own success might
be analyzed and upgraded. If it is profitable to develop excellence
in a telephone company, it is many times more profitable to develop
it in a life. Regardless of what the field of our endeavor may be,
success always centers its spotlight on high-grade things. And an
increase in the excellence of one's life goes far beyond any increases
that might be brought about in his finances or his telephones. Excellence not only improves and beautifies qualities in people, but it
also motivates the individuals concerned and it helps to bring about
their greatest accomplishment.

The idea of excellence comes very near to being the purpose of
life itself, and for that reason it runs through everything that we do.
Every business and every professional group and every worthwhile
social unit is conducting a constant and never-ending search for
quality. Quality is what we are most attracted to and what we are
most inspired by. It is what we want in an automobile, in a home,
and in a family. It is what we look for in everything that we do,
in everything that we are, and in everything that we ever hope to
become.

Probably no other theme has ever gripped the American imagination so intensely as the discovery of outstanding character qualities or genuine talent in unexpected places. We are thrilled when
someone from the slums becomes a scientific genius. We are delighted to hear of frail youngsters developing great athletic skills or
see poor boys become captains of industry. One history of excellence
tells of a group of humble, unlearned fishermen and tax collectors
who became saints and apostles.

One of the most important things about this quest for excellence
is that everyone is involved, and each may direct his compass
toward the goal of his greatest interest. It is one of the most revered

traditions in America that "anybody can become somebody." Our literature is filled with heroes, and every person has been given a divine gift in the form of a strong inclination to lift himself upward by following an ideal. It is a very profitable undertaking to hold in our minds the images of great thinkers, great doers, and great prophets. As we pay homage to the excellence in Abraham Lincoln's honesty and the devotion of the Apostle Paul, we become the beneficiaries of both. No one can hold a good idea in his mind or cherish a noble ambition in his heart without gaining something from it.

A hundred years ago Horatio Alger stimulated the ambitions of many young Americans with his "rags to riches" success stories. But excellence does not merely go from rags to riches. Its course also runs from "log cabin to President," from "plowboy to prophet," from "darkness to light," from "depression to happiness," and from "bad to good." Excellence encourages self-discovery, awakens ambition, arouses industry, inspires emulation, and improves every other form of accomplishment. Everyone has within himself a vein of greatness, and more often than not it is a touch of excellence that leads to its discovery. It is not unusual even for one who has won outstanding success to say, "I never dreamed that it could happen to me," or he says, "I didn't think I had it in me." But excellence has the power to create success or bring it to the surface. It also teaches us how to command the shaft in drawing out the gold.

While speaking on the campus of Stanford University in 1906, William James said, "The world is only beginning to see that more than about anything else the wealth of nations consists in the number of superior men it harbors." When God created man in his own image and endowed him with a set of his own attributes and potentialities, he desired to fill the earth with superior men. God does not want us to become entangled in those treacherous downdrafts that thrust so many people into a state of mediocrity and depression. Of course, the first step in producing excellence is to believe in it. So frequently people are ashamed to be outstanding. It often seems so much more comfortable to be mediocre. There is constant pressure pushing people downward toward being average. And when one has average goals and average ambitions, excellence becomes very difficult. Satan has invented an unprofitable satisfaction that makes people content in just getting by. This is the process by which so many people are forever prevented from finding life's proper meaning. Too frequently we join some "cult of easiness" or attempt to find happiness in apathy, aimlessness, and the pursuit of lesser things.

As a result we contract that most widespread disease in the world, which is some variety of the inferiority complex.

Sometime ago John W. Gardner wrote a great book under the title of *Excellence*. Its purpose is to help us orient our lives toward living at our best. He points out that while we have always paid the most pious lip service to the idea of excellence, yet we have seriously trifled with it in actual practice. However, there can be no real success and no real happiness without excellence, and there can be no excellence without effort.

Because every worthwhile thing in life is at stake, we should prepare our minds, our muscles, our hearts, our attitudes, and our spirits themselves for the promotion of excellence. The most profound utterance was given to this philosophy by Jesus himself, who said, "Be ye therefore perfect, even as your Father which is in heaven is perfect." Certainly God did not intend that those whom he had created in his own image and endowed with his own potentialities should waste their lives in failure. We must not send back to God a life that has only been half used. Certainly the greatest waste there is in the world is not the devastation that goes with war; it isn't the cost of crime; it isn't the erosion of our soils, nor the depletion of our raw materials, nor the loss of our gold supply—the greatest waste there is in the world is that human beings, you and I, live so far below the level of our possibilities. Compared with what we might be, we are just partly alive.

Excellence is a curiously powerful word. It can overcome all of life's downdrafts. As we absorb the spirit of excellence, we can perform almost any miracle. When we develop a strong, deep feeling about it, the most vigorous work becomes easy and greater amitions and more worthwhile interests follow in their course.

Excellence means different things to different people. To some, it means to become a great scholar or a fine athlete, or to develop a noble character. To some, excellence may symbolize the golden age of Greece, or it may make us more aware of the problems of our own day and help us to weave into our own aspirations those specific activities necessary to create that better world that we ourselves expect to help build.

The greatest power drawing us upward is the pattern of excellence in him who was ordained to be our example. The mission of the Son of God was to redeem us from death and to help us reach that necessary pinnacle so that God's will could be done on earth as it is done in heaven. When this kind of quest is accompanied by the proper amount of searching, aspiring, and longing, it produces an affinity for good that can bring us back to God. For this purpose the Creator has placed within us "an upward reach," "an improvement instinct," "a divine urge for superiority" that should have our constant encouragement.

When enough strength is given to this ambition to do our best, it gives dignity and character to our work, and brings pleasure to our hearts, happiness to our families, and eternal glory to our souls. And whether one may be a janitor, a judge, a surgeon, a technician, or just a plain human being, his life to be complete must have excellence. When anyone does a slovenly, dishonest, or half-hearted job in anything, he lowers the general level, and to that extent he becomes a regrettable burden upon his society.

Of course, excellence not only involves competence. It also implies the highest standards and the greatest devotion. Only when we cherish what Whitehead calls the "habitual vision of greatness" do our lives find their most satisfying fulfillment. And as we make greater demands upon ourselves, we entitle ourselves to look forward to more vitality and greater happiness. Any individual who lives at less than his best cheats himself, and no society that is passive, inert, and preoccupied with its own comforts will long endure.

This idea of quality should never be ignored, either in the most humble activities or in the most exalted places. The biggest problem of our present world is that we do not pay enough attention to excellence. For some reason most people are actually crowding toward the bottom levels of life where only the lower prizes are available. Jesus pointed out, and history has proven, that it is the broad road leading toward death that is the most heavily traveled. So many serious problems arise in all phases of our lives when our ambitions are aimed below our best.

The ten plagues were sent upon the people of Egypt because their lives lacked sufficient quality. But the history of our entire earth from Cain to the present day is largely made up of a long series of plagues, famines, pestilence, earthquakes, wars, and disease that we have attracted to ourselves because we have not lived up to the Lord's required standards. The people who will live upon the earth during the one thousand year millennium will be those who have made the greatest progress in this quest for excellence. Even in heaven, people will be happy and successful according to the measure of their excellence.

In writing to the Corinthians, the Apostle Paul describes the three general degrees of glory in which we will live after the resurrection and final judgment. They are called the "celestial," the "terrestrial," and the "telestial." Paul compares them in brightness to the sun, the moon, and the stars. Then he says, "For one star differeth from another star in glory. So also is the resurrection of the dead." Certainly the Lord intended this comparison to stimulate our ambition, and to help us to provide ourselves with such abilities and motivations as would bring about our highest glory.

Thomas Jefferson once pointed out that at the same time that life is trying to educate us, it is also sorting us. He said, "The geniuses will be raked from the rubbish." Jesus expressed this same idea in his account of the goats being separated from the sheep and the tares being sorted out so that they could be tied in bundles and burned. Of course, the causes of whatever happens to us can be found inside ourselves. To help us develop excellence, a divine program by which we might work out our eternal exaltation has been given to all men, and after the dropouts have been eliminated, the rest will be classified according to their degree of excellence. We are sometimes like the indolent student whom the professor described by saying that he had great gifts but he was too lazy to unwrap them. What a great tragedy when we fail to unwrap those divine gifts of faith, courage, industry, of which excellence is composed. In developing these traits we must *want* in capital letters.

Jesus said, "Ask, and it shall be given you; seek, and ye shall find; knock, and it shall be opened unto you." (Matt. 7:7.) And we must ask loud enough and seek hard enough and knock long enough to get the right answer.

An ancient American prophet once said, "God grants to every man according to his desire." This is still God's program for accomplishment. If our desires are weak, our industry will tend to fail and our achievement will be small. There is an old saying to the effect that you can't keep a good man down, but that is just not true. Some of the very best men are presently being kept down by those traits of mediocrity, ignorance, sin, sloth, and the other natural enemies of excellence. We must turn on enough faith and develop enough ambition to carry us above our present questionable level. We need more excellence in our precepts, more excellence in our motivations, more excellence in our drive, more excellence in our preparation for life, and more excellence in our ambition to live it at its best.

Captain Cook shows us the spirit of excellence when he says about his early-day voyages of discovery, "I had an ambition, not only to go farther than any man had ever been before, but I wanted to go as far as it was possible for any man to go." Suppose that in the journey of our lives we set our goals to go as far as it is possible for anyone to go. Then we would be within reach of that great goal set by the Master, wherein he said, "Be ye therefore perfect, even as your Heavenly Father is perfect." What a thrilling opportunity to dedicate our lives in a quest for the excellence required for such an accomplishment.

Abdication

A N INTERESTING WORD THAT MAY HAVE SPECIAL SIGNIFICANCE FOR
some of us is the word abdication. It means to renounce or to
relinquish some important right or power. It describes a formal
withdrawal from something, and often involves the forfeit of substantial holdings. One of the best ways to develop excellence is to
renounce our failures and to withdraw from evil. But to withdraw
from good things is also much more common in our lives than we
might realize. And we may be able to serve our best interests by
thinking about some of them before they take place.

The dictionary gives the classic example of this situation by citing
one of the most dramatic events in the history of our world. It took
place when the English King Edward VIII relinquished his right to
the British throne in order to marry an American divorcee. His
instrument of abdication was sent to Parliament on December 10,
1936. In this document the King said, "I, Edward the VIII, King of
Great Britain, Ireland and the British dominions beyond the seas,
Emperor of India, do hereby declare my irrevocable determination
to renounce the throne for myself and my descendants, and it is my
desire that effect should be given to this instrument of abdication
immediately. In token whereof I have hereunto set my hand this
tenth day December, 1936, in the presence of the witnesses whose
signatures are subscribed. (Signed) Edward R. I."

Because of the particular reason for his abdication, the official
instrument did not include the customary phrase, "By the Grace of
God," and it also omitted one of the king's most important titles,
that of "Defender of the Faith."

Edward's birth on June 23, 1894, was heralded on the front
pages of every newspaper in the realm, and town criers hourly
announced the progress of his delivery. He was born heir to a kingdom that governed one-fourth of the world's people, and covered
one-fourth of the surface of the earth. His destiny would seat him
upon a throne, place a crown upon his head, and put a scepter in
his hands. It would also make him head of the Church of England.
As Edward was growing up, he wore velvets and satins; he attended
the best schools with guards at his side; he received his training from

the best tutors, and his royal environment kept him continually aware of his own tremendous future.

When Edward was 17, his grandfather, Edward VII, died, and when his father, George V, came to the throne on July 13, 1911, young Edward was made Prince of Wales. It has been said that no crown prince in history ever had such thorough training for the throne than did he. And it is probable that a more popular crown prince never lived. He was idolized in his country and throughout the rest of the world. His friendly, democratic ways, his sense of diplomacy, and his good sportsmanship made him a great favorite of everyone. In August 1911, one week after the outbreak of World War I, he joined the first battalion of Grenadier Guards and in November was appointed aide-de-camp to the Commander-in-Chief of the British expeditionary force in France. Shortly after the end of the war, the Prince began a series of travels that took him all over the world, and he was referred to as the "super-salesman" of Great Britain. Finally, at the death of his father, he ascended the throne on January 20, 1936.

With his vast experience and his tremendous popularity, his reign was expected to be an extraordinary one in every way. And for the first few months, everything went along smoothly. As his popularity grew, the entire world wished him well. But in the summer of 1936 some new influences were introduced into the picture. In August he began a several weeks' yacht cruise in the Adriatic. Among his guests was Mrs. Wallis Warfield Simpson, the wife of a London shipbuilder. Mrs. Simpson had already had a previous marriage and divorce. Then in London on June 10, 1931, she had been introduced to the future king. A friendship and then a romance developed that was soon to rock the British empire. When Mrs. Simpson made application for a divorce, the gossip began to flow thick and fast. But the idea that the king, who was also the head of the Church, would contemplate such a marriage was unthinkable. On October 20, 1936, Prime Minister Stanley Baldwin called on the King and asked him to put an end to these unpleasant rumors. But the report came back that the King was contemplating a morganatic marriage with Mrs. Simpson, as soon as her divorce was final. A morganatic marriage is one in which a member of a royal family marries an inferior who can never acquire her husband's rank. And the children of such a marriage can not succeed to the throne nor acquire any of the titles or property of the royal parent.

To avoid the developing problems, the King finally decided to abdicate! The abdication bill was passed by both houses of Parliament the next day and was signed by King Edward at 1:52 o'clock that afternoon. Then the short reign of the most thoroughly prepared king was ended. That night at 10:00 p.m. from Windsor Castle he broadcast his farewell address. Among other things he said, "A few hours ago I discharged my last duty as King and emperor, and now that I have been succeeded by my brother, my first words must be to declare my allegiance to him. This I do with all my heart. But I have found it impossible to carry the heavy burdens of responsibility and to discharge my duties as King as I would wish to do without the help and support of the woman I love—therefore I now lay down my burden and quit public affairs altogether. It may be some time before I return to my native land, but I shall always follow the fortunes of the British race and empire with profound interest, and if at any time in the future I can be of service to His Majesty in a private station, I shall not fail. And now we all have a new King. I wish him and you his people happiness and prosperity with all my heart. God bless you all—God save the King."

Then, just after midnight, he left England to begin a lifetime of voluntary exile. He was given the title of Duke of Windsor by his brother, the new King. This was accompanied by an income to provide for his support. The former King and Mrs. Simpson were married on June 3, 1937.

We do not know what the satisfactions or regrets of this abdication may have been. We do know that it was precipitated by an illicit love affair in direct violation of God's command from Sinai saying, "Thou shalt not covet thy neighbor's wife." We also know that the bad example sent repercussions from one end of the world to the other. In commenting on the omission of the royal title "Defender of the Faith" and the phrase "by the Grace of God" from his abdication message, the Prime Minister said that everyone would feel better if Edward were to act as though he was aware that such things existed.

Edward is now a wrinkled old man; his features indicate that he has been carrying a very heavy burden. He gave up his kingship, his country, his church leadership, and his friends to live in a foreign land. During these long years Edward must have often reflected upon his life as it could have been, and Mrs. Simpson must also have frequently recounted the chain of events that she had set in motion, and grieved over their consequences. She had left two husbands and by her charms had motivated a third man to give up the leadership of the greatest empire in the world. In his exile, Edward's importance, his influence to do good, has largely been destroyed. And he abdicated the natural destiny that he was born to serve.

And yet in only a little different way, every man is born a king. In recounting his great vision of the final judgment, John the Revelator said that God hath made us all kings and priests unto him forever. (Rev. 5:10.) The gospel of Jesus Christ puts our feet on the king's highway, which is designed to get us ready for our own divine destiny. The royal road to power, importance, happiness, and eternal exaltation is found along that strait and narrow way on which the master himself walked and which he talked so much about. The King of Kings and Lord of Lords has set up that eternal goal that the children of God may some day hope to become like the parent, and our biggest problem is often our own numerous abdications. Far too many of us also fall in love with the wrong things. It is very easy for us to want those things that have been forbidden. We frequently fall in love with unrighteousness and liquor and ease and sin, and thereby we abdicate from that eternal possibility that says "every man a king." It is so easy to renounce our birthright as the children of God and relinquish our divine rights as heirs of the King of Kings.

To forfeit our greatest privileges and powers, we don't always need to spell out a written abdication instrument to be acted upon by parliament. We can accomplish the same thing by a mere default, or we may relinquish our rights or forfeit our own substantial holdings by an almost unconscious withdrawal from righteousness. We can abdicate our greatest blessings by carelessness or thoughtlessness or heedlessness. And we automatically write our own message of withdrawal when we forget God, ignore his commandments, become bitter, critical, inactive, or fall in love with evil. When we renounce God's plan of life and salvation, we lose his blessings, and then the scepter of our office is turned over to someone else.

Edward VIII is the only king who has ever voluntarily abdicated the British throne, but millions of people are constantly forsaking their heavenly birthright to live in a foreign land.

We remember that in the antemortal council in heaven, Lucifer abdicated his position as the Son of the Morning to become a devil and live a life of misery, evil, and hell. Judas abdicated his position as an apostle of Jesus to become a suicide and fill a lonely grave in a Potters field. Some have abdicated in favor of immorality, alcoholism, atheism, and sloth.

An unpleasant thing about abdication is that like Edward VIII, most people not only relinquish their own blessings, but they do it on a morganatic basis where they also sign away the rights of their offspring. God said that the sins of the fathers would be visited upon the children to the third and fourth generation.

The idea of abdication reminds us of the experiences of Mark Anthony. After the assassination of Julius Caesar, the Roman empire was divided into two great war camps, one led by the conspirators and the other by Anthony and Octavius Caesar. During the long hard war that followed, Mark Anthony distinguished himself as the greatest military leader of his time. Armed with his convincing speech, the power of his logic, the courage of his leadership, and his own self-discipline, he became the most powerful man in his world. He took upon himself the hardest tasks. He lived for weeks on a diet of insects and the bark of trees. He endured the greatest privations with wondrous good cheer. He won the unquestioned loyalty of his men, the acclaim of the people, and finally won the war. Now Mark Anthony found himself in the place where the great Julius Caesar had once stood as master of the world.

But when the need for struggle was past, Anthony became idle. He went to Egypt and fell in love with the bewitching Queen Cleopatra. He became a victim of the soft luxury and perfumed elegance of the Egyptian court. His great mind became clouded by the fumes of wine. His personality began to disintegrate, and Mark Anthony had soon abandoned his better self. Then he lost the power of his leadership, the loyalty of his men, the acclaim of the people, and the support of Octavius. Finally a guard of soldiers was sent to arrest Anthony and bring him back to Rome in chains. Anthony avoided arrest by thrusting a dagger into his own heart, and as he lay dying he recounted to Cleopatra that there had been no power in the world sufficient to overthrow him except his own power. He said that only Anthony could conquer Anthony. Then, contemplating the arrival of the Roman soldiers, he made his last speech to Cleopatra, which William Haines Little has put into verse. He said, "Let not Caesar's servil minions mock the lion thus laid low. 'Twas no foeman's arm that felled him, 'twas his own hand struck the blow. He who pillowed on thy bosom, turned aside from glory's way, when made drunk with thy caresses, madly threw a world away."

Anthony and Edward VIII each threw away his own world. But when we throw away the love of righteousness and abdicate as the heirs of God, we also throw away the greatest of all worlds, which is the Celestial Kingdom. Then we abdicate our eternal glory not only for ourselves but sometimes we also throw away those benefits that belong to our children, as they will probably follow in our footsteps. Yet no power can overthrow us except our own power, just as "only Anthony can conquer Anthony." Only Edward VIII could sign his own abdication instrument, and only we can throw away our own eternal blessings.

May God save the King, and may God save us, the heirs of the King of Kings, by protecting us from the great sin involved in the abdication of righteousness.

America the Beautiful

A NUMBER OF YEARS AGO EUGENE BURDICK AND WILLIAM LEDERER wrote a book entitled *The Ugly American*. This title represents an attitude about Americans and America in the minds of some people. Many of us *do not* present the most attractive picture of ourselves, and it is natural that ugly activities in Americans will reflect unfavorably in the American image. There is a feeling among many people that in recent years, a deterioration in our conduct has seriously impaired the elegance of our reputation. This fact has more than ordinary significance in view of the large amount of available evidence that this great nation was established by the direct design of God upon the foundation principles of freedom and righteousness. In 1835 a French visitor, Alevis De Tocqueville, published a book based on his study of the United States. In it he made this challenging statement: "America is great because she is good, and if she ever ceases to be good she will cease to be great." Of course, each individual American citizen is obligated to bear his fair share of responsibility, not only for his country's political image, but also for her social, moral, and spiritual welfare. The great empires of the past have fallen because of the ugliness that has been allowed to become a part of their national inheritance. And while it may not be very important what Mr. Burdick and Mr. Lederer may think about America or any other people, yet every nation must rise or fall according to the kind of image it presents in God's sight.

Sometime ago a woman in a divorce court described what it was like to be married to an ugly American. For 29 years her husband had scoffed at religion. He had dominated her every move and had denied her many of her normal liberties, including her freedom to worship and her freedom to live a righteous life without being humiliated and made to feel that she was something less than a human being. Her husband assumed the privilege of depriving his wife of her right to go to church. Because of his high affinity for those kinds of deceit and misrepresentation that he felt would be helpful to him, she had lost all of her confidence in his sense of fairness and integrity. He set his children an ugly example in alcoholism, nicotine addiction, profanity, atheism, and extreme antagonism toward God. He was not only an ugly American; he was also an ugly Christian, and an ugly father and an ugly husband. For 29 years this woman had submitted to his evil in an unsuccessful attempt to win a peaceful coexistence of right and wrong in their home. As a consequence, the lives of all family members became distorted with evil, as all were molded more or less into his moral image.

If we sing "God Bless America" as criminals and delinquents, we should not expect our prayers to be answered very enthusiastically. There is not much point in praying for a drunken America or a profane America, or an atheistic America. After God had finished his work of creation, he looked out upon the world and called it good. And, of course, his vision included America. Certainly God, who sees the end from the beginning, did not provide the unmatched fertility of our soils, our great rivers, our magnificent forests, our lakes of oil, and our mines filled with valuable metals without having a desire to bless the people who would live here. We also know that he wants to build a beautiful America, filled with beautiful Americans and beautiful Christians. The word Christian was first used in Antioch to designate the followers of Christ, and Christianity is one of the characteristics of America. In thinking about the beauty of America, we might remember that we have far more Christians in this country than does any other nation in the world. Our nation was built on Christian principles, and certainly our present and future success depends upon Americans following the Master. One cannot very well be a great American without living the qualities of Christian beauty in his life.

Recently, while standing in one of the garden spots of America, I tried to imagine how many billions of buckets of paint God must have used to beautify our mountains, our landscapes, our homes, and our flower gardens. Our red apples, yellow peaches, purple grapes, blue plums, black cherries, and many colored flowers impress us with the fact that God loves color and harmony. We might also wonder about the other billions of buckets of perfume, taste, and nourishment that he has put into the flowers, fruits, and other things to delight the senses of man. Certainly he used the greatest skill in making them so wonderfully attractive. But God reserved his greatest beauty to put into his own children inhabiting every land and nation. But America is a land where human dignity and voluntary righteousness are attempting to find their fullest expression. And while there are many variations of ugliness in Americans, yet there are also many whose lives are filled with beauty.

God promised to spare the little city of Sodom if fifty righteous men could be found therein, but it has required many more than that number of righteous lives to account for the great lavishness with which God has blessed America. America itself has many beautiful things about it. Even after carefully acknowledging all of her faults, America is still by long odds the greatest nation ever known upon the earth.

America is beautiful for her many freedoms and for her stable government. America is beautiful for her lack of blood purges, gas ovens, dictatorships, and political revolutions used by so many nations as the instruments of government. America is beautiful for her sacred regard for human life and human dignity. America not only has the largest number of people claiming to be Christians of any nation, but she also has the largest percentage of Church attendance. America sends out more religious missionaries and makes a far greater effort to help other people economically than all of the other nations in the world combined. We buy more Bibles in America than all the rest of the world put together.

The United States is the center of the world's learning, culture, inventions, material progress, and scientific achievement. Our national flag represents a way of life that is the envy of the world. We pledge our allegiance to that flag and to the republic for which it stands. We also vow our wholehearted support to this greatest nation under God, which he has made indivisible in order to more effectively provide liberty and justice for all. Our national motto declares our belief "In God We Trust," and so far as we practice this motto, our land will be free and our lives will be successful. It is much more than a coincidence that for almost two centuries we have remained free amid the great turmoil and slavery of other nations. Someone has said that in America it is "believe it or not," whereas in so many countries it is "believe it or else." We live without the necessity of "having a dictator's foot on our necks or an oppressor's hand over our mouths."

Many years ago Katherine Lee Bates wrote a poem that reflects the spirit of America. It is entitled "America the Beautiful." And inasmuch as the successes of America and Americans are so dependent upon each other, we might weave in between the lines some sentiment about those beautiful Americans who under God have helped to make America great, and who are responsible for much of the continued national and individual success that we presently enjoy. With our many blessings in mind we sing:

Oh beautiful for spacious skies,
For amber waves of grain,
For purple mountain majesties
Above the fruited plain!
America! America!
God shed his grace on thee
And crown thy good with brotherhood
From sea to shining sea.

Oh beautiful for pilgrim feet,
Whose stern impassioned stress
A thoroughfare of freedom beat
Across the wilderness!
America! America!
God mend thine every flaw,
Confirm thy soul in self-control,
Thy liberty in law.

Oh beautiful for heroes proved
In liberating strife,
Who more than self their country loved,
And mercy more than life!
America! America!
May God thy gold refine
'Til all success be nobleness,
And every gain divine.

Oh beautiful for patriot dream
That sees beyond the years.
Thine alabaster cities gleam,
Undimmed by human tears.
America! America!
God shed his grace on thee
And crown thy good with brotherhood
From sea to shining sea.

It must be very pleasing to God when we love our country and try to build up her great free institutions. We can develop our own appreciation by reminding ourselves of the many benefits that we enjoy as well as the many obligations that come to us as a consequence of living in this great, free land, which has been so highly favored.

Recently a retired soldier, age 42, gave up his job to re-enlist in the army. A friend said to him, "Don't you think that you have done enough for your country?" He answered, "Can anyone ever do enough for his country?" What price would be too great for anyone to pay for American freedom and American opportunity, or who could do too much in order to keep these blessings alive and vigorous in our land and in our hearts!

During the first century of our national existence Abraham Lincoln said, "We have been the recipients of the choicest bounties of heaven. We have been preserved these many years in peace and prosperity. We have grown in numbers, wealth and power as no other nation has ever grown." Then he mentioned our perennial problem when he said, "But we have forgotten God, we have forgotten the gracious hand that preserved us in peace and multiplied and enriched and strengthened us, and we have vainly imagined in the deceitfulness of our hearts that all of these blessings were produced by some superior wisdom or virtue of our own. Intoxicated by unbroken success, we have become too self-sufficient to feel the necessity of redeeming and preserving grace, too proud to pray to the God who made us. It behooves us then," said the President, "to humble ourselves before the offended power to confess our national sins, and to pray for clemency and forgiveness."

Abraham Lincoln was speaking as the President of the United States, but he might have said those same things if he had been speaking as a prophet of the Lord. We feel the spirit of the prophets as we hear President Lincoln say, "Whereas it is the duty of nations as well as men, to own their dependence upon the overruling power of God, to confess their sins and transgressions in humble sorrow, yet with assured hope that genuine repentance will lead to mercy and pardon, and to recognize the sublime truth, announced in the Holy scriptures and proven by all history, that those nations only are blessed whose God is the Lord; and inasmuch as we know that by his divine law, nations like individuals are subjected to punishments and chastisements in this world, may we not justly fear that the awful calamity of civil war, which now desolates the land, may be but a punishment inflicted upon us for our presumptuous sins to the needful end of our national reformation as a whole people?" If only those nations are blessed whose God is the Lord, then above all we must continue to deserve them.

America can be beautiful. She can be the most beautiful nation in her repentance and in the reformation of her national life. Our society will always have problems as long as some of us as individuals continue to show ourselves as ugly Americans or ugly Christians.

And we must do far more than merely follow the master with our lips; our hearts also must be beautiful. We must have God's doctrines clearly in our minds, and we must follow him by keeping all of his commandments. We would like to be well regarded by other nations, but it is far more important that we be on good terms with the God of this land, who is Jesus Christ.

It is hoped that at this 191st anniversary of our nation's birth, all Americans will join together in expressing their appreciation for the greatness, goodness, strength, and beauty of America. As we repledge our love, loyalty, and support, may we ask God to make us good Americans and good men and women, for only as Americans are good can they be beautiful, and our divine destiny itself requires a beautiful America and some 200 million beautiful Americans. I pray that God will help us to achieve both of these ends.

American History

To MANY PEOPLE, THE HISTORY OF AMERICA BEGAN ON OCTOBER 12, 1492, when a spark of light from an Indian campfire shined through the darkness into the eyes of Christopher Columbus. But long before that time the western continent had already had an important history.

In times past, we have considered the western continent as a "new world," and a kind of after-thought of creation. However, it is indicated from ancient American ruins and hieroglyphics that a great civilization once flourished here. Some more specific information about our continent came to us with the publication of the Book of Mormon. This is an inspired volume of ancient American scripture having the greatest possible importance to us and to our day. From this authentic record, written by God's ancient American prophets and supplemented by some modern-day revelations, we have learned that America has had a wonderful past and will have an even more brilliant future. The people who occupied this land had attained heights of excellence far surpassing that which existed here when Columbus arrived.

In fact, it has been revealed that the cradle of civilization was not located in Asia, as has been supposed by many, but in the very heart of what is now the United States of America. The Garden of Eden was located in the area we know as Jackson County, Missouri. The Lord himself has identified this locality as the place where Adam called his posterity together and blessed them three years prior to his death. (D&C 107:53-56, 116; 78:16.) And this is the place also designated by the Lord where the new Jerusalem will be built to serve as one of the Lord's capital cities during his thousand-year millenial reign upon the earth. (D&C 45:66-67; Ether 13:3-8.) We have a total recorded world history of 5,967 years, 4,000 of which passed before the birth of Christ, and 1967 since, and only about one-fifteenth of the total has passed since Columbus. It seems hardly reasonable that God would go to all the trouble to create this earth and then allow its richest and most productive part to go to waste until almost the winding-up scene.

It was some 1,656 years from Garden of Eden days to the flood of Noah's time. The large posterity of Adam had spread out from its Garden of Eden center, and this land was covered with people when God sent the flood to destroy all except Noah and his family. Nearly a year later, Noah's ark landed at Mount Ararat in what we have known as Armenia. But knowing what we do about ocean currents, we might well understand that the ark had traveled some distance from where it had taken off so many months earlier.

The Bible also says, "And God made a wind to pass over the earth." (Gen 8:1.) There is another factor involved inasmuch as the scriptures indicate that in the days of the flood there was no Atlantic Ocean dividing the continents. In giving the account of creation as recorded in the Bible, God said, "Let the waters under the heaven be gathered together *unto one place,* and let the dry land appear; and it was so." (Gen 1:9.) Originally the land was all together. It was not until the days of Peleg some time after the flood that the earth's land areas were broken up to form the continents as we now know them. (Gen 10:25.) But in any event, we have the sure word of the Lord that civilization first began in America, and it was the *second* beginning that took place at Mount Ararat in Asia more than sixteen centuries later.

However, it wasn't very long after the flood before wickedness again took over the people. But this time, instead of destroying them, the Lord confounded their language at the Tower of Babel. The Bible says, "And the Lord scattered them abroad from thence upon the face of *all* the earth." It was only natural that one of these dispersed groups should be led back to America. And of this we also have a definite authentic record. A part of the Book of Mormon contains an inspired account of a special group called the Jaredites, who from the confusion at Babel were specifically selected to resettle in the newly created western hemisphere. Their leader was described as a large and mighty man highly favored of the Lord, and referred to as "The brother of Jared." On one occasion the Lord talked with him out of a cloud for a period of three hours. (Ether 2:14.) This reminds us of the talk the Lord had had with Moses before sending him forward toward his own promised land.

Among other things, the Lord said to the brother of Jared, "I will go before thee into a land which is choice above all other lands of the earth. And there will I bless thee and thy seed, . . . and [I will make thee] a great nation. And there shall be none greater than the nation which I will raise up unto me of thy seed, upon all the face of the earth." (Ether 1:42-43.)

This pre-Columbus American civilization lasted here for approximately 2,000 years. It was the contemporary of Assyria, Babylon, Persia, and the other great nations of that day. And the Lord himself said that no nation of that day was greater than the one flourishing in ancient America. In some ways this *Jaredite* nation was very similar to the *Israelite* nation that the Lord established in Palestine at a later date. One point of similarity is that both of these groups had inspired prophets to give them God's word and record their history.

God has always been very anxious to build up a righteous people. It was for this purpose that he called Abraham to leave his idol-worshipping ancestors and start over in the new land of Caanan. God promised great things to Abraham if his posterity would serve God. They were told that they could have their own government, that they would be a favored people, a royal priesthood, a holy nation, living in a chosen land. Based on their righteousness, their bodies should be immune to disease, and God would bestow upon them unimagined blessings of health, happiness, and prosperity.

God specifically forbid them to give up their freedom or allow any king to rule over them. The Israelites had periods when they were faithful and prosperous. But in many respects their record presents a rather miserable spectacle of disobedience to God. In the days of Samuel they clamored for a king, and again the Lord cautioned them about the evil of dictatorships, but they refused to listen. Finally God said to Samuel, "Hearken unto the voice of the people in all that they say unto thee: for they have not rejected thee, but they have rejected me, that I should not reign over them." (I Sam. 8:7.) It doesn't take many evil kings to do a nation irreparable damage.

The wicked King Ahab and his idol-worshipping queen Jezebel brought so many idolatrous priests into Israel that for a time Jehovah worship was almost blotted out. In his later years, even King Solomon, who had seen God twice, joined his idolatrous wives in worshipping idols; and he led many other people into idolatry.

It was primarily because of the wickedness of their kings that the people of Israel were finally divided, and both segments were carried away to live in foreign servitude to pagan nations. The Lord also told the Jaredites that they must have no kings. It seems a small wonder that the Lord should get sick and tired of having his people led away time after time by selfish, ungodly dictators. The Book of Mormon says, "God had sworn in his wrath unto the brother of Jared, that whoso should possess this land of promise, from that time henceforth and forever, should serve him, the true and only God, or they should be swept off when the fulness of his wrath should come upon them." (Ether 2:8.)

We have a substantial interest in this ancient nation and what its people did; for, like our own founding fathers, they played an important part in making *our* America what it is today. It was to them in that long-ago time that God made his everlasting decree that no kings should be permitted to rule here, and this decree still governs us. It was God's divine pronouncement recorded in these pre-Columbus scriptures that from that time henceforth and forever, this land should be free from captivity and from all other nations under heaven if they would but serve God. And for many years our ancient predecessors prospered under this decree. Then they failed to maintain their righteousness, and their entire nation was wiped out in a long civil war. After their destruction, another colony was brought to these shores from Jerusalem about 600 B.C. This group were members of the house of Israel and were led by a prophet by the name of Lehi. They flourished here for nearly a thousand years. Then, because of their wickedness, the members of one of their factions were cursed with a dark skin. (II Nephi 5:21.) However, this group later became the more righteous part of their civilization, and when their last great battle took place in 384 A.D., the few white survivors were absorbed by the victors.

When Columbus arrived here he found a group of near-naked, half-savage redmen. However, this once great civilization had left us one of our greatest possible resources in their inspired scriptures. It covers the combined period of pre-Columbus American history from 2200 B.C. to 384 A.D. Because of their unrighteousness, their prophets had foreseen and foretold their own destruction. But their prophets were permitted to look forward beyond their own time to our own day, just as the prophets on the eastern continent were permitted to do. These early American scriptures foretell that Columbus would be moved upon by the Spirit of God to rediscover this continent. (I Nephi 13:12-14.) We know that Columbus himself believed that he was an instrument of the divine will and was being directed by God. These ancient American scriptures also foretell the rise and power of the great American nation that we now know as the United States, and that it would be established under an inspired constitution written by wise men that God would raise up for that very purpose. (D&C 101:77-80; I Nephi 22:7.)

This prophetic scripture is especially emphatic that no kings should rule in this great modern American nation, and that this choice land had been set apart by God as a sanctuary of freedom. It is no mere coincidence that the Lord brought to our shores a group of freedom-loving, God-fearing pilgrims and pioneers to be the foundation of this great, free, Christian nation.

Like Christopher Columbus, the founding fathers believed that they were being directed by God. George Washington said, "The singular interpositions of Providence in our behalf have been such as could scarcely escape the attention of the most unobserving." In his inaugural address on April 30, 1789, President Washington said, "Every step by which we have advanced to the character of an independent nation seems to have been distinguished by some token of providential agency." And the Bible bears this out by saying, "Except the Lord shall build the house, they labor in vain who build it." (Ps. 127:1.) How else can we account for the outstanding leadership of the United States of America and the fulfillment of many Book of Mormon prophecies concerning our own country that are presently taking place before our very eyes?

Certainly we still need improvements, and yet in a very remarkable way America is discharging her divine mission. Think what a different world this would be if there had never been a United States of America. If any Communist combination of nations should win world dominion, then none of our other problems would ever again seem very important. For as Emerson has said, "Of what avail is plow or sail, or land, or life, if freedom fail!" How gratefully therefore we should sing and pray our gratitude to God.

My country! tis of thee,
Sweet land of liberty,
Of thee I sing;
Land where my fathers died,
Land of the pilgrim's pride,
From every mountain side,
Let freedom ring!

My native country, thee,
Land of the noble, free,
Thy name I love;
I love thy rocks and rills,
Thy woods and templed hills.
My heart with rapture thrills
Like that above.

Let music swell the breeze
And ring from all the trees,
Sweet freedom's song;
Let mortal tongues awake;
Let all that breathe partake;
Let rocks their silence break,
The sound prolong.

Our fathers' God to thee,
Author of liberty,
To thee we sing.
Long may our land be bright
With freedom's holy light.
Protect us with thy might,
Great God, our King!

And may our lives be such that America may continue to be the land of the free and the home of those who serve God.

The American Mission

J AMES RUSSELL LOWELL ONCE SAID THAT "NO ONE IS EVER BORN into the world whose work is not born with him." In the grand counsel in heaven, Adam and Eve were selected to become the progenitors of the race of mortals that were to live upon the earth. The scripture also says that God knew Jeremiah before his earth life began and that his work was cut out for him, as God had ordained him to be a prophet unto the nations before he was born. (Jer. 1:5.) Jesus himself was foreordained to come into the world to redeem it from sin. (I Peter 1:20.) And Henry Van Dyke could have been speaking for many others when, in referring to the particular work that life had given him to do, he said,

> This is my work, my blessing not my doom;
> Of all who live, I am the one by whom this work
> Can best be done in the right way.

It is also true that certain *nations* have been organized for a particular purpose and have been given a specific mission to perform. Ancient Israel was given an assignment to be a holy nation and to keep Jehovah worship alive in an idolatrous world. It was the job of the Israelites to set the proper example, showing men and women how to live at their best. But in these latter days a great modern American nation has been established by God and has been given a divine mission of the greatest consequence. Even if our only means of judgment were "by its fruits," it would still be perfectly clear that God had a special interest in America and had assigned it an important role for these latter days.

We know that from the very beginning America has been a land specially dedicated to freedom. It was founded by liberty-loving pilgrims and pioneers who were led here by God to escape the tyranny and oppression of other lands. Our national symbol is a great statue of liberty standing on Bedloe Island in New York Harbor at the gateway of America, beckoning hitherward outcast and homeless people. This great lady holds aloft the torch of freedom, and on a tablet at the base of this statue is inscribed a characteristically American philosophy, which in part reads as follows:

Give me your tired, your poor,
Your huddled masses yearning to be free,
The wretched refuse of your teeming shores—
Send these, the homeless, tempest tossed to me;
I lift my lamp beside the golden door.

We know that on many occasions in world history God has made
a special effort to establish a great world power out of freedom-
loving, righteous people. And as far back as the council in heaven,
he made a firm commitment to free agency for all mankind. It was
the contest between the philosophies of freedom and compulsion that
caused Lucifer to rebel against God and to be banished from heaven.

Force and coercion are still the primary cause of much of the
trouble that is presently taking place in the world. A long string of
dictators, including Genghis Khan, Alexander the Great, Caesar,
Napoleon, Stalin, Hitler and their present-day successors, have always
sought to dominate other people. And the philosophy of "by their
fruits ye shall know them" definitely puts the dictators in the camp
of Satan. What a happy exception it is, therefore, to see the world's
strongest present-day nation as the leader in science and culture,
taking an exactly opposite course in its dedication to the idea of
promoting the freedom of all mankind. In times past those nations
like the Philippines, Cuba, Japan, and Germany that have fallen
into American hands have been rehabilitated, given training and
gifts, and set free. But we have a more sure way of knowing about
the divine mission of America even than by merely judging her by
her fruits.

In 1830, when the United States was a small, young nation, an
ancient volume of pre-Columbus scripture known as the Book of
Mormon was translated into English. From this source, supplemented
by some modern-day revelations, we learn the history of America
from the time of Adam to the present. We also learn of the divine
decrees of God concerning this land, and the important coming
events that will yet transpire here. America is the place where the
New Jerusalem will be built to serve as one of God's capital cities
during his millennial reign following the glorious second coming of
Christ. The tenth Article of Faith says, "We believe in the literal
gathering of Israel, and in the restoration of the Ten Tribes, that
Zion will be built upon this the American continent, that Christ will
reign personally upon the earth, and that the earth will be renewed
and receive its paradisiacal glory."

God's messages about America make clear what was pointed out in Abraham Lincoln's proclamation of 1863, that these blessings were not produced by our own superior wisdom or virtue, but God's own hand has been the instrument in shaping the course of America. The scriptures are clear, and history testifies that God rules in the affairs of men. And even at this moment God is making ready to cleanse the earth of its sin and to redeem it from the unpleasant state in which it has lived for nearly 6,000 years, since the fall of man. But still the international power struggle among ungodly men goes on attempting to dominate men's minds and to get possession of as much of the earth as possible.

And now we are even conducting a battle for possession of the moon. "But the earth is the Lord's," and soon he will take personal physical possession of it and establish a perfect theocratic government here where everyone may live righteously, successfully, and happily. Then no one will say that God is dead, or that revelations from him have ceased, or that it doesn't matter any more what we do. For then Christ will reign over the earth in person as King of Kings and Lord of Lords. Then every knee shall bow, and every tongue shall confess that Jesus is the Christ.

In the meantime, most people are going along as did those of Noah's day to whom the Lord himself compared us. (Matt. 24: 37-39.) But during this final period of preparing the people, the Lord wants at least one place where freedom prevails, where righteousness can be taught, and where everyone is at liberty to worship God according to the dictates of his own conscience.

There are some who say that America is declining in her moral concepts and is losing the sense of her divine mission. But at least on a basis of comparison this is not so. A few years ago the United States was just one great nation among a group of many other great nations. But the relative importance of American leadership has actually been greatly increased in recent years, until now it stands almost alone at the top of the list of nations and has no close competitors. And while we may do many things wrong and certainly we have some serious sins, yet where is there any other nation to compare with her?

The Christian religion itself was once exclusively located in Asia, but now its center of gravity has also passed to America. The people of the land where Jesus labored so hard to establish his Church not only put him to death, but comparatively very few of those who live there now have even accepted, let alone retained even a small part of the Christian faith. In fact, there is a very small percentage of Christians in any of the large nations except America. We buy more Bibles in America than in all of the rest of the world put together. The United States has six percent of the world's people and seven percent of its land area. In these particulars America is far below such nations as Russia, China, and India. And yet the United States gives more economic aid in feeding, clothing, and otherwise assisting needy peoples than all other nations combined. And it is also the American mission to keep freedom, righteousness, and human dignity alive in the world and make them available to all other interested peoples. God has said, "And this is my work and my glory, to bring to pass the immortality and eternal life of man." But we have now been invited into God's firm to assist in that work in which he himself spends his entire time. It now becomes our work and our glory to bring to pass the immortality and eternal life of man.

The Communist nation that comes second to the United States in power is on a much lower level so far as its standards of education, Christianity, economic production, and genuine help to others are concerned. Russia also plays a completely different kind of role among the nations. Its mission is very largely one of evil. It functions as the world's troublemaker. It is carrying on the philosophy of force that was originated by Lucifer in the council of heaven. It is trying to destroy Christianity and wipe from the earth all belief in God, which is directly against the divine purpose. As goals to be accomplished, Russia places "domination" far above truth and righteousness. Lenin effectively represented the general philosophy of Communist leaders when he said, "It is moral to tell any lie, break an agreement, violate any law, liquidate any individual or group or do anything else that will advance the cause of Communism."

This was followed up by Khrushchev's threat of burying us. And we know they would if they could. But how strangely this philosophy would sound under an American label, and how poorly it compares with the American point of view expressed by Abraham Lincoln, when he said, "With malice toward none, with charity for all, with firmness in the right as God gives us to see the right, let us press on to finish the work we are in, to bind up the nation's wounds and to care for him who has borne the battle, for his widow and his orphans."

Where should we look for the source of this strangely different philosophy if not to God, the author of all good? A revelation from him says that the Constitution of the United States is an inspired document written by wise men that he himself had raised up unto this very purpose. And it is based on justice and fairness for all men. It was given in the spirit of Jesus' teaching his disciples to pray, saying, "Thy kingdom come, thy will be done in earth as it is in heaven."

Just before his crucifixion Jesus looked beyond the apostacy and the dark ages that followed his rejection. He described many of the conditions that would exist in the latter days, and he foretold some of those events that should immediately precede his own glorious second coming to the earth. After foretelling such things as the wars and difficulties between the nations, he said, "And this gospel of the kingdom shall be preached in all the world as a witness unto all nations, and then shall the end come." (Matt. 24:14.) To prepare the way before him, the gospel of Jesus Christ could not very well have been restored in Russia or China, as those nations are trying to blot out the Christianity that they already have. The gospel could only have been restored in a free society where righteousness and fairness were part of the national philosophy.

John the Revelator also proclaimed the restoration of the gospel in the latter days, when he said, "And I saw another angel fly in the midst of heaven, having the everlasting gospel to preach unto them that dwell upon the earth, and to every nation, and kindred, and tongue, and people, Saying with a loud voice, Fear God, and give glory to him; for the hour of his judgment is come: and worship him that made heaven, and earth, and the sea, and the fountains of waters." (Rev. 14:6-7.)

It is the testimony of The Church of Jesus Christ of Latter-day Saints that the angel has flown and that he came to America, and the message is now going forth for the last time before the final winding-up scene takes place. No one knows the day nor the hour that the Lord will come, but Jesus gave us his sign when he said, "Now learn a parable of the fig tree; When his branch is yet tender, and putteth forth leaves, ye know that summer is nigh: So likewise ye, when ye shall see all these things, know that it is near, even at your doors." (Matt. 24:32-33.)

America and Americans must not fail in this divine mission. We already know from several big-scale experiences about what happens when nations or men turn their backs on freedom and righteousness and God. That act has caused the downfall of all of the peoples of the past. But in the present we may be held to an even more strict account, as it is said that "where much is given, much is required," and no nation has received as much as we have. In 1852, Daniel Webster made a prophetic statement before the New York Historical Society about these eternal principles on which our national greatness depends; he said, "If we and our posterity shall be true to the Christian religion, and if we and they shall live always in the fear of God and shall respect his commandments, we may have the highest hopes for the future fortunes of our country. It will have no decline and fall, but it will go on prospering and to prosper.

"But if we or our posterity shall reject religious instructions and authority, violate the rules of morality and recklessly destroy the political constitution which holds us together, no man can tell how sudden a catastrophy may overwhelm us, that shall bury all of our glory in profound obscurity. Should that catastrophy happen, let the horrible narrative never be written. Let its fate be that of the lost books of Livy, which no human eye shall ever read, or the missing pleiad of which no man can ever know more than that it is lost and lost forever."

And may God help us to be great Americans, and faithfully carry forward that divine mission which he has assigned to us.

The Badlands

SOMETIME AGO PRESIDENT DAVID O. MCKAY TOLD AN INTERESTING story about an event that took place in South Dakota back in 1933. On July 18 at about three o'clock in the afternoon, the Cornell family discovered that their young son Alfred was missing. Apparently he had wandered away from camp and had disappeared into the famous Badlands. He was bareheaded, barefooted, and dressed only in a pair of coveralls. The Badlands of South Dakota are noted for their dangerous pitfalls, treacherous ravines, rattlesnake pits, and as a lair of other dangerous animals.

When it was discovered that Alfred was missing, the parents began an immediate but unsuccessful search. Later in the evening, neighbors and friends joined in the hunt, which continued throughout the night. Early Wednesday morning, a neighbor rode sixteen miles to spread the alarm about the lost child. Farmers, housewives, sheep men, cowboys, business and professional men, storekeepers, Boy Scouts and Girl Scouts, and officers of the law responded to the call for help. They all gathered at a predetermined place to hear Sheriff Thompson give his instructions. He said:

"We are going out into the Badlands to find and bring back the little Cornell boy. The best way I know of to guarantee success is for all of us to form into one single line and then all advance together. Each man, woman, and child of us will be spaced only a few feet from each other. Every hole and ravine and cave along the way must be thoroughly searched. Every bush must be examined as we go. If our line is not broken, every square yard will be effectively scanned. This is the only way to make sure that nothing will be missed. I don't know how long our search will take, but Alfred Cornell is somewhere out there in the Badlands, and when we turn back, the little fellow will be with us. We can only hope that we shall not be too late. I have appointed some of you as deputies to ride on horseback to make sure that there will be no slip-up, and if I know anything about the people of this state, there will be none. Now let's get going."

The line was formed at 6:30 Thursday evening, and just before dark, the boy was found. His legs and feet were badly bruised and inflamed. His father and mother rushed to him. As the mother clasped him in her arms, she said, "Alfred, how do you feel?" "Fine," answered the plucky little fellow, as he burst into tears. When this long line of human beings saw that the boy had been recovered alive, a great shout of gratitude arose from over 200 throats. By their cooperation they had found that which was lost. They had answered the challenge; they had overcome the obstacles of the Badlands and had saved a life.

Our world is filled with similar or even greater challenges, and all of the badlands are not located in South Dakota. Life is made up of the opposites of good and evil, and all around us life has its badlands. On one hand we have areas and conditions of life that appear to resemble the Garden of Eden, and on the other hand there are danger areas that are infested with serious problems and destructive evils. Our earth has its temples of God, and in most cases the dens of vice are not very far away.

In thinking of various Badlands I remembered the emotions that I felt many years ago while reading Sir Arthur Conan Doyle's *Sherlock Holmes, Story of the Hound of the Baskervilles*. The story has its setting out on the moors of England at night. The dense English fog gave the moors an unworldly and ghost-like atmosphere. The treacherous quicksands and other hidden dangers always made the moors an unsafe place to be, particularly during the nighttime. But Mr. Sherlock Holmes had been employed to try to solve the mystery of a giant unearthly hound that had recently been known to roam the moors at night. The animal had already destroyed several people who, because of some need or their lack of wisdom, had ventured out onto the moors at night. Some people had heard the baying of this unearthly hound, and in the night others had caught fleeting glimpses of this demon dog with phosphorus-appearing jaws and terrifying eyes as he sped through the darkness on some mission of destruction. Some believed that a supernatural hound of hell had been turned loose by an evil power to bring death to certain people who were unable to keep out of his way. Therefore, if we were making up a list of the world's Badlands we might add this section of the English moors.

Some time ago while returning from California we stopped at the graves of the Donner Party in the high Sierra Nevada mountains near Lake Tahoe. In 1846 a company of about one hundred people under the direction of Jacob and George Donner had been making its way to California when it was trapped by an early snow at what has since been called the Donner Pass. The heavy snowfall made it impossible for them or their animals either to move forward or to turn back. Their meager supply of food was soon exhausted. In trying to keep themselves alive, they ate everything they could find, and finally they resorted to eating each other. Almost the entire company perished in the cold and snow before help could reach them. Since then, well-engineered highways, powerful snow-moving machinery, and better methods of transportation have decreased that particular hazard. But this tragic spot is still marked by the graves of many people, and a historic monument points out one of the danger spots of earlyday America.

Two years after the tragedy of the Donner Party, gold was discovered at Sutter's Mill near Sacramento. In the spring of 1849 hundreds of people from eastern parts of the United States put their earthly possessions in whatever kind of conveyance they could get and headed for California, seeking gold. Many loaded themselves down with their prized possessions and the keepsakes that they did not want to leave behind them. But some had not adequately counted on the hazards in crossing what was then the great American desert. As food and water became more scarce and as their animals began to weaken, they began discarding their grand pianos and treasured pieces of furniture, and finally some of their most urgent necessities had to go. Many of the gold-seekers died on the desert. Later, when their bodies were discovered, some were only a short distance from the waterholes that could have saved their lives.

The case of the Forty-Niners is not the only one where people have given up their lives to the badlands of the desert. We have other instances of thirst and madness possessing people's lives because they could not find the waterholes in time. Still others have lost their lives in the badlands of cold and of famine and of disease.

But all of the badlands where our interests have been jeopardized have not been physical in their nature. In fact, the problem is primarily not in the land at all, but in the people. God said to Adam, "Cursed be the ground for thy sake." The earth is in a fallen state because of the acts of the people who do live and have lived upon it. Over four thousand years ago, the Lord commanded Abraham to get out of the badlands of Ur of the Chaldees. He said, "Get thee out of thy country, and from thy kindred, and from thy father's house, unto a land that I will shew thee: And I will . . . bless thee, and make thy name great; and thou shalt be a blessing." (Gen. 12:1-2.)

Abraham had a nephew, by the name of Lot, whom the Lord asked Abraham to take along with him. Finally, Lot was settled with his flocks and herds in the great well-watered Jordan Plain, which was one of these Garden of Eden places. As the Bible says, "It looked like the Garden of the Lord." (Gen. 13:10.) But Lot got a little bit too chummy with his neighbors, the Sodomites, whom the Bible says were exceedingly wicked. Finally, Lot moved into their city with them. When the Lord decided that because of their wickedness the cities of Sodom and Gomorrah must be destroyed, he sent two angels to rescue Lot and his family, and they barely got them out of town in time. The Bible says, "Then the Lord rained upon Sodom and upon Gomorrah brimstone and fire from . . . heaven; And he overthrew those cities, and all the plain, . . . and that which grew upon the ground." (Gen. 19:24-25.)

As a substitute for the idea of badlands, the Lord has often used the word "Babylon." This is a term to designate those areas where conditions are not conducive to the spiritual welfare of people. In many places throughout scripture the Lord makes such statements as "Go ye out of Babylon," "Flee from Babylon," "I will not spare any that remain in Babylon." (D&C 64:24.) In fact, the promised destruction that hangs over the present world if we do not repent makes what has happened in other badlands seem like a summer picnic in comparison.

In teaching about the time just prior to his second coming, Jesus foretold that many would reject the teaching of the gospel, and he said, "Verily I say unto you, It shall be more tolerable for the land of Sodom and Gomorrah in the day of judgment, than for that city." (Matt. 10:15.) Our primary present-day concern seems to center around the badlands of the mind, the badlands of the personality, and the badlands of the spirit.

Our Pilgrim forefathers came to this continent seeking God and righteousness where they could enjoy religious liberty. But in this enjoyment many have become entangled in the dreadful quagmire of evil. Ten million Americans are now struggling in the quicksands of alcoholism; and it seems that the more we struggle with our problem, the deeper we sink into its mire. There are ten million more individuals who are already wading out toward this awful death pit and may soon be in beyond their depth. The cancerous deaths of some of our nicotine addicts are far more painful than any of those who had their throats torn open by the Hound of the Baskervilles. Because of our proneness to do evil and our willingness to forget

God, a thick fog of spiritual darkness more bewildering and confusing than any that covered the English moors often settles over our minds, making it impossible for us to tell good from evil. Then, when we become as "blind leading the blind," we all fall into the ditch together. Wherever we go we hear evidences of the awful scourges of profanity, dishonesty, and disbelief that desolate our land.

The dangers from high mountain passes and dens of rattlesnakes do not presently cause us serious concern. But as in the days of Adam, our own evil is still bringing a curse upon our land, making it a less profitable place to live.

After World War I, the youth of America and the western world were called the "Lost Generation." They had been caught in the maelstrom of the war and its jazz era aftermath, until they had lost their sense of direction and the meaning and purpose of their lives. With our present-day signboards and highway markers, we are not presently in great danger of being physically lost, and we may feel that the parable of the lost sheep doesn't seem to fit us any more either. With our good educations and high standards of living, we seem so capable and self-sufficient—we think we know our way around. And yet there is an attitude in the air that prompted Jesus himself to compare us with those who lived in the days of Noah. The people of Sodom and Gomorrah didn't understand this story about the badlands until the fire and brimstone was pouring down upon them. Even with our perfectly marked and brilliantly lighted highways we may still get lost if we lose our sense of gratitude and appreciation. Our love of material things is still a serious rival to our love of God. The shadows of the marketplace may still darken our path as much as they did the contemporaries of Jesus. There is still serious danger when we wander in the badlands of our own sins.

We need to join hands in righteousness to protect ourselves against the dangers that lie at every turn. The reason the little Cornell boy was saved was because someone was afraid. The reason that the people of Sodom and Gomorrah were lost was because they were unafraid and even unaware of their own danger.

There is an interesting Hebrew word called "iniquity" that we ought to be more afraid of. Basically it means perversion. It means that one is twisted or crooked in his thinking. We are iniquitous when we are too content with our own assumed competence; when we indulge in any degree of iniquity, we run the risk of losing our souls in some badlands of our own making. President James A. Garfield made a certain statement so frequently that it came to be regarded as his personal motto. He said, "There are many things that I am afraid of. One is, I am afraid to do an evil thing." And on the other hand, Solomon said, "Fear God, and keep his commandments, for this is the whole duty of man." God has commanded us to stay away from the badlands. No one has ever been bitten by a rattlesnake who didn't first get too close to it. God will bless our lives if we join hands in righteousness and make certain that we do not break the line.

Beauty, God's Mark of Virtue

ONE OF THE PROBLEMS THAT BOTHERS OUR PRESENT-DAY WORLD is the letdown in those soul qualities that manifest themselves in an inferior personal appearance and contribute to a worsened behavior. Our civilization has successfully survived the stone age, the iron age, and the scientific age, but certain important present-day values seem to be threatened by what might be called the "age of the Beatles," or the "age of the Nothings," or the "age of the unclean and the irreverent." Many people were upset when one of the Beatles gave it as his opinion that members of his group were more popular than Jesus Christ. But the fact that certain people are popular at all may be a cause for some serious concern. Queer dress, unsightly dirt, uncut hair, and other forms of ugliness in one's personal appearance may be signs of things that we should try harder to avoid.

Some people always seem to want to dress up as someone else. In the past, masquerade balls have been popular. But it seems it would be more profitable to take some noble role rather than play the part of a clown or a ne'er-do-well. We feel a sense of gain when we remember the fairy godmother who lifted Cinderella out of the dirt and drudgery and sent her to the ball dressed as a beautiful delightful princess. But considerable damage can be done when we reverse this upward trend and send ourselves to the ball of life masquerading as beatniks or sloppy Joes. Apparently many girls and boys think it is smart or that it is an effective technique for their rebellion to dress themselves in cut-off shorts, patterned after some hillbillies from the comic strip. The name given to one of these funny strip idols is Moonbeam McSwine, whose chief associations are with pigs. In trying to outdo their hillbilly models, some of our young people sew artificial patches on their clothing to give them the most dilapidated, unkempt appearance possible. But this is also a technique for poisoning their own drinking water, so to speak. Hats largely went out of style sometime ago, but now neckties, shoes, and even shirts seem to be following suit.

Recently a printed program outlining a three-day religious convention for young people specified in two places that everyone was expected to come fully dressed in proper clothing. They did not want the influence of this convention spoiled by improper dress. It is likely that a letdown in personal appearance has far more than physical significance. When ugliness gets its roots into one part of our lives, it may soon spread to every other part. And it is not far from a sloppy personal appearance to a sloppy personal attitude and an inferior personal performance. Every ambitious salesman needs to know the importance of being clean and properly dressed. A displeasing personal appearance will not only adversely influence the prospect, but it also tends to destroy the salesman's morale as well. In many cases whole groups of people are being drawn downward by their own self-created environment, and so you can frequently tell one's mental and moral condition by his personal appearance. A great culture once flourished upon this western continent; but after the fall of their civilization had taken place, Columbus found them as a group of near-naked semi-savages, with rolls of tobacco leaves burning in their mouths.

Our abandonment of neckties, shoes, shirts and the pride formerly shown in our personal appearance may indicate that we are again approaching the bottom part of our civilization's cycle.

Recently a marriage counselor told of trying to save a marriage in which a sloppy wife, with uncombed hair and an unkept person, insisted in going around in dirty slacks without shoes or stockings. Her physical appearance indicated an undesirable social and marital state. Anyone desiring to give their own marriage a boost, or help their business to prosper, or cause an upsurge in their general success, should give some thought to keeping himself clean, appropriately dressed and in good personal condition. Or if someone desires to have the spirit of the Sabbath day, he should take a bath, have his hair cut, and put on his best clothes. Every human being operates as a unit. The feelings and attitudes that are in control in one department may soon carry over into the others. Aristotle summed up this situation by saying that a good physical appearance was better than all of the letters of recommendation in the world.

Good actors live the spirit of the parts they play, and their faces, minds and clothing are made up accordingly. Sometime ago an interesting article appeared in the paper in which it was reported that the man who had been taking the part of Judas in the famous Oberammergau Passion play had just committed suicide. The paper also noted that this was the *third* Judas who had committed suicide. Because Judas played an ugly part, it cost him his life. We should also be particularly careful that there is an adequate amount of beauty in that part in life that we select for ourselves to play. If we dress like Moonbeam McSwine and live with the fleas, our spirits will tend to arrange themselves accordingly. The boy who plays at being a bank-robber will be a different kind of person than the boy who plays at being a patriot. And the young people who get great satisfaction in playing the role of beatniks or deadbeats or tramps or scarecrows or hell's angels may someday find themselves at some undesirable destination, as our subconscious minds take us seriously and answer our prayers accordingly.

It is significant that this deterioration in our dress should correspond in time with the increase in hoodlumism, vandalism, educational dropouts, and mental distortions. When the government undertakes to build an effective army, great stress is placed upon the soldiers' dress. The government puts all of its recruits in uniform. Then it insists on high standards of appearance and requires that each soldier must stand inspection every day, to see if his shoes are shined, his uniform is pressed, and that all parts of his person, his attitude, and his equipment are in first-class order. A first-class soldier with a dirty rifle, a negative attitude, and a sloppy uniform is a contradiction, as every soldier is made up in one piece, and it is impossible to put him up in several different personality packages. It was recently reported that a check had been made on several of these beatnik young men who had been taken into the army. When they were given haircuts, uniforms, and baths, and when some of the other symbols of their rebellion were removed, they began responding in a normal way again.

Washington Irving said, "It is the divinity within, that makes the divinity without." But this important law works in both directions. If we patterned the soldier's uniform and his training after some ludicrous funny-paper hillbillies and made the army look as ridiculous and dirty as possible, we would probably not develop a very strong fighting force. But every individual, both old and young, should be concerned about getting more beauty and more dignity into his personal life. The Lord probably had this idea in mind when, in trying to revive ancient Israel from the depression and misery of their captivity, he said to them, "Awake, awake; put on thy strength, O Zion; put on thy beautiful garments, O Jerusalem, the holy city: for henceforth there shall no more come into thee the uncircumcised and the unclean." (Isa. 52:1.)

The poet was also preaching the need of being well dressed inside and outside when he said:

If thou of fortune art bereft,
And if thou hast but two leaves left to thee,
Sell one and with the dole
Buy hyacinths to feed the soul.

Someone added to this philosophy by saying that if he found himself in a strange city hungry and nearly broke, he would spend his money for a shoeshine. To add beauty to one's life and to develop a hunger for an uplifting part to play in life can work wonders in anyone's success.

The dictionary gives two major conceptions of beauty; one is found primarily in the object itself. Beauty always excites a sense of pleasure and delight. It appeals to and stimulates the aesthetic tastes and instincts. The second result of beauty is in the uplifting effect it produces in others. Schlegel said, "There is no more potent antidote to a low sensuality than the adoration of beauty." Aristotle said, "Beauty purifies the thoughts, as suffering purifies the passions." Bancroft said that "beauty is the sensible image of the infinite. Like truth and justice, beauty lies within us. Like virtue and the moral law, beauty is the companion of the soul."

It is an interesting fact that God is the author and chief patron of beauty. This earth itself is a place of boundless beauty and endless fascination. You get a feeling of the infinite when you get the glory of the sunrise in your mind and the calm peace of the sunset into your heart. God painted the sky and the earth with beauty. Think of the inconceivable variety, color, and design in the flowers. God dresses his creations in beauty, and who can imagine the Creator himself as having a distorted personality or dressed in slovenly, unattractive attire?

Although God has made his creations beautiful, yet he has placed the greatest of all of the fountains of beauty within the human heart itself. Every generous thought or generous deed is a thing of beauty, a great ambition; an invigorating faith is a joy to behold. Homer said that beauty was a glorious gift of nature, and Ovid said that it was a favor bestowed by the gods. When one's soul is inspired, or when he is gracious, kind, generous, and helpful, his countenance lights up, and his features take on a more radiant attractiveness. In his prayer, Socrates said, "Make me beautiful within." We make ourselves beautiful by holding in our minds and hearts beautifying thoughts. We have all seen plain people who have become beautiful by the workings of a radiant spirituality. A godly spirit will make the plainest body beautiful. Great mental and spiritual qualities transform our bodies into their likeness. And this great "law of sympathy" also works in both directions.

Shaftesbury says, "The most natural beauty in the world is honesty and moral truth. For all beauty is truth. True features make the beauty of the face, true proportions the beauty of architecture, true measures the beauty of harmony and music. By having something noble to do and something worthwhile to live for gives expression and symmetry to the body and greatly expands the capacity of the soul."

On the other hand, when people deal in brutality, vulgarity, and crime, it is not long before the ugliness and unhappiness become visible on the face. Emerson said that "beauty is the mark that God sets on virtue." Tuckerman said, "The soul by an instinct stronger than reason always associates beauty with truth."

It is only natural that heaven, the home of goodness, should be the place of the greatest beauty and happiness. In trying to describe heaven, the Apostle Paul said, "Eye hath not seen, nor ear heard, neither hath it entered into the heart of man the things that God hath prepared for them that love him." There is a hymn entitled "Beautiful Zion, Built Above," which gives us the spirit of heaven as it is described in the scriptures. We sing:

> Beautiful Zion, built above;
> Beautiful City that I love;
> Beautiful gates of pearly white:
> Beautiful temple—God its light;
> He who was slain on Calvary,
> Opens those pearly gates to me.

> Zion, Zion, lovely Zion,
> Beautiful Zion,
> Zion, city of our God!

> Beautiful heaven, where all is light;
> Beautiful angels clothed in white;
> Beautiful strains that never tire;
> Beautiful harps thro' all the choir;
> There shall I join the chorus sweet
> Worshipping at the Savior's feet.

Beautiful crowns on every brow;
Beautiful palms the conquerors show;
Beautiful robes the ransomed wear;
Beautiful all who enter there;
Thither I press with eager feet—
There shall my rest be long and sweet.

Certainly we would not want to enter heaven in the uniform of a beatnik.

We are told in the scripture that God himself is such a glorious being that no one in his natural mortal state could live in his presence. A modern-day revelation was given in November 1831, in which God said, "For no man has seen God at any time in the flesh, except quickened by the Spirit of God." He said, "Ye are not able to abide the presence of God now, neither the ministering of angels; wherefore, continue in patience until ye are perfected." (D&C 67: 11, 13.) We remember that when Moses came down from visiting with God on the Mount, the glory of God rested upon him to such an extent that the people could not endure his presence. And the scripture says that he put a veil over his face until he had finished speaking. (Exod. 34:33.)

Our own beauty and righteousness will also attract some of God's glory into our lives now, and inasmuch as we are getting ready to visit his celestial presence, we should clean up our minds and hearts and always be dressed in appropriate clean clothing. And our prayer is that God will help us to ennoble our lives with that kind of beauty which is God's mark of virtue.

Blindness

ONE OF THE IMPORTANT TEACHINGS OF JESUS HAD TO DO WITH the fact that so many people have eyes that can't see, we have ears that don't hear, and hearts that fail to understand. In our material as well as in our spiritual affairs, many of life's greatest benefits are lost, merely because we fail to build alertness into our lives with an effective kind of observation and attention. Isaiah described the situation of many of us, when he said, "We wait for light, but behold obscurity; for brightness, but we walk in darkness. We grope for the wall like the blind, and . . . we stumble at noonday as in the night." (Isa. 59:9-10.) But Isaiah was not speaking only of those who are physically blind; we are also susceptible to an unprofitable kind of spiritual and moral blindness. We usually think of physical light as being one of the most worthwhile and interesting of all of God's blessings. It is partly for this reason, that we have made sightseeing one of our most common and pleasant forms of recreation. Over and over again, we admire beautiful landscapes, and sometimes a brilliant sunset can almost take away our breath. We try to preserve the image of other beautiful things by painting them on canvas.

It is interesting to try to imagine what it must have been like when, in the beginning, that brooding, unbroken darkness covered creation. Then, by contrast, we might try to feel the delight arising in our souls when, in that march of eternal progress, God first said, "Let there be light." Suppose that we try to understand what it would mean to have physical darkness fill our personal lives. An unknown blind boy helps to stimulate our appreciation, as he says:

THE BLIND BOY

What is that thing that you call light,
  Which I can ne'er enjoy?
What are the blessings of your sight?
  Please tell a poor blind boy!

You talk of wondrous things you see,
  You say the sun shines bright;
I feel him warm, but how can he
  Make it day or night?

My day or night myself I make,
Whene'er I sleep or play;
And could I ever keep awake,
It would then be always day.

With heavy sighs, I often hear
You mourn my hapless woe;
But with sure patience, I can bear
A loss I ne'er can know.

Then let not what I cannot have,
My cheer of mind destroy;
Whilst thus I sing, I am a king,
Although a poor blind boy.

Unfortunately, we usually don't adequately appreciate our vision until we lose it. John Milton was one of our most famous blind men. In his early years he planned to write a great poem. He said to a friend that he was pluming his wings for a flight. His goal was not set on some easy object like the moon; rather, he said that he desired to put in words some ideas that would reach from heaven to hell. However, Milton never got started on this great project until after he had lost his sight and found himself with no other employment. Then he prayed that inasmuch as the great blessing of physical vision had been denied him, that God would grant him spiritual sight, that he might see and understand the things of God. He said:

So much the rather thou celestial light shine inward,
And the mind with all her powers irradiate.
There plant eyes, all mists from hence purge and disperse,
That I may see and tell of things invisible to mortal sight.

Finally his great literary masterpiece was completed; he called it *Paradise Lost,* and someone has appropriately pointed out that Milton never saw paradise until he lost his eyes. His first wife died; and after he had become totally blind, he married again. He often thought about his wife and wondered what she looked like. One night he saw her in a dream. She was dressed all in white. He thought he had never imagined anyone or anything quite so beautiful, but as he was about to embrace her, he was awakened; then he said, "Day brought back my night." In writing of this experience, he said:

Vested all in white, pure as her mind,
Love's sweetness, goodness in her person shines so clear,
That nothing could have rendered more delight,

But, O, as to embrace me she inclined, I waked,
She fled and day brought back my night.

When Milton was asleep he could see, but when he was awake
he was blind. In the nighttime he had eyes; in the daylight he
he couldn't see. He mourned the great loss of his sight by saying,

Light, the prime work of God in me extinct,
With all her various objects of delight.

The great blessings of wisdom had been completely shut out at this
important entrance of his mind.

Some have wondered what it would be like for one who had
been blind all of his life, to be suddenly granted the gift of sight.
Those who have had clear vision since birth and look on sight as
the most important of the senses might well imagine that a blind
person suddenly given sight would cry out with delight at the new
world of brilliant color, filled with all sorts of interesting objects and
people to which he had just been admitted. But James T. McCay
says that such is not the case. In his book, *The Management of
Time*, he quotes Professor J. Z. Young, an authority on the human
brain, saying, "When the patient opens his eyes for the first time, he
gets little or no enjoyment; indeed, he finds the experience a rather
painful one. He reports only a spinning mass of lights and colors.
He is quite unable to pick out objects by sight, or to recognize what
they are, or to identify them by name. He has no conception of
space with objects in it, although by touch he may know the objects
themselves, as well as their names. One might think it natural that
it would take a little time to learn to recognize things by sight; but,
it doesn't take just a *little* time, it takes a very long time, sometimes, running into years."

"A blind man's brain must be trained in the rules of seeing. We
ourselves may not be conscious that there *are* any such rules, as we
ordinarily think that we see naturally, but actually we have learned
a whole set of seeing rules during our childhood. If any blind man
or anyone else desires to make effective use of his eyes, he must
train his brain not only to recognize objects, but also to understand
their meanings." Professor Young says that this can be done only by
great thoughtfulness and persistence. One week after one man had
begun to see, he was shown an orange; he didn't know what it was.
When asked what its shape was, he said, "Let me touch it and I
will tell you." After touching it, he quickly said that it was an
orange, and that it was round. When shown a triangle, he described

it as round; when the three corners of the triangle were pointed out to him, he said, "Ah yes, I understand now, that one can also *see* how a thing feels."

Some of us who are troubled with spiritual blindness may have even more serious problems. Like the blind boy, we may feel no loss for those things that we do not know, even though they may be very important.

The story is told of one man who was greatly enjoying the marvelous beauty of the earth, the glory of the landscape, the grandeur of the mountains, and the brilliance of the sunset. Then, suddenly, he was startled by hearing on the sidewalk behind him the tap, tap, tap of a blind man as he felt his way with his cane. This seriously disturbed the sightseer's enjoyment. He was depressed because this blind man was missing the beauty that so delighted him. Then he remembered what Jesus had said about those who had eyes but couldn't see. And he wondered to what extent he may be one of these. Then he wrote some lines, in which he said:

> I pitied him in his blindness,
> > But can I boast, I see;
> Perhaps there walks a spirit close by,
> > Who pities me.
>
> Some spirit who hears me tapping
> > That five-sensed cane of mind,
> Amid such unguessed glories,
> > That I am worse than blind!

Blindness usually comes to us in some kind of fraction. In the moral and spiritual areas of our lives, very few people are ever totally blind. More frequently, our vision gets distorted so that we see the wrong things. Mental triangles seem round, and spiritual black spots may look as if they are white, and evil may appear to us to be good. Even the most observing people sometimes develop these mental and spiritual blind spots. The dictionary says that there is a point in the retina where the optic nerve passes through the inner court of the eyeball, which is not sensitive to light, and consequently we get a physical blind spot at that point. The dictionary compares these physical blind spots to those areas where a radio station gets poor reception. Similarly there are some spiritual and mental areas in people where discernment fails, and where understanding and discrimination don't always operate on a sound basis. These blind spots sometimes involve a loss of our greatest abilities and pleasures. Many serious tragedies often develop because we are unable to effectively interpret those moral situations in which we find ourselves. To see something from a distorted or false point of view is frequently more serious than not seeing anything at all. And sometimes we are led astray by an illusion coming from some narrow personal interest.

A very interesting and constructive story was written some time ago by John Godfrey Saxe entitled "The Blind Men and the Elephant." This spectacle of six blind men going to see an elephant was intended to remind us of some of our own experiences and shortcomings. These men of Indostan were wise men from the East. And each saw this strange animal, the elephant, from his own personal point of view. Each responded according to his own limited experience. Each handled his own difference of opinion in a way that is characteristic of most of us. Mr. Saxe says:

It was six men of Indostan
    To learning much inclined,
Who went to see an elephant
    (Though all of them were blind),
That each by observation
    Might satisfy his mind.

The First approached the elephant,
    And, happening to fall
Against his broad and sturdy side,
    At once began to bawl:
"God bless me! but the elephant
    Is nothing but a wall."

The Second, feeling of the tusk,
    Cried: "Ho! what have we here
So very round and smooth and sharp?
    To me 'tis very clear
This wonder of an elephant
    Is very like a spear!"

The Third approached the animal,
    And, happening to take
The squirming trunk within his hands,
    Thus boldly up and spake:
"I see," quoth he, "the elephant
    Is very like a snake!"

The Fourth reached out his eager hand,
    And felt about the knee:
"What most this wondrous beast is like
    Is mighty plain," quoth he;
" 'Tis clear enough the elephant
    Is very like a tree."

The Fifth, who chanced to touch the ear,
    Said: "E'en the blindest man
Can tell what this resembles most;
    Deny the fact who can,
This marvel of an elephant
    Is very like a fan."

The Sixth no sooner had begun
    About the beast to grope,
Than, seizing on the swinging tail
    That fell within his scope,
"I see," quoth he, "the elephant
    Is very like a rope!"

And so these men of Indostan
    Disputed loud and long,
Each in his own opinion
    Exceeding stiff and strong;
Though each was partly in the right,
    And all were in the wrong!

Mr. Saxe has left it for us to see through this odd picture the great world of contending souls in which we live. Each of us is deciding the great questions of life within the narrow limits of that light and truth which he personally possesses. Each of us is loath to accept the equally accurate experience of others. The spender does not always understand the miser; the idler cannot well appreciate the diligence of the hard worker. The brewer and the tavern keeper contend against sobriety and abstinence; the Communist and the free man are continually at sword points. Even those religious denominations with common aims and objectives are often at variance with each other. Men have often burned their fellow men at the stake, in the name of the very God of love that both groups claim to serve. But so frequently we look at life through our own limitations and appetites. We often identify God's will with that particular code which we most desire to believe. And in this simple picture of the contending blind men, we see a model of our own great world in miniature. From the deeper meaning of the picture, this great truth crowds in upon us: that when we fail to get the whole truth, two men may differ from each other and yet both may be perfectly honest.

The best way to see things accurately and clearly is to look at them from God's point of view. And if we are to see accurately, we must keep the obstructions of selfishiness and sin out of our eyes. The blind spots caused by our personal interests, or the distortion brought about by our rationalizing and wishful thinking, can eventually even cause the destruction of our souls. The average man will love God more when he has enough facts to understand him better. And we will also have a more generous appreciation for our fellow-men when we see things in their truest perspective. We might help ourselves toward this condition by letting into our souls a little more of the spirit of that great command given on the first day of creation, wherein God said, "Let there be light."

Born Again

O N ONE OCCASION NICODEMUS, A RICH AND INFLUENTIAL MEMBER of the Sanhedrin, asked Jesus what was required to inherit eternal life. To answer this question effectively was the purpose for which Christ had been born. Jesus said to Nicodemus, "Except a man be born again, he cannot enter into the kingdom of God." Because Nicodemus did not understand, he made further inquiry. Then it was made clear that the Master was not talking about a physical rebirth, but a rebirth that took place in the minds and hearts of people. Jesus required his followers to be baptized in water; then, by a baptism of the spirit, the believers might come forth in a newness of life.

Baptism and the laying on of hands for the bestowal of the Holy Ghost takes place only once. But we may repent, change our ways, and get a renewal of life as often as we desire. Life at its best involves a constant perfecting of attitudes, knowledge, skills and habits, causing a continual upgrading to a higher plane of life. Louise Fletcher Tarkington once said:

> I wish there were some wonderful place
> In the Land of Beginning Again
> Where all our mistakes, and all our heartaches,
> And all of our error and sin
> Could be dropped like a shabby old coat at the door
> And never put on again.

This process of turning our lives upward is probably the greatest opportunity we ever have. New Year's is not the only time to make resolutions, and our lives may be purified and charged with new energy at our own command.

Many years ago Harold Beebe wrote an interesting book entitled *Twice Born Men*. It includes some specific accounts of men who had been born over, and they had been born better the second time. But growth is a gradual process. Neither virtues nor abilities are ever acquired fully developed. But each day should give us some increase. Our lives may begin anew each morning on a higher level of excellence. One day may see the birth of a stronger faith; the next, our courage can be reborn with new power; another day finds us in possession of a more vigorous industry, or some greater devotion becomes alive in us. Jesus said, "Except a man be born of the water and of the spirit, he cannot see the kingdom of God." But these sacred initiatory rites are just the beginning of our journey toward eternal exaltation. Then, as the days come and go, we add line upon line and precept upon precept. It was not given to Jesus nor is it given to us to meet the foe, to fight the battle, and to overcome once and for all in a single encounter. The way of success requires the elimination of some vice today and the planting of some virtue in its place. Then, as our objectives are increased and our ambitions are vitalized, our lives turn upward toward more worthwhile things. Then, as we are born into a richer, happier life, we become new people. We might find great profit in reliving the experiences of some of our great twice-born men.

We remember Saul of Tarsus on that day when he left Jerusalem headed for Damascus. On the way he beheld a heavenly vision, under the weight of which he fell to the earth. Upon the recovery of his strength, he said, "Lord, what wilt thou have me do?" Then, in the light of his greater understanding, he made some New Year's resolutions of his own and Saul of Tarsus became a new man. And he was a much better man after he had been born the second time. Now he had new objectives and new ambitions. He had repented of his sins and had been baptized. He had acquired some new attitudes and new drives. In the process of this important change, he even received the new name of Paul. But he did not stop with these changes. Thereafter, throughout his long life, Paul was constantly renewing himself as well as helping others to be born again. Many years after his experience on the Damascus road, he said to the members of the Church at Ephesus, "Put off . . . the old man, which is corrupt according to the deceitful lusts; And be renewed in the spirit of your mind." He said, "Put on the new man, which after God is created in righteousness and true holiness." (Eph. 4:22-24.)

The old man in us that needs to be put off may be a "man of sin" or "a man of hate," or a man who is idle, dishonest, or unfaithful. We need to be born again with our deformities eliminated and our virtues strengthened. A few new good habits can by themselves make a new man. On one occasion, the Lord asked someone to answer this question. He said, "Will a man rob God?" Then, giving his own answer, he said, "Yet ye have robbed me. But ye say, Wherein have we robbed thee? In tithes and offerings. Ye are cursed with a curse: for ye have robbed me, even this whole nation." (Mal. 3:8-9.) If the people were robbing God, then, by not paying their tithing, and if we are doing the same thing now, then we are robbing God now, and we need to be born again. When we lay off our disobedience, our dishonesty, and our love of evil, and stop trifling with God, we will come out of our new birth feeling like real Christians. The great principle of repentance, which is such an important part of a new birth, is something far more than merely feeling sorry for our mistakes. It also includes an aggressive attitude of elimination. Then we put off the old man and dress ourselves in more righteous clothing. When the crowing of the cock reminded Peter of his triple sin of denial, he did not need to be baptized again. First he "went out and wept bitterly," and then he made up his mind to make a new beginning. After the weak, wavering Peter had been reborn enough times, he became Cephas, the rock, the stalwart, the great Christian disciple and chief of the apostles.

The other day a man came in to talk about an occupational problem. In the past he had been a good man, but someone had persuaded him to try to make a living selling a shoddy, second-grade product. Because of his former reputation for honesty, his friends who now trusted him were betrayed. Some people sin by denying God, but he had sinned by denying his own honor. And in a hurry he needed to get himself born again with a better company, a superior product, a repairing of the injury, and a greater sense of trusteeship. When we sponsor any philosophy or any merchandise, we should be prepared to give to our clients our personal guarantee of honor based on some sound arithmetic and good judgment, that what we recommend is of the highest quality and that we are working in their interests.

Christ sponsored no Christianity that was second-rate in quality, there should be no second-grade Christians among us either on Sundays or on Wednesdays. The philosophy of "let the buyer beware" is not a Christian doctrine, nor can it be practiced by any honest men. God has accused those who were not paying their tithing of robbing him, but those who use personal friendships or religious influence or the ignorance of the client to promote inferior goods and ideas are not only robbing their fellowmen, but they are also robbing themselves.

Mohandas K. Gandhi once said that there were 999 men who believed in honesty for every honest man. It would be difficult to find anyone who did not "believe in honesty," and yet we remember Diogenes, who went around ancient Athens with a lighted lantern in the middle of the daytime trying to find just one honest man.

Those who only "believe" in honesty are not honest. They must also practice it. Alexander Pope said, "An honest man is the noblest work of God." What a thrilling challenge for a dishonest man to be born again, providing that this time he could be born honest. For only as we fashion ourselves in the mold of honesty can we prevent a distortion of that great moral image in which we were created.

While we are being born over, we should make sure that we are born with a little more vision, a little more purpose, and a little more self-control. However, with us it sometimes requires, as it did Paul, a kind of shock treatment to bring us to our senses. The prodigal son needed and received a pretty good jar while in the swine pastures of the far country. Some people only make up their minds to start over after they have landed in a hospital or a jail or been overcome by some disaster. Fortunate are they who have this vitalizing experience of a new birth as early in life as possible. Abraham Lincoln was born again as he absorbed the great Bible ideals and attitudes before the open fire. It was his better self that made him contend with the boys planning to build a fire on the back of the mud turtle. Lincoln once interrupted his journey to put a baby robin back into its nest. These things may sometimes sound trivial, but they are the keys of character. But, in addition, the greatest events often swing on little hinges.

I once knew a ten-year-old boy who playfully threw an apple at a robin. His aim was better than he had anticipated, and the bird was killed. This experience had a revolutionary effect upon the entire balance of his life, as a new concern for God's creatures was born in him.

Many years ago, for a grade school play, we were required to memorize some lines that I have always remembered. I don't know who the author was, but the experience that prompted him to write these lines caused at least one part of his feelings to be born again. He said:

> I used to kill birds in my boyhood—
> Bluebirds and robins and wrens;
> I hunted them up in the mountains,
> I hunted them down in the glens.
>
> I never once thought it was sinful—
> I did it only for fun.
> I had rare sport in the forest
> With the poor little birds and my gun.

But one beautiful day in the springtime
I spied a brown bird in the tree,
Merrily singing and chirping,
Happy as a bird could be.

I raised my gun; in a twinkle
I fired; my aim was too true—
For a moment the little thing fluttered,
Then off to the bushes it flew.

I followed quickly and softly;
And there to my sorrow I found,
There close by a nest full of young ones,
The old bird was dead on the ground.

I picked up the bird in my anguish;
I stroked the wee motherly thing
That would never more feed her dear loved ones
Nor dart through the air on swift wing.

I judged from the vow of that moment,
When my heart with such anguish was stirred,
That never again in my lifetime
Would I kill a poor innocent bird.

One of our biggest problems is that while we all may have many wonderful experiences and think many good things, yet they sometimes don't go deep enough into our machinery to bring changes about in our lives. After King Agrippa had listened to a testimony from his prisoner Paul, the great Christian missionary, he said to Paul, "Almost thou persuadest me to be a Christian." Then Paul said, "Would God that not only thou, but all those who hear me this day were both almost and altogether such as I am, except these bonds." The answer of the great King Agrippa indicated that he didn't quite have what it took to be born again. He wasn't quite ready to make a clean start on a new page. But so many of us are like that. Many people are "almost" ready to do something, but not quite. We make New Year's resolutions without quite enough power to get them into operation. We want to be honest, but it never quite gets to be convenient. We allow our ignorance, indifference, and procrastination to stand in our way and prevent this thrilling experience of a second birth.

In Walter Malone's poem entitled *Opportunity*, he encourages us with ideas of the new birth possibilities that are always before us. He said:

They do me wrong who say I come no more
When once I knock and fail to find you in,
For every day I stand outside your door
And bid you wake, and rise to fight and win.

Wail not for precious changes passed away,
Weep not for golden ages on the wane!
Each night I burn the records of the day;
At sunrise every soul is born again.

Laugh like a boy at splendors that have sped,
To vanished joys be blind and deaf and dumb;
My judgments seal the dead past with its dead,
But never bind a moment yet to come.

Tho' deep in mire, wring not your hands and weep;
I lend my arm to all who say, "I can!"
No shamefaced outcase ever sank so deep
But yet might rise and be again a man.

Dost thou behold thy lost youth all aghast?
Dost reel from righteous retribution's blow?
Then turn from blotted archives of the past
And find the future's pages white as snow.

Art thou a mourner? Rouse thee from thy spell;
Art thou a sinner? Sins may be forgiven;
Each morning gives thee wings to flee from hell,
Each night a star to guide thy feet to Heaven.

God has not only given us a star to guide us to heaven, but he
has also given us a great set of gospel principles to make our success certain. And while the most valuable and necessary experience
in life is to be born, it is probable that coming next on our list is
the experience of being "born again." We can be born with our
sins washed away, born with our spirits enriched and our ambitions
strengthened. We can be born with enough faith and industry to
become like God. To be born again means that we are ready for
the best of eternal life to be born in us.

Collectors

THE MOST INTERESTING OF ALL SUBJECTS FOR STUDY, CONTEMPLA-
tion, and improvement is ourselves. And yet we probably
know less about ourselves than any other thing. If someone were to
ask us questions about science, invention, or history, we could answer
them, but if they asked us to write our an analysis of ourselves and
tell them about our mind and soul qualities, we may not give very
good answers. For example, why is it that we do as we do, when
we believe as we believe? We don't know very much about our
ante-mortal past, or how much, if any, of it has carried over into our
present. One of the most important things to be remembered about
ourselves is that we are children of God, formed in his image, and
endowed with a set of his attributes. We should also keep in mind
that we are heirs to God's glory, and through a divine growth process
the obedient offspring of God may hope to eventually become like
the parent. To help us realize our fullest potentialities, we are born
into this life with certain natural tendencies, and one of the most
meaningful of these is what someone has called the "collecting
instinct." Without any special instructions or education, we all start
out in life as collectors.

To demonstrate this natural law, suppose that you turn any small
boy upside down and shake him a little bit. You will probably find
that a whole collection of colored rocks and broken glass, marbles,
chalk, pieces of string, and an occasional chicken foot will drop out
of his pockets. Then if you set a detective on his trail, you will also
discover some pack rat characteristics as he leads you to a cache of
valuables that he has stashed away without any particular reason
for doing so being known to him. As this boy becomes older, he
will upgrade the quality of his collection. He will possibly get possession of a dog, a gun, and a fishing pole. If the subject of your
study happens to be a girl, you will find that her collection includes
dolls, dishes, handkerchiefs, and dresses. She will also have some
hope chests filled with all kinds of accumulated treasures.

These collecting abilities all seem to be in the human package
as standard equipment at birth. Inasmuch as these tendencies are
presents from the Creator, we assume that they were meant to serve

a good purpose, and that he intended that they should be developed by us and directed into the most productive channels. As these fundamental abilities are being enlarged, we begin collecting incomes, savings accounts, real estate, life insurance policies, and stocks and bonds. But a very fundamental part of this acquisitive instinct is directed toward the collecting of knowledge, abilities, virtues, and skills. We collect friends and memories. Jesus was trying to stimulate our collecting activities in the right direction when he said, "Seek ye first the kingdom of God and his righteousness, and all of these things shall be added unto you." The kingdom of God is sometimes thought of as "a place" or "an organization," but it has also been referred to as "a condition." Jesus said to one group of people, "the kingdom of God is within you." There is a note in the King James version that says that he meant "the kingdom of God is among you," and that may be what he did mean. But it may also be true that the kingdom of God is within you. Certainly faith, courage, and determination can only exist inside of people. In fact, it doesn't really matter very much what is ahead of you or what is behind you, because all of the most important things are inside of you. When Jesus mentioned "God's righteousness," he was thinking of something that should get inside of us. For before any of us can get into the kingdom of God, it is necessary for the kingdom of God to get into us.

Someone once said that it doesn't help a person very much to go through college unless the college goes through him. One might be baptized into the Church every twenty minutes with little avail unless he gets the Church into him. Jesus mentioned "talents" and "things," and we should remember that "things" always follow "talents." If we can collect enough "talents," the "things" will come as a natural consequence. That is, when we have collected an effective combination of education, industry, attitudes, skills, and habits we are pretty well on our way to any projected success. It is very important that a good collector should also be a wise discriminator. Otherwise we may someday discover that we have an assortment of such wrong things as headaches, distraught nerves, weak wills, vain regrets, bad reputations, tobacco breaths, and cancerous lungs. Bad men are most easily distinguished from good men by the kind of habits that they have stored away in their personalities. Even the finest collecting instinct may backfire and become a liability unless the person possessing it quickly discards those things that are undesirable. A fisherman catches all kinds of fish in his net, and he may occasionally get a turtle or an octopus; or, to change the figure, we might compare our success to success in the mining industry. Before ore has value it must be run through the refinery. A good smelting operation is one that retains the gold and discards the dross.

It is a general rule in life, and in mining that no ore comes pure. And the place of discrimination and good judgment in life is to help us to separate the good from the bad. Then we can take the gold into our life's treasury and throw the dross away. For this same purpose farmers have combined harvesters to separate the chaff from the wheat. The chaff is thrown away and the wheat is put in the bin. A good conscience and a sound reasoning ability are life's threshing machines. When God created us as he did, it was his thought that as we moved through our world of opposites where good and evil were growing side by side, we should save the wheat but discard the tares to be burned. In agriculture or in life, we are not likely to find many fields where some tares are not inclined to grow among the wheat. Throughout the universe there are disease and health, right and wrong, success and failure, growing side by side, and over all God has erected a sign saying, "Thou mayest choose for thyself." This collecting instinct with its powerful urge to acquire is indispensable to success, but it is just as necessary that we also develop our ability to discard.

A good fisherman may throw back everything that he doesn't want. It is not necessary for a miner to go through life burdened down with the dross. A farmer is not required to put the chaff in the bin; and one of the greatest privileges of life is that we may throw back anything that would bring discord or ugliness to our lives, and yet we may collect the good things to our heart's content. It is a great idea to collect stamps, autographs, butterflies, silverware, tapestries, or paintings. It is wonderful to own land, build barns, develop factories, and store up goods. We may select the occupation offering us the highest challenge, the finest opportunity for service, and the greatest reward of money in the bank. Then what a thrilling idea that in addition we can acquire the most satisfying collection of abilities, virtues, character, qualities, and personality traits. We also have the inestimable privilege of selecting a life's companion and collecting a family of capable, righteous children who in turn are good collectors. Because the primary compensations of our lives depend upon our skills as collectors, we should therefore decide as early in life as possible what it is that we want to collect. Suppose, therefore, that we make up our own individual collection list.

I suppose that in a place of high priority we would have a notation to collect and hoard as much good health as possible. It is reported that John D. Rockefeller, the world's first billionaire, offered to give his chauffeur half of his wealth if the chauffeur would exchange stomachs with him. If a good stomach is worth a half a billion dollars, what would a sound heart, a clean mind, a good pair of lungs, a stable nervous system, and a righteous soul be worth?

In February 1833, the Lord gave to the Prophet Joseph Smith a revelation that is recorded in the eighty-ninth section of the Doctrine and Covenants. The Lord said that tobacco, liquor, tea, coffee, and some other things were not good for people, and that it is pleasing to God when his children abstain from using them. Just think how many billion-dollar lungs, how many billion-dollar hearts, how many billion-dollar minds, and how many billion-dollar nervous systems could be saved if we had the good judgment to obey God and discard all of our evils. Some of the most important parts of our religion are the "thou shalt not's" of the Ten Commandments. For when our minds are definitely settled about those things that we *don't* want, then we can effectively begin to collect those things that we do want. Only when we have definitely decided that we don't want ignorance are we in the best condition to obtain a good education. The first thing that Adam and Eve were asked to decide after they were placed in the Garden of Eden was whether or not they would eat the fruit of the tree of knowledge of good and evil. After they had eaten, God said, "Behold, the man is now become as one of us, to know good and evil." And I would like to point out in passing that the right kind of knowledge still tends to have that effect upon people. It still tends to make man become as God. In addition to our many opportunities in formal education, we also have a limitless number of good books filled with a wealth of wisdom and inspiration. God has not only honored us with the privilege of choosing for ourselves, but he has arranged a vast inventory of knowledge from which selection may be made. And we may collect to our heart's content. If the chauffeur's stomach was worth a half a billion dollars to John D. Rockefeller, how much would Abraham Lincoln's honesty be worth to us? But without any expense we can include in our collection of virtues the integrity of Mohandas Gandhi, the determination of Winston Churchill, the courage of Joan of Arc, the manhood of George Washington, the wisdom of Ralph Waldo Emerson, the fairness of Benjamin Franklin, the industry of Thomas A. Edison, and the religion of Jesus Christ. We can collect a reverent spirituality, a thankful heart, a loyal devotion to right, and effective ability to do good, a sound understanding of the gospel, and a deep appreciation of the finest things in life. What an exciting possibility that we may also increase the value of our collection with a virtuous heart, an enthusiastic attitude, a cheerful personality, a willingness to serve, and a set of the finest habits!

Some of our material things are subject to the law of diminishing returns. An increase in financial wealth sometimes has a decreasing ability to serve our needs and make us happy. For example, John D. Rockefeller may not have been ten times more happy with ten billion dollars than I would be with one billion. Riches are not always what they seem to be to those who don't have them. Emerson once said, "I would that everyone was rich that he might know the worthlessness of riches."

It is unwise to devote too much time or energy to something that does not bring a corresponding return. Jesus gave us an idea for a vastly increasing rate of return when he suggested laying up for ourselves treasures in heaven. Treasures in heaven have many advantages. They are more satisfying and a lot more permanent. William James once said that the greatest use of life is to spend it for something that outlasts it. The real value in collecting is to collect those treasures that will last forever. In this connection it is interesting to remember that poverty and riches alike are largely of the spirit. These last forever. Someone pointed out one of the shortcomings of earthly riches by saying, "You can't take them with you." And someone else has added that with taxes as they are, you can't even keep them while you are here.

Another weakness of earthly riches is that they may not be negotiable in that realm where we are going to spend our eternal lives. Suppose, therefore, that we follow this more profitable suggestion of laying up treasures in heaven and center our attention upon the religion of Jesus and his program for our eternal progression. The greatest of all of our human concepts is the immortality of the personality and the eternal glory of the human soul. Throughout eternity you will be yourself and I will be myself, with quickened senses, amplified powers of perception, and vastly increased capacity for reason, understanding, love, and happiness, all of which we may develop now. Our machines wear out, our barns fall down, and our substance goes back to the dust, but our finest collection of personal qualities will have eternal life. The wonders of personality are so unlimited that we even think of God himself in terms of them.

Real wealth is not so much what we have as what we are. We don't work merely to acquire, but to become. Success in life isn't just what you can get out of it, but it is what you can become by it. Jesus said, "He that hath eternal life is rich." Stamps, butterflies, stocks, mortgages, and real estate may sometime lose their value, but our treasures in heaven will continue to provide us with success and happiness forever, and I pray that God will help us to make the most of our wonderful collector's instinct.

Commandments

SOMETIME AGO IN NEW ZEALAND WE ATTENDED THE TRADITIONAL Maori celebration that is sometimes held to welcome visitors. One of their braves did an elaborate and significant war dance before the advancing strangers. As this warrior made his nearest approach to the visitors, he issued a challenge by dropping a tree twig on the ground in front of them. If the newcomers picked up the twig, it signified that they came in peace and desired to be friends. However, if they left the branch lying on the ground, it indicated that they were unfriendly and came as enemies. Among the most important of all virtues to the Maori are kindness and friendship. One may have many other faults and weaknesses, but if he is kind and sincerely desires the happiness of others, then many of his other sins may be forgiven. Of course, kindness and friendship are universally held in very high esteem. These great, warm, friendly emotions are also badly needed to promote the happiness and peace needed in our world. In all of our human relations it is very important that we understand the motives that actuate those with whom we associate.

Even when a child is receiving a parental spanking, it makes a great difference what motivation is prompting the parent. Spite, hate, or revenge can produce quite a different result than if the child understands that the parent believes that he is acting in the child's best interests. One old puritan parent is quoted as saying to his son before the licking began, "It is not with any illwill I bear thee, but for the good of thy soul."

However, we sometimes do each other great harm when we leave the twigs representing our love lying on the ground so that our friends think that we come as enemies. Our employers, parents, friends, the government, the church, and even God are sometimes called upon to take some disciplinary action or present some message when there is a risk of causing hurt feelings or doing some kind of soul damage. In fact, it is sometimes surprisingly difficult to distinguish between our friends and our enemies. For example, it is traditional that we acquire our worst bad habits from our best friends. From the top of Mount Sinai God said that the sins of the fathers would be visited upon the children. Because of the power of an evil example we might understand what Jesus meant when he said that "a man's foes shall be they of his own household."

On the other hand, Jesus taught kindness; he said that we should love our enemies. There is more than one reason why we should do this. To love our enemies is one way to keep the destructive emotion of hate out of our hearts. Another reason is that it is usually our enemies who provide our lives with challenges and keep us awake and on our toes. There is another good reason why we should love our enemies, and that is that we made them ourselves. Sometimes people live in doubt as to whether or not God himself is our friend. Occasionally *he* also has some parental duties where he must choose between using the rod or spoiling the child. However, we frequently do ourselves great harm when we imagine that God comes to us as an enemy.

One of the important parts of Christian religion comes under the heading of "commandments." And frequently when someone gives commands they sound like enemies. Ordinarily we don't like anyone who scolds us or appears to be ordering us around. And when we read the scriptural accounts of some of the things that the ancient prophets said to the people who were getting off the track, we may be impressed that they were being a little bit rough. Of course, this frank direct language has several important advantages. One is that it is so definite and clear that everyone knows exactly what is meant. Jesus himself was a very kind, gentle person, and yet he said some things to the Pharisees and others that were not couched in the most gentle language. For this reason some people have taken sides with the Pharisees.

Sometime ago a prominent minister declared that in his opinion the Ten Commandments no longer served as an effective basis for our religious teaching. His criticism was that they are negative in attitude, dictatorial in spirit, and gave people the idea that the church was some kind of a wet blanket. He said he felt that these harsh "Thou Shalt Not's" were not in good taste in our day. He didn't say whether or not he believed that such things as dishonesty, immorality, and false religions mentioned in the commandments were in good taste, but he did feel that the commandments themselves were outmoded and no longer useful.

Another religious leader said that the tone of these stern "Thou Shalt Not's" was much too harsh for our present-day sensitivities. He suggested that the spirit of the Ten Commandments should be modified and toned down a little bit, and instead of using the word "command," we might substitute some softer word such as "advise" or "suggest" or "recommend."

This may be what we are actually doing with our own children. There is a psychology that says that we should not offend them with any hard distinctions between right and wrong. Many people have felt that our moral standards for our children and also for ourselves are a little too harsh and are in some need of revision. In fact, for some time we have actually been making some rather radical revisions. Presently we are in the process of adopting the philosophy of "the new morality." In many cases this actually means *immorality* or no morality at all. But as these revisions are being made downward, we are multiplying our divorces, producing a bumper crop of juvenile delinquents, and reaping a harvest of mental, spiritual, and veneral diseases. Because some have decided that feelings of guilt are harmful to the personality, they are contending that standards should be made low enough that those with bad habits will not be made to feel uncomfortable. Some people who have conflicts with their conscience may feel that God is their enemy, and that the new morality is their friend and the one who approaches with good intentions. However, merely because we can smother our conscience and reject God as our enemy does not prove that we are right or that these kinds of activities are in our own best interests.

There is another softening-up process going on in our society under the title of "progressive education." We are sometimes afraid to point out a student's errors or let him know exactly where he stands for fear of upsetting him or causing him to get discouraged. In his great book *The Return to Religion*, Dr. Henry C. Link makes a contrast between his own religious home training and that of his children, who were allowed to choose for themselves. Dr. Link says, "We were taught that certain things were right or wrong because God said so. But we could only tell our children that things were right or wrong because we said so." This does not build the same kind of personality strength. Without the pressures of a religious training in actual Christian doctrines, children do not acquire the same basic moral values in life that the Christian-trained parent accepts automatically, even though he no longer credits the divine origin or the teaching itself. The parents who destroy the authority of God in the minds of their children set themselves an impossible task, as they themselves must then take over the responsibility.

Then, as the child grows older, he comes more and more under the influence of the conflicting authority of society, the school, the neighbors, the gang, and the community. When the child finds that his own parents are vacillating, uncertain, and frequently in error, his defenses are destroyed, and he has little left to cling to or to believe in. It is pretty difficult for any parent or anyone else to replace God as an authority on right and wrong. We need some fixed point to work from, some immovable north star by which we can take our directions, and God provides the only fixed truth and certain point of reference that there is in the universe. Our human authorities who speak on their own responsibility and out of their own limited judgment and experience are always changing their minds. In telling us how they view various subjects, they often say, "This is *my* view," or "It seems to *me* to be thus and so." A psychiatrist says, "*We* are coming to believe," and a minister says, "I would consider it to be so." But as one important line in the scripture says, "there is a way that seemeth right to man, but its ends are the ends of death."

How refreshing, therefore, to feel the firm, solid authority of the word of God, saying, "Thou shalt not." "Thou shalt not steal." "Thou shalt not bear false witness." "Thou shalt not commit adultery." We can absolutely depend upon it that God is *not* about to join some organization for the promotion of the new morality or for toning down the spirit of the Ten Commandments or for that type of progressive education that keeps everyone in the dark. Jesus did not even tone down his statement to the unprofitable individual who was afraid and buried his talent in the ground. Jesus said to him, "Thou wicked and slothful servant." If our sensibilities are weak enough and if they are combined with a sufficient tendency toward rebellion, then such a statement may injure our morale. But at least we would know where we stood, and we would also know where God stood. These solid, rigid commandments should give us some strength in our backbones. It should be reassuring to know that God is the same yesterday, today, and forever. If we are doing those things that he so vigorously disapproved from Sinai, then we can be pretty sure what he is thinking about us.

It was said of Jesus, "He speaks as one having authority and not as the scribes." We can't imagine Jesus being confused about the differences between right and wrong. Jesus was not a speculator nor a theorist nor a wishful thinker. He didn't base his doctrines on some unproven hearsay or untried experiment. He didn't guess. He always did what was right. He said, "My doctrine is not mine, but his that sent me." (John 7:16.) When the young lawyer came to Jesus and asked "What must I do to inherit eternal life?" Jesus didn't vacillate or equivocate or speculate. He gave him the only answer that could be given, as there is only one right answer—not a thousand, as we sometimes try to make ourselves believe. If "command" is not a very good word for God to use in these important matters, then suppose that we try to find a better one, when our eternal welfare and happiness is at stake. How would we like to have a vague, indefinite God who wasn't sure of his ground?

An engineer was once fired from his job. He asked why. The president said, "You allowed us to take a course of action on which we lost a substantial amount of money." The engineer said, "But surely you remember that I specifically advised you against that action." The president said, "Yes, I know that you did, but you didn't pound the table when you did it."

No one can accuse God of not pounding on the table. He came down to the top of Mount Sinai in fire; and to the accompaniment of lightning and thunders, he gave his Ten Commandments. There is nothing negative about any one of them. Each is about as positive as it could possibly be, and certainly no one should doubt that God knows his business and that he means exactly what he says. We also know that his laws are still in force, and that the Ten Commandments are not about to be modified. It is very unlikely that God has any plans for watering down the principles of the gospel or for changing his eternal program because it may possibly offend someone.

However, we don't need to worry very much about the Ten Commandments unless we are violating them; and if we are, then we had better look out. If we are too much pained by the word of the Lord, we might remember that "it is the hit bird that flutters." If *our* sensibilities are offended, we might find it more profitable to change our conduct to fit the law rather than hope that God will change the law to suit our sensibilities. God is much wiser than we are. He is more interested in *our* welfare than we ourselves are. And God has the vision to see every end from its beginning. Some people get drunk because they cannot see the alcoholism contained in the whiskey bottle, or the failure that is inherent in weak sensibilities. Far better than we do, God knows about the terrible waste involved in failure and sin. He also knows that man has polluted, befouled, perverted, and misused every good thing that he has ever put within our reach. Any vacillation or wishy-washiness in our righteousness causes trouble for us. It is most desirable that we should strengthen our over-sensitive feelings so that we will not be offended by hearing God's great laws that are given in our interests. Neither should it be necessary to have a lot of sickly sweet sugar coating on every elementary truth that God gives us. He himself has made an unwavering commitment to righteousness under all circumstances, and that is exactly what he wants us to do.

There is another rather "harsh" scripture in which the wise man Solomon said, "Fear God and keep his commandments, for this is the whole duty of men." This phrase "fear God" is one that is frequently used in the scriptures. Some "fear" is bad, and some is good. The kind intended by this scripture is a Godly fear that is made up of concern, reverence, awe, love, and worship. It is a part of what Shakespeare calls the "fear" that reason leads.

The scripture says that the fear of the Lord is the beginning of wisdom. To fear God indicates our good judgment and the faithful reverence that makes us *love* to keep his great commandments. They are designed by him to help us become the kind, honorable, righteous children of whom he can be proud, and may God help us to feel that great pleasure that comes from his loyal service.

Devotion

S OMETIME AGO I HEARD THE HEAD OF A GREAT SALES ORGANIZA-
tion say that no one can predict a salesman's sales success by
knowing his intelligence quotient, or his education, or his heredity,
or who his friends are, or even what his aptitude is. While all of
these are important, yet the determining factor in every worthwhile
success is a character quality that this great leader referred to as
"devotion."

This interesting meaning and the great traits of conviction, love,
and stick-to-itness of which it is made up is one with which every
salesman and every American and every husband and every Christian
should get on a more intimate basis. The dictionary describes devotion as "an eager inclination," a "strong attachment," "an ardent
love," a "loyal affection," "an animated zeal," "an abiding fervor."
Above I.Q. and above aptitude and above education and above need,
every good salesman and every good Christian and every good man
should have a strong belief in the cause that he represents and an
unwavering commitment to do his job in the best way it can possibly be done.

Elbert Hubbard once said, "If you are going to work for a company, in heaven's name work for it." And he might have said that
if you are going to get married, first get a strong attachment and
then be prepared to do whatever is necessary to make this important
relationship an outstanding success. Now if you take upon yourself
the name of Christ, in heaven's name magnify your calling. The
Lord said to the Laodiceans, "because thou art lukewarm, I will
spew thee out of my mouth." Nothing is so miserable as this trait
of always being in-between, where one is neither one thing nor the
other.

One man recently said that he didn't love his wife, but he also
confessed that he didn't love his parents, nor his children, nor his
enemies, nor his friends. He didn't love his job, nor his country, nor
God, nor life itself. His miserable existence was concerned only with
his own amusement and comfort. Like so many others, his tragedy
is summed up by the fact that he lacked devotion. When this superb
virtue is translated into life, one gets an eager inclination to do right,

a strong loyalty to his part of the world's work and a profound attachment for God. Devotion gives one a sincere enthusiasm about life and an ardent love for those to whom sacred vows have been taken. An animated zeal to improve one's self and a religious fervor to promote his spiritual ideals lift anyone up to greatness. In every worthwhile field, including the worship of God, one's greatest need is a stability of soul. The good book says, "He that wavereth is like a wave of the sea, driven by the wind and tossed," whereas steady, devoted, unwavering strength can make anyone almost all powerful in any of life's situations.

From the scriptures we learn that Job was a very successful, wealthy, and happy man. His vast possessions, great prestige, and fine family made life very satisfying. Then in quick succession he lost his wealth, his health, and his family. Job was afflicted with every kind of adversity, and the most dreadful sores kept him in constant and complete misery. Finally some of the people closest to Job suggested that he give up. In their words, they said, "Curse God and die." That is about what most people do when things go seriously wrong. But Job could not be overthrown even by the most severe problems. Of the Creator who had permitted these disasters to overwhelm him, Job said, "Though he slay me, yet will I trust in him." (Job 13:15.) Then he said, "While I live I will not remove my integrity from me; while breath is in me and the spirit of God is in my nostrils, my lips shall not speak wickedness, nor my tongue utter deceit. I will hold fast to my righteousness and will not let it go, so long as I live." (See Job 27:3-6.) And we might say hurrah for Job; we like to see someone who is stronger than anything that can happen to him. The kind of attitude Job had will make a champion out of anyone in any situation among any kind of company.

When real, solid devotion lies at the center of life, then our lives themselves become outstandingly worthwhile. It was devotion that made Nathan Hale stand up before the enemy firing squad and say, "I regret that I have but one life to give for my country." Devotion is that quality that makes husbands and wives faithful to each other, in spite of the differences, whereas the members of that breed having lesser devotion may be drawn off the track by every new infatuation that comes within range. For lack of this basic trait of human character, each new day sees new families broken up and the welfare of small children disregarded. Frequently parents bring children into the world and then abandon them spiritually and materially merely because some different emotional breeze is blowing upon them. We must be more than outwardly devoted—this great quality must be internalized to get its greatest power. Someone has pointed out that most people are "Bible Christians"—that is, the Christianity is in the Bible rather than in them.

It has been said that it doesn't help anyone very much to go through college unless the college goes through him. When one gets into the Church, some benefits accrue to him more or less automatically, but it isn't until the Church gets into him that the really important things being to take place. A young man once said to Mozart, "Will you teach me to write symphonies?" Mozart said, "You are too young to write symphonies." "But," the inquirer said, "you were writing symphonies when you were fifteen years younger than I am." Mozart said, "But I didn't have to ask anyone to teach me." Mozart's desire to learn had been given power by being internalized; and when one internalizes dedication, it places every success within his easy reach.

It is perfectly astounding how undreamed-of mental and spiritual faculties rush to our assistance when we get our whole souls committed to some unwavering aim. What a tremendous power a firm resolution gives! How it multiplies every faculty of the mind, and stimulates every function of the body! A firm resolution to achieve will dissolve all of the obstacles that deter the efforts of the fainthearted. Sometime ago I read about a business that manufactured compasses. In a great supply room there were thousands of compasses of every size and description. Because their unmagnetized needles had no responsibility, they were pointing in every direction. But as soon as the needles were magnetized, each received its own peculiar power. From that moment on, every needle pointed straight toward its star, and was constant and true forever after. A magnetized needle does not point toward *every* heavenly body. They may all try to attract it. The sun may dazzle it; the meteors may beckon it; the stars may twinkle at it, trying to win its affection; but the magnetized needle, true to its instinct, with a finger that never errs in sunshine or in storm always points constantly toward its star.

And so it is with our success. When we can be equally true to the aim of some unwavering purpose, we have it made. Other luminaries may try to distract us from our course, but if our lives are dedicated to their missions, then no moon that shines with borrowed light and no meteors that dazzle but never guide can ever turn the needle of our purpose from the north star of its ambition.

This persistent, steadfast, constant, unwavering devotion to a great purpose without whimper or complaint, without suit for relief or release, can be one of the most inspiring characteristics of human personality.

Think, if you will, of Paul the Apostle, as he sits in his prison cell in Rome awaiting his execution. He is an old man. For over thirty-five years he has turned neither to the right nor to the left, but said, "This *one* thing I do." He had no sidelines, made no excuses, and indulged in no wasteful startings and stoppings. Instead, he always had that sure and steady quality of always being there, of always going forward, of always keeping in focus the one great aim and purpose of his life.

How different his career from what might have been expected thirty-five years before, when he was a young and influential member of the Sanhedrin with everything to make his career promising: friends, position, influence, and education.

Then had come that day on the road to Damascus when "suddenly there shined round about him a light from heaven:

"And he fell to the earth, and heard a voice saying unto him, Saul, Saul, why persecutest thou me?

"And he said, Who art thou, Lord? And the Lord said, I am Jesus whom thou persecutest; it is hard for thee to kick against the pricks.

"And he trembling and astonished said, Lord, what wilt thou have me do?" (Acts 9:3-6.)

For three days Saul was without sight, without food, without drink. But the Lord had said, "He is a chosen vessel unto me, to bear my name before the Gentiles, and kings, and the children of Israel:

"For I will shew him how great things he must suffer for my name's sake." (Acts 9:15-16.) And from that day onward, Paul ceased not to carry forward with his utmost vigor his assigned task.

After thirty-five years, he counted his manner of life by saying, "In labours more abundant, in stripes above measure, in prisons more frequent, in deaths oft.

"Of the Jews five times received I forty stripes save one.

"Thrice was I beaten with rods, once was I stoned, thrice I suffered shipwreck, a night and a day I have been in the deep.

"In journeyings often, in perils of waters, in perils of robbers, in perils by mine own countrymen, in perils by the heathen, in perils in the city, in perils in the wilderness, in perils in the sea, in perils among false brethren;

"In weariness and painfulness, in watchings often, in hunger and thirst, in fastings often, in cold and nakedness.

"Beside those things that are without, that which cometh upon me daily, the care of all the churches." (2 Cor. 11:23-28.)

Of all of his experiences, this last must have been the most wearisome—the care that comes from within the Church. People sometimes get tired and want to quit, or they lack the enthusiasm to supply their own initiative and must be encouraged and helped and coaxed. It is easy to fight the battles from without, but the real heartbreak comes when the wavering is from within. But there was no wavering in Paul. He would go on, and on, and on, alone if need be, and on his own power.

When we consider the ability that Paul had developed for sustained, continued effort in one direction, it is small wonder the Lord said, "He is a chosen vessel unto me." This might also be said of many others if we could learn to stick to our convictions as energetically and as enthusiastically and as long. He says that "his bodily presence was weak, and speech contemptible." He mentions his "thorn in the flesh," but men can get along without money, without name, and without influence; your appearance may be poor, and your speech may be faulty, but all that will be as nothing if you know where you are going. We have never heard of Paul taking a vacation or being afraid of wearing out. He was on fire with his determination and never lost sight of his goal.

It is an interesting thing, which he must have thought about, that there is nothing mentioned in all the Revelations about resignations. Occasionally he must have thought of the ease and comfort and affluence that might have been his, and it must have occurred to him long before thirty-five years had passed that he had "served his term" and would be "entitled to a release." But that was not for him. And it is not for us. There can be no such things as a release in the work in which Paul was engaged. He and we must continue to go on and on, and at an accelerated pace. We can't work out our salvation in two years or ten years or twenty years. "Only he that endureth to the end shall be saved." Paul said of himself, "I fight on, lest I myself should be a castaway."

Just before the end of his ministry, Paul wrote a letter to Timothy, a young man in whom he had a special interest. He calls him "his son in the gospel," and after exhorting Timothy to the utmost of diligence, he expressed the realization that his own mission had been completed. He said, "For I am now ready to be offered, and the time of my departure is at hand. I have fought a good fight, I have finished my course, I have kept the faith." (2 Tim. 4:6-7.)

How inspiring such words can be when they come at the end of such a life of outstanding devotion and constancy. Paul was to go soon to Rome to be beheaded. But even in his death, his determination never faltered, and the fervor of his faith showed no sign of any decrease from that first day when blinded and stunned he had said, "Lord what wilt thou have me do?" I like to think of Paul on *that* day, when the axe of the executioner granted him the final release from his earthly labors, when he should go to stand a second time before Jesus of Nazareth; and I imagine that there will be very few, if any, men who will ever stand before their maker with greater cause to rejoice than he. And when we come to that point in our lives and have cause to reflect on the fight we have fought and the course we have run, how insignificant will be the money we have made or the ease we have enjoyed or the affluence we have attained.

Life was never intended to be only a pleasure trip. It is a mission, a conquest, a testing, and how bitter must be the final remorse of any wasted life. My prayer is that God will help us to develop the courage, the industry, and the devotion to live God's answers to the great Apostle's question, saying, "Lord, what wilt thou have me do?"

The Discipline of Language

THROUGH ITS MONTHLY LETTER, THE ROYAL BANK OF CANADA recently sent out an article entitled, "The Discipline of Language." It pointed out the power that can be generated when words are properly used and understood. The function of some words is to inform, some provide entertainment, and some give encouragement. Some words persuade, some give cheer, and some may be used to defend a way of life. When we fail to use our language effectively communication breaks down and our lives themselves tend to become inferior. Confucius once said, "If our language is not correct, then what is said will not be what is meant; if what is said is not what is meant, then what ought to be done will remain undone." But whether one is speaking, writing, or learning, the ability to pass ideas effectively from one to another is almost all important, as this is the process by which we teach, sell, inspire, and motivate.

The foundations of civilization itself are laid with words, and they underlie every activity in life. They are the indicators of our humanity, the measurement of our ability, and the tools of our success. Words convey affections, give expression to prayers, vitalize our ambitions, and record our progress. Our standards of living, our mastery of science, the quality of our faith, and the effectiveness of our know-how all come about because of our ability to get our ideas over. It is also true that the faulty use of words or the failure to communicate between family members, business associates, or the representatives of nations is a most serious menace to our every success and happiness.

After a prominent and very capable candidate for a high political office had been defeated in an election, he said, "I did not communicate." If the voters had been able to crawl inside his mind and discover what he thought and how he felt and what he was, he might have been able to get more votes. Unfortunately, most people are not mind readers; and when we lack the ability for effective communication, the darkness continues, so far as we are concerned.

The tremendous divorce carnage that desolates our society is largely a result of breakdown in communication. It is pathetic how little some husbands, wives, and children know about the hopes, ambitions, needs, and desires of each other. In the usual marriage relationship some giant Berlin walls are built between husband and wife, as well as between parents and children, with the result that the understanding that is able to get across is below the required minimums. One of our most common complaints is that someone doesn't understand us. Most hates, fears, disagreements, frigidity, mental and physical cruelties are the results of misunderstanding.

Because every human being needs love, acceptance, instruction, and encouragement, we should be able to cast ourselves into words. And just as we need food, rest, breath, and drink every day, so we need words of inspiration, love, enlightenment, discipline, and correction every day. Some words of restraint and caution also serve a most important need. We can keep disorder and confusion out of our affairs by making sure that we are not misinterpreting the word signals or misusing the blueprint of those ideas by which we live.

In business or in life, few inefficiencies are so serious as poverty in our language. Every time a business man does not express himself clearly and meaningfully, he loses business for his firm and wastes his own time. Husbands and wives fail each other for this same reason. The key to almost every success is the word "communication." Even the greatest thoughts for which one has no words are often valueless. And those ideas and ambitions that are kept locked in the mind have no way of producing a pleasure or making a profit. When traveling in a foreign land, one must learn to use the currency of that country if he hopes to enjoy its benefits. But the currency of life is language; and whether we are traveling or staying at home, we must have a good supply of negotiable words and know how to use them if we would receive the maximum value from life. For words are the basic currency in all of our exchanges.

It is through words that we gain knowledge, stir up ambition, arouse spirituality, and instill faith. Words are the tools of thought that we employ even with ourselves. They represent things, feelings, and activities. Words come in different colors, sizes, intensity, and shades of meaning. And we need to be as artistic and as scientific as possible, not only in their employment but also in their interpretation. Of course, to be completely exact is impossible, inasmuch as no idea or thing can ever be precisely or adequately represented by mere verbal symbols. A friend and an enemy would probably use different words to describe our conduct. It is frequently difficult to translate ideas from one language to another. We also have problems in translating our perception into language or our ambitions into words.

Suppose that you tried to find words to explain what salt tasted like to one who had never tasted salt. Or how would you describe terror or anger to one who did not already know these emotions? Or how could you explain the difference in the pain of a toothache from that of a finger smashed in the door of your automobile, to one who was ignorant of both these experiences? In the holy scriptures God has tried to make clear to us the difference between eternal happiness and eternal misery. But even the significance of *his* words may go over our heads with very little understanding coming from the most descriptive words that even God knows how to use. We have a tremendous price exacted when we have to get the lesson from a personal experience rather than from the less expensive way of understanding that we get from words. Sometimes it is pretty difficult to enlighten our children in the most simple differences between wrong or right, without their having to fall back on the wastefulness of a personal experience. How unfortunate are those young people who have to learn the consequences of dishonesty or sloth or immorality from personal experiences. Or how effectively can we shape an idea for a business associate or develop an ideal for a student, or how can we understand in advance the blessings and emotions connected with celestial glory? In spite of the best intentions, we have some of our most serious problems with our communication. But because words are the best tools that we have, we should learn to make the best possible use of them by keeping our language of thinking and communicating under the most careful discipline.

The workmen engaged in building the tower of Babel were craftsmen, skilled in their trades. If God had taken away their tools, they would have made some more; if he had deprived them of their skills, they would have learned them over again. But when he took away their means of communication with each other, then the building of the great tower was immediately abandoned. And so it is with the building of a successful business or a loving family or a happy life. When communication breaks down, progress comes to a standstill in many departments of our lives.

Of course, our words must be genuine and sincere and should always be supported by an adequate performance. Because our actions always speak louder than our words, we can develop our greatest ability for expression by translating every word into its highest form of activity.

Many people fall down because of the discord that is sometimes permitted between deed and creed. And because no one really lives as well as he knows how to live, our most serious shortcoming is our failure to translate our ideas and ambitions into their higher denomination of *works*. The central fact of life is that everyone, including God, will judge us primarily by what we do. No one is much of an expert in guessing at the meaning of words that haven't been spoken, or of deeds that remain unperformed. Even if we are equipped with the most adequate vocabulary to express every shade of thought and meaning in exactly the right word combinations, yet these words would have little value unless they were accompanied by an intensity of feelings that could be translated into its most appropriate activity.

Often we let a wealth of words lie inert and unemployed; or sometimes because of our own voluntary weakness in translation and communication, we allow coarseness or poverty to characterize that which might have been expertly and powerfully done. Because every word has its own particular shade of meaning, there are actually no synonyms. Words may have a great deal in common, but there is something about each one that makes it unique. Words sometimes change in meaning to us as our own attitudes and behavior change. The word "love" may describe many things, from one's appetite for liquor to his adoration of God.

One of our greatest tragedies is that we are not on an intimate basis with great literature, which can be a very profitable kind of visual communication. We can choose from among the authors those who have a comparable spirit to that which we would like to develop. As we devour the words of William Shakespeare, John Milton, Winston Churchill, and Ralph Waldo Emerson, we may acquire some of their superior skill as architects of language. They not only organized great thoughts, but they were effective as trans- lators and were masters of expression.

During the critical days of the Second World War, Winston Churchill made a number of great speeches. And probably more than anything else these speeches were responsible for saving the world from the mechanized might of the Nazis. In a communica- tion to the British people, Churchill said, "We shall not flag nor fail! We shall go on to the end. We shall fight in France, we shall fight on the seas and the oceans, we shall fight with growing con- fidence and power in the air, we shall fight on the beaches, we shall fight on the landing grounds, we shall fight in the fields, and in the streets. We shall never surrender." The great qualities of courage and determination that existed in Churchill's life were translated into words and broadcast to the people of the empire. Then in the hearts of loyal Englishmen they were changed back into the original virtues exhibited by Churchill.

Suppose we were to translate the Apostle Paul's famous sermon on love into our own lives, or suppose we were to appropriate for our own use the great ideas from the Sermon on the Mount or the Ten Commandments or the Lord's Prayer. Or suppose that we were to communicate the expression "Father, thy will be done" into the working machinery of our lives. Those who can effectively read, memorize and love the great scriptures can use them to lift themselves up to God.

The right words with appropriate feelings can discipline our lives to achieve the destiny that God has marked out for us.

Disciplined language demands more than merely adding words to our vocabulary. It is also a matter of forming attitudes and breaking slovenly habits of thought. It inspires us to avoid using second-rate words and ineffective idea combinations merely because they are handy. Our individual words and meanings should always fit the occasion. The electronics engineer does not use his trade language in explaining to his wife how to change a fuse. Sometimes we use a particular jargon that makes understanding difficult and communication ineffective. Our words often transform us into their own image. There are several willful language offenses that we are guilty of. One is obscurity and confusion. Sometimes we use negative words, which represent negative thoughts. There is a great inventory of profane and ugly words that lead us away from our goals. This misuse of words and the abuse of ideas can cause a quick deterioration to take place in our own language, and then a serious negation takes place in our communication. When we fail to say our prayers or when we use speech to pervert our commitments to God, our language is misused, our abilities are weakened and our ideas themselves may go down in value.

Without proper discipline and adequate exercise, our language takes on a kind of flabbiness or formlessness or mindlessness. When we are not living at our best, our expression may deteriorate into what the late James Thurber called "our oral culture of pure babble." Our expression and our performance depend to some extent upon each other. Some of our greatest ideas come during expression and our expression is best when we are living at our best. Expressions of patriotism increase our love of country. Even thinking is handicapped without expression. Someone was once asked what he thought about a certain thing, and he said, "I don't know; I haven't spoken on it yet." We need to do more speaking about God and success and faith as we clarify our thoughts and give them power in speech. We need selected exercises in reading, and we need disciplined practice in thinking and speaking. Language itself may be enriched by the insight, imagination, and experience of those generations that have gone before us. We need to see how acknowledged masters use words, ideas, and emotions. The more we immerse ourselves in the work of the great writers of good language, the broader and more accurate our vocabularies will become and the more vigorous our activities. As the lives of great people have passed by, some of their ideas have been put down on paper, and we can help to build our own lives by using the tools that they have developed. And above all, our constant prayer should be that God will help us to be able to effectively communicate with him both in our expression and in understanding his reply.

Doubting Thomas

O NE OF OUR MOST INTERESTING ACTIVITIES COMES FROM STUDYING other people. People are helpful to us for different reasons. The constructive use to which some people put their lives serves as an example for us to follow. And the weaknesses of others teach us about those things that should be avoided. The lives of great sinners as well as great saints are fascinating; and each has a contribution to make, if we will only seek it out. We may take the best from such men as Winston Churchill, Abraham Lincoln, Thomas A. Edison, Ralph Waldo Emerson, Mohandas Gandhi, and George Washington, and with equal benefit be repelled by the worst in Nebuchadnezzar, Jezebel, and Herod the Great. Each human being is unique, as life makes no duplicates, and each has a different focus as well as a different mixture of virtues. Moses was unlike Abraham. Cain and his brother, Abel, made the opposite kinds of marks in the world. And there will never be anyone else like the Apostle Paul.

Each individual life also contains some contradictions. Peter denied the Lord three times, and yet he was such a model of faith that he was called Cephas the Rock, the chief apostle. John was noted for his loving disposition and Judas for his betrayal. Judas allowed his weakness to carry him too far, but he later suffered so intensely for his sin that he returned the betrayal money and went out and hanged himself. If only Judas had repented before it was too late, his life might have been remembered for its good.

But all of our heroes have weaknesses. None of the Twelve were able to stay awake to sustain Jesus during his hour of suffering, and when the shepherd was smitten, the sheep were scattered. One member of the Twelve attracts our special interest with a characteristic that he held in common with many people. This apostle is sometimes referred to as "Doubting Thomas." In some ways he was the opposite of Peter. It seemed so easy for Peter to believe. When Jesus suggested that all of the Twelve would be offended because of him, Peter said, "Though all men shall be offended because of thee, yet will I never be offended." He said, "Though I should die with thee, yet will I not deny thee." (Matt. 26:33,35.) Peter always seemed so sure of himself.

But with Thomas, faith took root more slowly. After the resurrection Jesus appeared to the apostles assembled in Jerusalem during the absence of Thomas. And when they told him that they had seen Jesus alive, Thomas just wouldn't believe it. He said, "Except I shall see in his hands the print of the nails, and thrust my hand into his side, I will not believe." Later Jesus said to Thomas, "Reach hither thy finger, and behold my hands; and reach hither thy hand, and thrust it into my side: and be not faithless, but believing." Then in addressing a statement to Thomas which has a general application for everyone, Jesus said, "Thomas, because thou hast seen, thou hast believed: blessed are they that have not seen, and yet have believed." (John 21:25,27,29.)

Doubt continues to be one of the most serious problems troubling this restless earth, and our world itself is full of doubting Thomases. We doubt God, we doubt the scriptures, we doubt our opportunities, we doubt truth, we even doubt ourselves. The dictionary says that to doubt is to waver in one's opinion or judgment. It is for one to be uncertain in his belief, and to hesitate in his faith. It is to be unable to make up one's mind between some affirmative and negative proposition. To doubt is to question and withhold confidence, or it is to distrust and deny approval. One in doubt is apprehensive and refuses to accept. Doubt is the opposite of the great success qualities, such as knowledge, assurance, conviction, and certainty. Of course, some forms of doubt can be very helpful if properly used. There is "a doubt that wisdom leads" that can make one into an inquirer and investigator. An earnest scholar in doubt about his graduation becomes more diligent in his studies. A suitor in doubt about the intentions of his beloved is stimulated to improve his position, and sometimes when a devout seeker after truth has doubts about God, he may become more thoughtful in his search for understanding.

To be free to learn, it is sometimes necessary for the mind to be kept open, without any undue pressures from either side. But serious problems may arise if our mental gear shift gets stuck in a neutral position. Then, like Aesop's mule, we may be unable to make up our minds and may starve to death midway between two piles of hay. Doubts may become so chronic that our minds may reject everything that does not conform to what we already believe. If we were trying to criticize Thomas, we might reason that he should have believed in the resurrection of Jesus even before it took place. Jesus had given the disciples a considerable amount of instruction on this subject; and, in addition, the resurrection had been one of the acknowledged principles of the gospel from the beginning. Ever since the days of Adam the prophets had looked forward to the resurrection. But apparently Thomas disregarded these considerations. Then he not only denied the testimony of one witness, but he also doubted the testimony of his ten most trusted fellow workers.

But the difficulty is still with us; and in this all important matter of living successfully, doubt continues to be one of our biggest problems—this in spite of the fact that we not only have the information possessed by the early members of the Church, we also have the judgment of time, shining upon the life of Christ. But we also have some new witnesses. The resurrected Jesus has again appeared upon the earth to reestablish among men a belief in the God of Genesis, the God of Calvary, and the God of the Resurrection. The Prophet Joseph Smith reports his own personal manifestation when he says, "I saw two Personages, whose brightness and glory defy all description, standing above me in the air. One of them spake unto me calling me by name and said, pointing to the other— *This is My Beloved Son. Hear him.*" Then the young prophet received instructions about the part he was to play in the great gospel restoration of the latter days.

Our *reason* should testify that Joseph Smith was telling the truth; otherwise how could he have accomplished what he did? Since that time the world has been given three great volumes of new scripture outlining in every detail the simple principles of the doctrines of Christ. One of these is the Book of Mormon, an ancient American volume of scripture, in the front of which is a signed testimony of three men who bear their solemn witness that this ancient record is true. In one sentence they say, "And we declare with words of soberness, that an angel of God came down from heaven, and he brought and laid before our eyes, that we beheld and saw the plates, and the engravings thereon; and we know that it is by the grace of God the Father, and our Lord Jesus Christ, that we beheld and bear record that these things are true."

Inside the book itself, a sacred promise is made by the Prophet Moroni as follows: "And when ye shall receive these things, I would exhort you that ye would ask God, the Eternal Father, in the name of Christ, if these things are not true; and if ye shall ask with a sincere heart, with real intent, having faith in Christ, he will manifest the truth of it unto you, by the power of the Holy Ghost." (Moroni 10:4.)

These great events have taken place in our own interests, yet we frequently say with Thomas, "Except I see for myself, I will not believe." We sometimes also add that we will not even investigate. One man said, "I will not believe anything that I cannot understand." Such a person would have a very short list of beliefs, as no one completely understands even such common things as sunshine, or light, or growth; we cannot even see gravity or electricity or air. No one understands birth or death or how our hearts beat or what makes our minds work. We enjoy the benefits of a thousand things that we don't understand.

For reasons best known to himself, God has set this mortal life apart as a time when we should learn to walk a little by faith, and he has never followed the practice of giving his great truths to everyone personally. God talked to Moses face to face, but many of the people then did not believe. Many people have the attitude that unless the miraculous manifestation comes to them personally, they will not believe.

Recently a man expressed his desire for a fervent testimony of the truth of the gospel. But at the same time he pled guilty to the charges of alcoholism, immorality, lack of religious study, and Church absenteeism. However, he felt that if he saw some overpowering miracle performed, it would be easier for him to give up his liquor and his many other sins. He went beyond Thomas and said substantially, "Except I thrust my hand into his side, I will not quit drinking, or quit being immoral, or quit violating the Sabbath day."

Jesus approached the acquiring of faith from exactly the other direction. He said, "If ye shall do my will, ye shall know of the doctrine." If we live right, we can know many things with great certainty. Everyone can know that honesty is better than dishonesty. Everyone can know that it is right to be fair and to serve our fellowmen. We can have the most firm testimony about the value of the Ten Commandments, the Sermon on the Mount, the law of tithing, and the Word of Wisdom. We can also know that the other divine doctrines are not only true but that they also help us to live successfully, whereas if we steep ourselves in evil, we may lose our success and even the ability to tell right from wrong. So many of our problems begin when we fail to clear up our doubts by failing to make up our minds.

Shakespeare says, "Our doubts are traitors and make us lose the good we oft might win by fearing to attempt." When we succumb to these betrayers, we lose the most worthwhile values of our lives. It is easy for a sinner to believe that God is dead when that seems to be in his best interests. Some half believe that God is dead, and some don't care whether he is dead or not. Some can be so immobilized by this deadly neutrality of doubt that they can't believe, and yet they don't disbelieve. But either God *is* or God *is not*. There is no middle ground. It's all or nothing! If we do not accept him by design, we more or less automatically reject him by default. If we don't decide to get on the airplane, we automatically decide to stay off the airplane. It has been said that there is one folly greater than that of the fool who said in his heart, "There is no God," and that is the folly of him who says that he doesn't know whether there is a God or not. For only he who fails to seek fails to find.

There are many more people who suffer from unbelief than from disbelief. Some people are just not prepared to believe. And the religion of Jesus has always suffered more from those who did not understand than from those who opposed. It is our lethargic hearts rather than our sinful minds that most frequently stand between us and our salvation. Faith is a priceless possession, and Jesus said: "All things are possible to them that believe," whereas the scripture points out that "no man can be saved in ignorance." It could also be said that no man can be saved in indifference. Certainly no man can be saved in indecision. The benefits of believing are so overwhelming that to clean out our doubts should be a fairly simple matter. It has been reasoned that if one should err in believing the gospel of Jesus Christ to be true, he could not possibly be a loser by the mistake. But how irreparable is the loss of him who should err in supposing the gospel of Jesus Christ to be false. Someone has said:

> Suppose there is a Christ, but that I should be Christless.
> Suppose that there is a cleansing, but that I should remain unclean.
> Suppose that there is a Heavenly Father's love, but that I should remain an alien.
> Suppose there is a heaven, but that I should be thrust down to Hell.

We have everything to gain and nothing to lose by making up our minds on the side of faith, righteousness, understanding, and obedience to God. Ignorance, disobedience, indecision, and indifference all lead to a hazardous and costly doubt. It has been said that "he who is indifferent to his friend is ungrateful to his friend, but he who is indifferent to his Savior is unmerciful unto himself." The greatest idea there is in the world is that God lives and that man has a possible destiny to become like his eternal Heavenly Father. And may our united prayer be that God will help us to believe in our destiny and to achieve it.

The Earth's Sabbath

O NE OF THE OUTSTANDING MEMORIES CARRIED OVER FROM CHILD-
hood is my recollection of the Sabbath Day. Back in those
early times out on the farm, Sunday was a day completely set apart
from the rest of the week. From Monday through Saturday, our
attention was centered in the heavy labor involved in making a
living by the muscle power of men and animals.

But Sunday was different—it was the Sabbath. Sunday was the
day of rest. It was the day of the Lord. On Saturday night the
horses were turned out to pasture, and all work was suspended.
Saturday was also a kind of special house cleaning day to get things
and people ready for Sunday. Saturday evening was the deadline
in the preparation of Sunday School lessons. The final act of the
work week was concerned with that important ancient rite known
as the "Saturday Night bath." This was supplemented by a parental
issue of properly mended, clean clothing all laid out, ready for
Sunday.

This thorough physical and spiritual preparation also served as
our heartfelt acknowledgement of the Creator's program that the
Sabbath Day was supposed to be the high point of the week. It has
been said that our civilization would never have survived for half
a century if it had not been for this one day in seven when we live
at our best. This is the day when we put on our best clothes, read
our best books, think our best thoughts, and associate with the
people who mean the most in our lives. This is the day for which
we usually reserve the best meal of the week. And after we have
laid aside the cares that have concerned us during the other six days,
we go to the house of prayer and let our minds reach up and try to
comprehend the things of God.

The unit of life is the week, and each week of our earth's history
has been fashioned after that memorable first week, which was the
week of creation. As the scene opens on that first day, we feel the
brooding, unborken darkness covering the face of the deep, and
thrill at that initial forward step when, in the march of progress,
God first said, "Let there be light." (Gen. 1:3.) We follow the other
creative acts to the crowning scene, which took place during the

sixth day, when God created man in his own image and endowed him with a set of his own attributes and potentialities. Then, in summarizing the accomplishments of this period of creation, the holy record says, "Thus the heavens and the earth were finished, and all the hosts of them. And on the seventh day God ended his work which he had made; and he rested on the seventh day. . . . And God blessed the seventh day, and sanctified it." (Gen. 2:1-3.)

Then, in programming the world's mortal or temporal existence, God gave it a time allotment of seven thousand years, one thousand years to represent each of the seven days of creation. (D&C 77:7.) The first four thousand years began at the fall of Adam and ended at the birth of Christ. To this has been added the 1967 years that have passed since that time, so that on the divine calendar we are now living in the year of the world 5967, which is the late Saturday evening of the world's history. This divine time table, as well as God's signs of the times, indicates that the earth's Sabbath, which is the seventh one-thousand-year period, is about to be ushered in. After the creation, God looked out upon his handiwork and called it very good. The earth was then a paradise of beauty, peace, and plenty. Our first parents were placed in the beautiful Garden of Eden, where everything had been provided for their benefit. But at the fall of man the earth also fell. And in announcing the penalty for man's disobedience, God said, "Cursed is the ground for thy sake; in sorrow shalt thou eat of it all the days of thy life; Thorns also and thistles shall it bring forth to thee." (Gen. 3:17-18.)

We may think of this earth as a pretty wonderful place just as it is, but for nearly 6,000 years it has been operating in its fallen condition as a telestial world. Not only has it brought forth thorns, thistles, and noxious weeds out of the ground, but lawlessness, corruption, and every kind of disobedience have also flourished upon its face. Its surface has been made unproductive by deserts and waste places, while enmity and hate have been festering in the hearts of both men and beasts; and during all of this long, sad period, sin, suffering, and death have been the general portion of all mankind.

But the next one-thousand-year period will be the earth's Sabbath. This will be the period when the earth will rest and enjoy its sanctified state. For this period the earth will be renewed and regain its former status as a terrestrial sphere, with all of its paradisiacal beauty, glory, and righteousness fully restored. But first the earth must be cleansed. During its long history of sin and trouble, our earth has become soiled and dirty. And it must have its "Saturday Night bath" and be dressed in fresh, clean clothing in which it can appropriately live its best 1,000 years.

On several previous occasions God has attempted to cleanse the earth—once by a flood of waters in the days of Noah, and on other occasions he has used wars, famines, pestilence, and disease, trying to rid the earth of that wickedness that has defiled its face. But in preparation for the earth's Sabbath, God has indicated that fire will be the cleansing agent, and every corrupt thing will be consumed. (D&C 101:24.) On this subject Malachi said, "And the Lord, whom ye seek, shall suddenly come to his temple. . . . But who may abide the day of his coming? and who shall stand when he appeareth? for he is like a refiner's fire, and like fuller's soap." (Mal. 3:1-2.) Anyone who as a boy objected to having his ears scrubbed might look forward to this coming experience with some special anticipation.

The Lord has said, "For, behold, the day cometh, that shall burn as an oven; and all the proud, yea, and all that do wickedly, shall be as stubble: and the day that cometh shall burn them up, saith the Lord of hosts, that it shall leave them neither root nor branch." (Mal. 4:1.) Then will follow the long awaited seventh one thousand years. This will be a millennium of peace, when Christ will reign personally upon the earth as King of kings and Lord of lords. This change in the earth's status will be initiated at the glorious second coming of Jesus Christ, and after its purification, the new King will remove the curse from the earth and reinstate its former terrestrial magnificence.

This great millennial period, with its perfect government, has been a favorite theme of the prophets since time began. It should also be one of the most motivating influences in our lives. Over three thousand years ago the psalmist looked beyond the apostasy, the dark ages, and the wickedness and disbelief of our own day and said, "Our God shall come, and shall not keep silence: a fire shall devour before him, and it shall be very tempestuous round about him. He shall call to the heavens from above, and to the earth, that he may judge his people. Gather my saints together unto me; those that have made a covenant with me by sacrifice." (Ps. 50:3-5.) The Apostle Paul also speaks of this great event by saying, "The Lord Jesus shall be revealed from heaven with his mighty angels, In flaming fire taking vengeance upon them that know not God, and that obey not the gospel of the Lord Jesus Christ." (II Thess. 1:7-8.)

For this final one-thousand-year period, many sweeping changes will take place in the earth itself, as well as in the lives of the people who live upon it. The delightful paradisiacal condition of the earth with its Garden of Eden beauty will be restored. Its deserts and waste places will disappear, Satan will be bound, and there will be no more corruption, death, or disease, as we now know them.

About this change, John the Revelator said, "And I saw an angel come down from heaven, having the key of the bottomless pit and a great chain in his hand. And he laid hold on the dragon, that old serpent, which is the Devil, and Satan, and bound him a thousand years, and cast him into the bottomless pit, and shut him up, and set a seal upon him that he should deceive the nations no more, till the thousand years should be fulfilled: and after that he must be loosed for a little season." (Rev. 20:1-3.)

During this millennium the enmity among men and beasts will cease. (D&C 101:26.) Isaiah says, "The wolf also shall dwell with the lamb, and the leopard shall lie down with the kid; and the calf and the young lion and the fatling together; and a little child shall lead them. And the cow and the bear shall feed; their young ones shall lie down together; the lion shall eat straw like the ox. And the suckling child shall play on the hole of the asp, and the weaned child shall put his hand on the cockatrice den. They shall not hurt or destroy in all my holy mountain: for the earth shall be full of the knowledge of the Lord, as the waters cover the sea." (Isa. 11: 6-9.) Then no one will say that God is dead, or that his revelations have ceased, or that life has no purpose.

Many years ago Harry Emerson Fosdick wrote an interesting book entitled *It's a Great Time to Be Alive.* He pointed out some of the miracles and wonders that have made our age the most exciting since creation. And yet the magnificence of this coming one thousand years will make our day of wonders and miracles seem like the dark ages by comparison.

Of course, the Lord is not coming to the earth alone. As Paul said, "He will come with his mighty angels in flaming fire." And many of the righteous dead will then be resurrected and caught up to join the Lord and his company in the air. In speaking of this event, Paul said to the Thessolonians, "I would not have you to be ignorant, brethren, concerning them which are asleep . . . them also which sleep in Jesus will God bring with him. . . . For the Lord himself shall descend from heaven with a shout, with the voice of the archangel, and with the trump of God: and the dead in Christ shall rise first: Then we which are alive and remain shall be caught up together with them in the clouds, to meet the Lord in the air: and so shall we ever be with the Lord." (I Thess. 4:13-17.) What a great time this will be, to be alive!

And what a great time it will be when success, happiness, and peace shall cover the earth, and children will grow up without sin unto salvation. How meaningful, then, will be the Lord's promise through Zechariah, saying, "Sing and rejoice, O daughter of Zion: for, lo, I come, and I will dwell in the midst of thee, saith the Lord." (Zech. 2:10.)

Isaiah says, "And they shall build houses, and inhabit them; and they shall plant vineyards, and eat the fruit of them. They shall not build, and another inhabit; they shall not plant, and another eat; for as the days of a tree are the days of my people, and mine elect shall long enjoy the works of their hands. They shall not labor in vain, nor bring forth for trouble; for they are the seed of the blessed of the Lord, and their offspring with them. And it shall come to pass, that before they call, I will answer; and while they are yet speaking, I will hear. The wolf and the lamb shall feed together, and the lion shall eat straw like the bullock: and dust shall be the serpent's meat. They shall not hurt nor destroy in all my holy mountain, saith the Lord." (Isa. 65:21-25.)

Then men shall no more die and sleep in the earth, but they shall be changed in the twinkling of an eye, and shall be caught up, and their rest shall be glorious. "And God shall wipe away all tears from their eyes; and there shall be no more death, neither sorrow, nor crying, neither shall there be any more pain." (Rev. 21:4.)

What a great time to be alive, when Christ himself will be our law giver; and righteous men and women from both sides of the veil will live and reign with Christ for a thousand years in great success and happiness; and the new Jerusalem shall be built upon this the American continent. But what a tragic time it will be for those who fail to qualify. Suppose we should find ourselves among that group mentioned by John the Revelator, when he said, "But the rest of the dead lived not again until the thousand years were finished." (Rev. 20:5.)

A modern-day revelation says, "For . . . the Lord shall utter his voice out of heaven; . . . and the earth shall tremble, . . . and

[God] shall say to the sleeping nations: Ye saints arise and live; ye sinners stay and sleep until I shall call again." (D&C 43:18.) We cannot count on too much more time for procrastination, for while the scripture says that men will say, "My Lord delayeth his coming," yet the Lord himself has said that the allotted time will actually be cut short—otherwise no flesh would be saved upon the earth.

At the end of the seventh one thousand years, Satan will again be loosed for a little season before evil is completely banished forever. After the millennium, the status of the earth will again be increased to reach its final destiny as a celestial sphere on which the elect will live forever as members of that exalted order to which the Father himself belongs.

And may God grant us success in our part of this greatest of all of earth's enterprises.

False Witness

R ECENTLY WE HAVE HEARD A GOOD DEAL ABOUT A PROPOSED
political program called "The Great Society." This is a kind
of human betterment project, which contemplates a war on poverty,
a reduction in disease, and an increase in our physical comforts.
It anticipates an upgrading of our effectiveness and hopes for a
general elevation in our standards of living. But the success of any
great improvement program depends primarily upon our ability to
strengthen our moral qualities and center our focus on truth and
righteousness. This idea of a "Great Society" is one that we have
already had considerable experience with. This was the objective
in the minds of the Founding Fathers, when our nation was organized, and its system of laws established.

Under the law, when we have difficulties, we enlist the aid of
the court. But before the court can settle any problem, it puts the
testifiers on the witness stand. And each individual witness is required to take a solemn oath to tell the truth, the whole truth, and
nothing but the truth. Serious problems always develop either in
or out of court if these oaths are not kept. It is because so much
depends upon the truth that perjury has become such a serious
offense.

Of course, the American attempt to build a "Great Society" was
not the first one. Since time began, God himself has been working
on such a project, but even he has failed many times, and each
failure has been brought about because of some falseness in the
witnesses.

When the courtroom oath fails to carry over into life, our society itself begins to fall apart. Honesty and truth are the cement
that hold every real success together. This is also the base on which
all worthwhile knowledge and confidence must rest. And it is the
primary prerequisite in motivating every upward- and forward-
looking activity. Even one's judgment is no better than the quality
of his information. No logic is very dependable where truth is mixed
with falsehood.

As a pattern, we might think about that "Great Society" that
was instituted thirty-four centuries ago, when, from the top of Mount

Sinai, God outlined an order that he hoped to establish upon the earth. He promised that if the people would live ten great principles called the Ten Commandments, they would become a chosen generation—a holy nation, a royal priesthood, a peculiar people. He promised to make their bodies immune to disease. They would be able to triumph over all of their enemies. Their land would be one flowing with milk and honey. Then Moses went down from the presence of the Lord and put the people under covenant. They were sworn to believe in God and to live his laws. Each of these great commandments is of primary importance. But they all seem to center in number nine. In this great law, the Lord said to the people, "Thou shalt not bear false witness against thy neighbor." If kept, from this one Commandment alone might well materialize the greatest society. Every community success grows out of the quality of the personal honor of its individual members.

Many years after the attempt from Sinai had failed, Jesus again tried to reestablish God's kingdom upon the earth. As he closed his mortal ministry and ascended into heaven, he looked down on his disciples and said, "Ye shall be witnesses unto me, both in Jerusalem and in all Judea, and in Samaria, and unto the uttermost parts of the earth." This does not apply only to the apostles. We are all his children, and every child of God has been called to be a witness for him.

How productive our individual lives will be will be determined by how effectively we build the "Great Society" that God is still trying to establish among us. And all success will largely depend upon how well we discharge our obligations of truthfulness.

Every violation of truth is a stab at the very heart of our society. One of the most striking contradictions in our civilization is the fundamental reverence we profess for truth and our wholesale disregard for its actual practice. Our attempts for a peaceful coexistence between noble creeds and evil deeds have never been very successful. The conflict that results from our double standards gives both institutions and men split personalities. It produces innumerable wrongs among us and greatly weakens our society.

Recently, a bankruptcy proceeding resulted in some members of a small community losing over three million dollars. The investors were induced to venture their savings because the name of a well-known and highly respected citizen had been used and that great command given from the heights of Mount Sinai had been violated.

Consequently, the people not only lost their money, but much of their faith in human nature as well.

It is our responsibility to help to build the "Great Society" contemplated by the Savior of the world. And the religion of Christ allows us no deviation from truth and righteousness. Probably the most severe condemnation meted out by Jesus was upon the heads of those who professed one thing and practiced something else. In referring to them, he used such harsh terms as "hypocrites" and "vipers." Who can tell where even the slightest deviation from truth may take us. We should understand that a falsehood is a falsehood, no matter how small it is or how much it is adorned with truth or diluted with righteousness. The most serious falsehoods usually come wearing some kind of disguise, and it is always much harder to crush a half-truth than a whole lie. We may bear our false witness in the form of rationalizing, exaggeration, cowardice, sloth, silence, bad example, or just plain deceit.

Nothing gives such a blow to friendship as an untruth in a friend. Falsehood is also the greatest foe to love; it is the most effective destroyer of honor and the worst seducer of every worthwhile thing in life. Falsehood and error are the chief enemies of science. They are the greatest antagonists of religion. They are the mortal foes of every success. They also cause distressing financial burdens. It is in trying to discover the truth and get fairness established in our lives that we generate heavy court costs, lawyer's fees, policemen's wages, and the expenses of witnesses. The violation of truth is not only morally wrong, but it is also financially unsound and socially unprofitable.

As an assassin's weapon, a false witness against one's neighbor is more destructive than an Italian stiletto. But usually we do not stop with a false witness against our neighbors. By our attitudes, our bad example, and our silence, we bear false witness against our parents, our children, our friends, and even ourselves.

Recently, I talked with a man about a very costly and disagreeable circumstance that he had brought upon several other people. He made no attempt to deny his guilt; he based his case on his contention that no one could prove anything. As he manifested his willingness to let others suffer for his wrong, I thought, what a tragic waste of manhood! What a thrilling experience this man might have, if he would center his concern on truth, fairness, and a desire to make restitution, rather than upon evasion, escape, and repetition.

Some of the greatest joys of life are the joys of being, the joys of being genuine, the joys of being true blue. In political success, financial prosperity, or pure religion, one of our greatest opportunities is to build our lives on the ninth commandment. By long odds, the noblest work of God is still an honest man. And the opposite of truth always brings disaster. Jesus was crucified because of false witness. In this great tragedy the false witnesses of sin, ignorance, misunderstanding, disobedience, hatred, and betrayal all had their parts. Some of the disciples bore false witness by their absence, and some by their inaction. Peter bore a false witness by his denial, Judas by his kiss, and Thomas by his doubt. But false witness continues to be one of the most serious obstacles standing in the way of human progress. We frequently misrepresent the values of our goods in the market place. But we also misrepresent God in our own lives.

Our alcoholism, profanity, dishonesty, and immorality do not properly represent that great being in whose likeness we were created. We even misrepresent our own interests by deceiving ourselves. As we reationalize our sins, exaggerate our virtues, or color the evidence on which our decisions will be made, we are practicing a serious false witness and misleading our own souls.

In our self-created confusion, we make it so difficult even for ourselves to recognize right. And whenever we make a careful and factual examination of our words and attitudes, we discover that an exact statement even about ourselves is very difficult. If we desert the truth in trifles, how can we hope to trust ourselves in matters of importance? It may help us to exclude falsehood from our lives and to think of our breasts as being made of glass, for sometime our duplicities and infirmities will become as apparent to everyone as they already are to God.

I know a young man who is ruining his own and others' lives because he greatly exaggerates his own virtues and self-importance. He tolerates a serious selfishness and continually excuses his own weakness and sins. He takes credit for imagined abilities that are based on false assumptions. He always blames others when things go wrong. And for something to seem right to him, it needs only to appear to be in his own interest. But his problems are fast getting out of hand, and reason is becoming more and more difficult for him, as he is rapidly losing the power to undeceive himself. If falsehood had only one face, a liar would involve us in no danger, but "False Witness" has a hundred faces and a hundred figures all mixed up with some kind of rationalizing and self-interest.

As Colton says, "Falsehood is never so successful as when she baits her hook with truth."

When we get too involved with error, it becomes very difficult to distinguish between right and wrong. We can form the habit of dealing so loosely with the facts that all meaning may be lost. It is so easy to think illogically about those whose point of view is different from our own. It sometimes seems almost right to condemn those of our competitors who excel us in accomplishment.

Someone has said, "It is pretty difficult to judge fairly between two race horses, when we have our money bet on one of them."

Even the most serious lie can sound very logical when we want to believe it. However, most of us do not actually desire to be unfair; we merely allow our outlook to become so warped by envy, jealousy, prejudice, or self-interest that our judgment is distorted.

The Bible says, "The way of every man seems right in his own eyes," and an old proverb says, "There is not one guilty man in the penitentiary." These damaging varieties of false witness against ourselves not only make good judgment difficult, but frequently repentance itself becomes impossible.

One of the most serious kinds of false witness comes when we begin tampering with the yellow line that runs between right and wrong. When we rationalize, exaggerate, alibi, prevaricate, cover up the facts, and distort the truth, our possibilities for success begin a sharp decline. Or when we take judgment into our own hands, or attempt to dispense punishment by means of a whispering campaign, we commit one of the great sins. False witness brings on serious mental, emotional moral, and financial failure, one of the most serious manifestations of which is the heavy burden of evil that we lay upon our own souls.

The scripture says that "Satan is the father of lies," and to the extent that we deviate from truth, we join hands with him, and become his ally. Before we fully qualify for God's favor, we must cease witnessing for evil. False witness is a difficult sin to get rid of, as so frequently we are unaware of its contamination. If dishonesty smelled as awful as tobacco, or if it gave us the staggers like those of an alcoholic, maybe we would build better defenses against it.

What a thrilling idea that the God of heaven and earth is also the God of truth. He cannot lie. He permits himself no deviation from righteousness. But we are God's children. We are created in his image, endowed with his potentialities, and made heirs to his glory. What an exciting challenge it should be to follow his example in truth and honor.

Shakespeare was speaking about the most exciting kind of "Great Society" when he said, "This above all, to thine ownself be true and it must follow as the night the day, thou canst not then be false to any man."

Certainly one of the greatest opportunities of our existence is to surcharge our spirits with truth. Suppose, therefore, we go at regular intervals in imagination and stand before Mount Sinai, while again we hear the great God of creation say, "Thou shalt not bear false witness."

What greater objective could we have than to join with God in working out a realization of that great society in our chosen generation and build a holy nation, a royal priesthood, and a people peculiar for their righteousness.

Father's Day

ECENTLY I HEARD A MAN GIVING AN ACCOUNT OF WHAT HE CON-
sidered to be one of the most important days in his life. This
was a Father's Day remembered from many years ago when he was
just a boy. The family was having Sunday dinner with some especially invited guests. All had attended church that morning and had
heard an excellent sermon. At the dinner table an interesting discussion had taken place about some of the things that had been said.
There were also some very favorable comments about the excellence
of the life of the speaker. As the son listened, he was greatly impressed and was particularly proud of his father, who seemed to him
to be a very wise and a very good man. The son was not old
enough to understand everything that had been said, but he was
greatly pleased that his father so wholeheartedly supported the good
things said by the speaker. The entire situation seemed very favorable to the boy, and he remembered that he felt very good inside.
From this dinner table conversation he had received a substantial
inner strength. A love of goodness was transferred to him, and the
power of an ideal had been established in his heart that had remained there through all of the years since.

As this story was being related, I thought of many contrasting
situations where mealtime is used for destructive purposes. Sometimes at dinner time leaders are criticized, ideals are torn down, and
negative attitudes are frequently established in lives that are too
young to understand what is going on. The psychiatrists and others
later spend a lot of time digging down into these dark, subconscious
regions, trying to root out the hurtful things that have been buried
there. Think of the childhood injuries caused by parental conflicts,
where criticism, name-calling, tears, and bitterness make up the
mental part of the meal.

A psychiatrist recently told the story of an unstable patient who
had grown to be an occupational and social misfit. Before their
young family, his father and mother had tried to unsell each other to
the children. There were accusations of unfaithfulness and unfairness.
In bitterness, the mother had said to the children, "Your father
doesn't love us." They didn't understand exactly what that meant,
but they felt it was something pretty terrible. By the time his

parents were finally divorced, one of these children was completely confused. He had been filled with hatred for his father and had developed a distrust and bitterness about his mother. The strong parental foundations on which his life should have been built were almost completely destroyed. He now had nothing to tie to and no one to believe in. In seeking someone to take the place of his lost family, he had other serious disappointments and hurts; and he had lost confidence in everyone, including himself. The thing that we need more than nearly anything else in youth or in age is the association of good people with good ideas in which we can wholeheartedly believe. We need a lot of father's days with some good, stable, honest fathers in the middle of them. Certainly we should not be limited for our Father's Days to the third Sunday in June.

In 1935, Clarence Day, Jr., wrote a humorous play entitled *Life With Father*. And that is about the best title under which our general success could be accounted for. Under this title we might list the many wonderful experiences with good fathers that we carry in our memories and our subconscious minds that would constantly influence our lives for good and lead us to our eternal Heavenly Father. This result might well come from those magic Father's Days when some great experience is shared or some chord is struck or some light is kindled that is capable of illuminating all future time. Our early years are the times when experiences can be born and relationships can be established that are warm, pleasant, and stabilizing. When these are caught and closely held in the meshes of our minds, they can establish our success forever. Our fathers themselves may have long since passed beyond, but they have left behind them their "father's days," which continually stimulate our welfare. Then to be with them again in imagination, we have only to select from this wonderful assortment of experiences that remain in our memory. And as we relive some particular experience, we reabsorb the original good.

We may relive a family picnic or the memory of a family prayer when the power of our father's spirit seemed to reach up to God. Because we understand the goodness of his life, we know that God is hearing what he says. What a wonderful, uplifting experience to feel that our own father, so dear to us, has the same kind of standing with God. Then, next in order of thrilling experiences is to feel the love and respect that our parents have for each other. It greatly strengthens us to know that they are genuine and that no matter what may happen, we can count on them. Then we feel the great strength born during the family home evening, when our prayers and our faith are "all for one and one for all." A great person makes every occasion a great occasion. Yet in those important experiences that we remember so vividly with our fathers, they may not have been specifically seeking to instruct or inspire or enlighten us. But because they were the kind of people they were, they could do nothing else, for every place that they go and everything that they say and do makes someone else a little richer, a little better, and a little happier than he was before.

The third Sunday in June is a great day for many reasons. One is that it should be a symbol of every other day. It is also the special time when we try to honor and please that great individual who is the author of our lives. But the idea itself is such a great one that God has also set aside some special father's days. These are far more than mere holidays—they are holy days. These are the days when, by the excellence and happiness of our lives, we make a special effort to honor and please God, our Eternal Heavenly Father. These are those great days filled with rich spiritual experiences when we try to reach a high point in our lives. These are the days when we put on our best clothes and think our best thoughts. These are the times when we read the scriptures and live the ideals and ambitions that God has set up to direct our lives.

Recently I re-read the story of George Washington Carver, the great Negro scientist and teacher. This child of slavery, poverty, and struggle accepted his mistreatment without taking offense. He overcame all of the obstacles that he found in his way. He indicated to the world the unlimited possibilities of what a man can accomplish and what he can become. In a makeshift laboratory at Tuskegee, Alabama, Dr. Carver made some 300 commercial products out of the common peanut. He took in his hand this lowly part of creation and said to God, "Tell me, Great Creator, why did you make the peanut?" Then, to the amazement of the world, Dr. Carver made from the peanut a list of such things as soap, face creams, salads, cereal, milk, vinegar, butter, paint, oils, dyes, axle grease, shampoos, and hundreds of other useful articles.

But the primary purposes of God and the chief objective of man do not center in the peanut but in us. And well we might ask the great Creator to give us a vision of the highest purpose of our lives. Why did God make us and what does he want us to do about it? Who of us has the courage to understand his own unlimited possibilities if placed under the influence of God and our own good deeds? What greater father's day thought could one have than to understand that if we are sufficiently righteous, thoughtful, energetic, loving, and obedient, the offspring of God may hope to eventually become like the eternal parents? Thus we may fulfill the profound declaration when Jesus said to us, "Be ye therefore perfect, even as your Father in heaven is perfect."

Cecil B. DeMille, the famous motion pictures producer, was a man of some great talents and keen insights. He liked to get off by himself at times to think out a problem. On one occasion, he went out in a canoe on a lake in Maine and spent a whole afternoon quietly adrift. The canoe finally floated near the shore to a place where the water was only a few inches deep. Looking down, he saw that the bottom was crowded with some beetle-like bugs. As he watched, one of these water beetles came to the surface and slowly crawled up the side of the canoe. When it reached the top, it fastened itself to the wood and died.

Mr. DeMille soon forgot the beetle, and his thoughts went back to his own problems. Several hours later he happened to notice the beetle again and saw that in the hot sun, its shell had become very dry and brittle. As he watched, it slowly split open, and there emerged from it a new life in the form of a dragonfly. It left the old husk and took to the air on strong, capable wings, its scintillating colors flashing in the sunlight.

This new life could fly farther in an instant than the water beetle had crawled in his entire lifetime. Then the dragonfly circled back and swooped down to the surface of the lake. Mr. DeMille noticed its shadow in the water. The beetles below may have seen it also, but now their erstwhile companion was in a world beyond their comprehension. They were still living in their very limited sphere, while their winged cousin had gained all of the freedom between the earth and sky.

Then Mr. DeMille asked this interesting question, "Would the great Creator of the universe do that for a water beetle and not for a human being?"

We often forget the tremendous truth that God created man in his own image; he endowed us with a set of his attributes and also bestowed his potentialities upon us. God has said to us, "Ye are gods; and all of you are children of the most High." (Ps. 82:6, John 10:34.) He has planned for us to be kings and priests unto God and to reign with him forever. (Rev. 5:10.)

As we think seriously about what man is able to accomplish within the narrow limits of this life and what God can do for a caterpillar and a common water beetle, we should be able to lift our own eyes above the earth and believe more intently in those divine possibilities that he has outlined for our eternal lives. We should live a little closer to the source of our blessings with an effective focus on our eternal Heavenly Father. For as we depart from God and his righteousness, the lines of his image in us become blurred and indistinct by the corrosion or attrition of sin. Or if we center our affections on alcoholism, crime, immorality, and disobedience to God, we bring upon ourselves the tragic experience of departure from our eternal Heavenly Father.

Recently a young couple with their two small children spent a few days of their vacation with the wife's parents. One night, with the grandparents as babysitters, the parents decided to go to a show. When the little $2\frac{1}{2}$-year-old daughter discovered that her parents were about to leave her, she had a kind of internal panic. She loves her grandparents and enjoys visiting with them. But because she has a very special relationship with her parents, she didn't want them to leave her. They love her the most; they care for her daily needs; she kneels with them in family prayer. She belongs to them and is an actual part of them. She doesn't talk very plainly, but as her parents left she kept screaming and calling their names as loudly as she could. After they had gone, she cried and sobbed as though her little heart was about to break, and only after her strength had been exhausted and she had fallen unconscious in sleep did her sobs cease. But just suppose that we try to imagine what an eternal life would be like without God—what eternal failure could compare to a "life without Father"?

The Apostle Paul has described God's three degrees or subdivisions of glory. The highest of these kingdoms is the celestial— that is the order to which God himself belongs. This Paul describes as the glory of the sun. At the bottom of the scale is the telestial glory—this is the name of the lowest of the three degrees. This differs from the celestial as the twinkle of a tiny star differs from the blaze of the noonday sun. But this order contains a very large group, which is referred to in modern-day revelation by the Lord: "Where God and Christ dwell they cannot come, worlds without end." (D&C 76:112.) For them there will be no eternal father's day.

But God is not only our Father and our Creator. He is the source of all good. If it can almost break one's heart to be deprived of the presence of his parents temporarily, what might it be like to be deprived of God's presence throughout eternity by our own unworthiness? God's presence will be the place where the most important events will always be taking place, and where the most happy, satisfying experiences will be had. Our eternal Heavenly Father loves us in a way that we are presently unable to understand, and someday we will feel a love for him that we are now too immature to comprehend. In the meantime, we should follow that important scripture that says, "Draw nigh unto God, and he will draw nigh unto you." To this end may God help us to make the most of our wonderful Father's Days opportunities.

For Better or for Worse

I SUPPOSE THAT NO ONE WOULD EVER SERIOUSLY QUESTION THE FACT that the family is the fundamental unit of our society. By long odds, it is our most important organization with the greatest opportunities for good. But the family probably has the highest incidence of failure and causes more losses than any other of our legally constituted institutions. If we fail in business, the bankruptcy court will wipe out our debts, but who can wipe out the impairments of bankruptcy in a home? We have powerful political parties to check up on the government. We have a strong government to regulate business. We have thousands of policemen to see that we obey the law. But our family interests may be more seriously neglected than any of our other affairs.

One must demonstrate substantial leadership qualifications before he is appointed to manage an important business, and he may be bonded for faithful performance. But the management of a vital family unit is often carried on with little supervision by inexperienced people lacking in the basic character qualifications necessary for success. As children are added to the family, the job becomes more difficult and the liabilities are greater. Students who cheat in school can be expelled. Employees who don't earn their pay can be fired. When one breaks the law, he is picked up by the police. But what can be done for those who cheat in marriage or show themselves to be irresponsible parents? In marriage many men and women are causing deformities in their children and heaping misery and heartbreak upon each other with little hope of remedy. Unfair attitudes, immoral tendencies, and spiritual brutality within a family are sometimes very difficult to get at. The infirmities of selfishness, bickering, laziness, and irresponsibility often produce stomach ulcers, nervous disorders, instability, and actual physical death. For every 100 marriages, over 25 go through the bankruptcy proceedings of a divorce court. But many of the others suffer a kind of incompatibility that causes injury to the personality and damage to the soul. Our bad habits and irritating personality traits wear out our lives and load up our souls with psychiatric disease, inferiority complexes, and social disorders. Broken marriage vows leave the most unsightly scars on the lives of both the parents and children. Certainly one of the greatest opportunities of our lives is to discipline and educate ourselves for this basic role of being a successful family member.

I recently witnessed a marriage in which the principals joined their right hands and promised to accept and support and love each other "for better or for worse, for richer or poorer, in sickness or in health, until death do us part." Another couple made even stronger vows: not only "until death do us part," but also "for time and for all eternity." Jesus is a member of the first family of the universe. What would be gained by ending such a tremendous relationship after the few brief years of mortality? Before death had entered the world, God the Eternal Father said, "It is not good for man to be alone." I would not like to lose my wife and family here, and I cannot think of a single circumstance that would make it more pleasant to lose them hereafter. A good marriage consists not only in finding the right person, but also in being the right person. And certainly the great possibilities of marriage make it important that they turn out for the *better* rather than for the *worse*. Anyone who gets married automatically becomes the guardian of the welfare and happiness of the other. God, the author of marriage, ordained that these two should become one flesh. Neither one can be happy unless the other is also happy, and only as each spouse makes the needs and happiness of the other his primary consideration will the marriage turn out for the *better*.

When one begins to think only of his own interests and pleasures or when the welfare and emotional stability of children are disregarded, the most wonderful marriage possibilities go sour. One woman said that she married her husband for better or for worse, but because he was worse than she thought he was going to be, she was breaking up the family. Most marriages would be *better* rather than *worse* if even one spouse took full advantage of the opportunities of living at his best. "One man can, if he will, change the morale of a whole community." We might profitably spend some time figuring out ways to make marriage turn out *better* instead of worse.

One of the most important sub-headings for marriage success is for both to improve the quality of their religion. When human standards of belief are low in quality or antagonistic with each other, sores develop rapidly. A number of years ago an important book was published by Dr. Henry C. Link entitled *The Return to Religion.* Dr. Link was head of the Psychological Service Center in New York City. While getting his scientific education in psychology, Dr. Link had discarded many of his religious convictions in favor of what he considered to be a more intellectual approach to life's problems. But when he began his actual contacts with the personal problems of people, Dr. Link soon discovered that the best solution of almost all difficulties was to be found in the practice of the principles of religion of Christ outlined in the Holy Scriptures. In giving psychological tests to thousands of people, it was found that in almost all cases the needed therapy called for the practice of some basic fundamental religious principle. It was discovered that those who are actuated by religious motives had better social and physical health and significantly better personalities. They were not only happier and more successful, but they were also superior in almost every other way.

In a recent newspaper report a divorce judge indicated that of all of those divorces with which he had had to deal, 88 percent of the victims were not active in church and 45 percent claimed that liquor was one of the primary causes of divorce. He said that immorality, dishonesty, and selfishness were also very prominent factors in breaking up marriages. And everyone can give his marriage a turn for the better by eliminating from his life all of those practices that religion advises against. The basic qualities of kindness, faith, morality, and obedience to God are the foundation stones on which both religion and the good life are built.

Another primary technique for giving marriage a turn for the better is to improve our marital communication. During the courting period it is usually such fun to talk to each other. But people who engage in marriage counseling report that most married people in trouble know very little about the hopes, needs, and ambitions of each other. Some married people dread communication with each other much as a soldier of World War I dreaded an excursion through a no man's land that had been planted with land mines. When antagonisms are always triggering explosions that blow up in your face, then marital communication is discontinued. Or it may degenerate into a low grade of bickering and unpleasantness. Sores are sometimes formed that are never allowed to heal, but become more raw as they are picked and irritated. The problems of finances, bad habits, differences in religion, and child discipline cannot be solved effectively when sore spots are so raw that a shudder goes through the personality each time they are touched.

The one who yells the loudest is not always the one who wins the argument. The scripture says that it is the soft answer that turneth away wrath, and it is the cheerful heart that doeth good like a medicine. In winning India's indepencence from England by non-violent means, Mohandas K. Gandhi had a slogan of "Harmony in adversity and love despite differences." Any loving, thoughtful spouse can win more arguments than one who is bitter and resentful. One of the best-known ways to win is by yielding, and often the best way to advance is by retreating. The shortest distance between two points is not always a straight line. Sometimes we need to circle the field a few times and then come in from the other side. For a thoughtful, loving spouse, there are a lot of short-cuts to a straight line.

I know a salesman whose problems come primarily because he uses the straight-line, strong-arm kind of domination that almost always fails. He wins the arguments, but he loses the sales. He has never learned how to dim his lights effectively or use his reverse gears or the other winning techniques involved in the retreat. He doesn't understand the powers of praise, apology, and friendliness. Someone once wrote a play entitled *She Stoops to Conquer.* Frequently that is the spirit of every success. This is the same reason that automobile tires made of rubber last longer than tires made of steel. Because the rubber is more pliable, it gives way to the rocks and other obstacles that come up against it. Marriage partners also do better when they have a greater built-in "factor of tolerance." It is also the iron tire in marriage that gives the roughest ride and causes the most nervous breakdowns.

Jesus said, "Love your enemies, bless them that curse you, do good to them that hate you, and pray for them which despitefully use you, and persecute you." (Matt 5:44.) This is a success formula that can also be used successfully to make the marriage relationship take a turn for the better.

Recently a woman whose marital troubles had developed into some mental problems said how much she loved the President of the Church. Jesus said, "If you love your friends and hate your enemies, what do ye more than others?" Even the most undisciplined and unsuccessful love those that love them. It's easy to love George Washington and Abraham Lincoln and Joan of Arc, but a wife who can love her husband with all of his faults and failings is really entitled to some special credit. This is especially true if she generates the kind of love that will change his life for the better and lift him up toward God. It is easy to love someone when there are no problems to overcome.

Dante loved Beatrice. All of his life he wrote poetry to a beautiful woman whom he had spoken to only once in his life. Beatrice died in her 26th year. But in Dante's poems it was for Beatrice that he endured the fires of Hell, and it was for Beatrice that he made his way to the gates of Paradise. If Dante's love for Beatrice had been subjected to the grueling tests of domestic familiarity and family problems, his poems might not have amounted to much. Dante might have been happier and he might have given his own wife a lift if he had written a few love poems to her who stayed at home to train his children.

It is not proof of emotional superiority when one loves the movie glamour girls and hates the wife who cooks his meals and cleans the house. Often husbands forget that they personally selected their wives above all others to be their companions and the mothers of their children, and that they are finer people now than they were then.

One woman who had very bad financial relations with her husband said, "I have done everything I can possibly do. I can't do any more, and I am not going to try." Granted that she has a problem, yet no one has ever completely exhausted his every possibility. She has probably done everything possible so far as her particular system of arguing is concerned. She had tested to their limits the possibilities of nagging pressure and the invoking against her husband of those sanctions that were available to her. But there is a higher power of love that she has not tried. There is a program of returning good for evil and using some soft answers to subdue his stubborn personality. Anyone can get along with those who are kind, thoughtful, generous, capable, and loving. But when a loving, resourceful wife can persuade a husband who is unskilled in personality accomplishments to do what he should, then she is entitled to a gold star on her forehead. Almost every husband and every wife can make a spouse eat out of his hand if he just knows his business. More than about anything else, every woman and every man needs and wants love, kindness and admiration; each one also needs to see in his spouse those attractive traits that can be admired and looked up to. And the greatest of all the formulas for marital success is found in the words of Jesus, when he said, "As ye would that men would do unto you, do ye even so unto them." If we want hate, distrust, and argument, that is what we should give. If we want love and kindness, we should give love and kindness. Jesus pointed out the law when he said, "With what measure ye meet, it shall be measured unto you again." With this law under our belts, our marriages will turn out to be better and richer instead of worse and poorer. My humble prayer is that God will help us to live at our best and make the most of our eternal family opportunities.

Growth Rings

I N OUR BACKYARD WE HAVE A LARGE CROSS SECTION OF A PETRIFIED tree. It is like flint in hardness. The grains of the wood are still natural in appearance, with beautiful colors shining out from the tree's face. Apparently this particular section of tree has lain exposed to the elements for many generations, and the rains of the centuries have given it a brilliant luster so that it resembles the artificially polished, many-colored, jewelry-like pieces of petrified wood that are sometimes sold in novelty stores. Besides being filled with beautiful polished colors, the tree's yearly growth rings are all visible in its surface.

My interest in this tree was recently increased when I read a study made of the stump of a giant redwood. A count of its growth rings indicated that the tree was nearly three thousand years old. And to make the tree's history a little more graphic, those making the report had marked in a picture of the stump that particular growth ring that was being formed while some important historical event was taking place. Then some external drawings had been made showing the tree's size at various times throughout its history. One picture showed the tree as it was when the Revolutionary War was being fought. A slightly smaller tree indicated its size when Columbus discovered America. It was a little smaller yet at the time of the fall of the Roman empire. Even when Jesus was being born in Bethlehem this tree was an impressive giant, over a thousand years old. With some of these thoughts in mind, I sometimes look into the face of the tree in our backyard and wonder when it lived and how many great historical sights it had witnessed.

The growth rings themselves tell an interesting story of alternating periods of favorable and unfavorable living conditions. There were some years when the new wood added during that year was a quarter of an inch in thickness. Then a series of drouth years or other unfavorable conditions followed when the tree grew only a small fraction of that amount. I thought of the Bible's account of Egypt's seven fat years, followed by seven lean years in the days of Joseph.

Sometimes, as I try to read the history of my tree, I also think about the ups and downs in my own life, and the favorable and unfavorable experiences in the lives of other people. I thought, what an interesting experience it would be if we could see the year by year growth records as we are actually making them in our own lives. If we understood the amount and the consequences of our personal growth, we might be motivated more effectively to make each year's growing conditions as favorable as possible so we could produce a reasonable amount of new wood each year. No good businessman would neglect to keep an accurate year by year record of his financial progress. At the end of each year, he adds up the gains and subtracts the losses in order to discover what his net growth has been for that year. Most businessmen also have a graph showing the year by year progress made in their net worth.

Doctors keep records of their patients for shorter periods on hourly temperature charts and blood pressure reading sheets. The doctor also likes to know whether the patient is gaining or losing weight and how much.

God is also keeping some gain and loss charts for us. We remember that Belshazzar, the unrighteous king of Babylon, was found to be a spiritual lightweight on the Lord's scales. But Belshazzar himself knew nothing about it until the mysterious hand wrote his final score in the plaster of the palace wall. It said, "God hath numbered thy kingdom, and finished it. Thou art weighed in the balances, and art found wanting; thy kingdom is taken from thee and given to the Medes and the Persians." If Belshazzar had had some accurate way of recording his own gains and losses as he went along, he might not have been so badly taken off guard. Even those who handle important stock market operations would be lost without an accurate record of ups and downs. Men dealing with money or elections think it is very important to be able to see the actual gains and losses, booms and depressions, inflations and deflations, as they are actually taking place. When we can see trends and understand their significance, we are in a much better position to do something about them. Joseph was only able to save his people from starvation because he knew in advance that the seven good years would be followed by seven years of drouth, and because he was willing to do something about it. And Belshazzar could have prevented his own destruction if he had kept an accurate record showing in which direction he was going.

This information is just as necessary for us, and it would be interesting as well as helpful to see some graphic representations of our own spiritual peaks and valleys. If we were sufficiently advised about our own moral depressions, and the upswings and downdrafts in our conduct before God, then we could identify on our charts the influences that caused our highs and lows. We could then understand where and why they started, and when and how they were stopped. Then we could point to our graph and say, "Here is where I was at my best," or we might say, "This long valley of depression marks that difficult battle I had with myself." Then we would know the effect of a negative attitude or the cost of some bad habit. We could see where we stumbled over a particular obstacle or fell flat before some specific temptation. Certainly with such a graphic statement of profit and loss always before us, we could greatly improve the spiritual solvency of our lives.

If we are to reach a maximum of success, we must know what makes our effectiveness go up and down and, of course, we should also know what our scores are at all times and what should be done about them. The extremes of our fluctuations are illustrated by a recent U.P.I. dispatch reporting a kind of Horatio Alger success story in reverse. The newspaper headline said, "A Hero on Sunday, a Bum on Monday." It recalled that on the previous Sunday, 28-year-old John Dennis had rescued eleven-year-old Ronnie Perez from the tracks of the Long Island railroad freight yard. His clothing had caught fire, and while fifty passers-by watched the burning boy only Dennis had been willing to do anything about it. From his hospital bed Ronnie had asked his mother to thank Mr. Dennis, and he added, "May God bless him." But fifteen hours later Dennis was picked up by the police for robbing a Brooklyn service station. The arresting officer said: "Dennis was a hero in the morning and a bum at night." Judge Herbert I. Sorin said to Dennis, "I was very proud of you yesterday morning, but I am ashamed of you now." This is something like what God said to Belshazzar.

Our own indicators of success and failure may go up and down a little less dramatically, but just the same, if we were intelligently aware of our spiritual fluctuations and the changes in our moral temperatures, our lives could be kept under better control.

The Holy Scripture says that everyone will be judged according to his works. And the Supreme Judge of the world is not only all wise and all knowing, but he is also a good accountant, and he has an unerring record of our upsurges and our backslidings. We could make a much better final score if we kept track of it as we went along. It is very strange that so many people who get involved in some serious problems claim that they don't even know what is causing their difficulty and therefore they can do nothing about it. Some people actually become moral bankrupts and say they are not aware of the reasons for their insolvency.

One of our most unfavorable statements of position is described by the confused individual who says, "I'm all mixed up." It seems so easy to get our goals mixed up, and our directions mixed up, and right and wrong mixed up. We get our sins mixed up with our ambitions, and our faith mixed up with our inferiority complexes. We get too many civil wars going on inside of ourselves and sometimes we haven't the slightest idea of who is winning. How can it be otherwise if we fail to keep score and have no altimeter to register our ups and downs and no compass to tell us which way we are going? Someone has pointed out that there are actually five primary directions. There are north, south, east, and west, and the fifth direction is where we are now. Even the best compass may not help us very much until we get ourselves located, and the most accurate speedometer will be of little use unless we are headed in the right direction. We should first find ourselves, then get ourselves unmixed and headed toward the right goal at the right speed.

Self-preservation is said to be the first law of nature, and everyone's life is now at stake. We not only have a natural hunger to survive physically, but we have an even more important hunger to live eternally. For this purpose, God has given this self-preservation urge a natural companion, which has been referred to as our growth instinct. Everyone has an inborn yearning for improvement. At its best it is a natural hunger to be like God.

The Creator himself has implanted in every soul "an upward reach," urging him upward and onward forever. Every soul is homesick and restless for eternal life. The conscience of man is always encouraging him to be better than he is, and the still small voice of the spirit is like a radar beam guiding him heavenward. But in spite of all these uplifting influences, it is probably true that the most neglected resource in the universe is our own human resource. We have our automobiles regularly washed, shined, inspected, and repaired. We take the most scientific care of our crops and herds. But frequently we are far less thoughtful about ourselves. That is, we often fail to give ourselves the kind of education that we should have, and frequently we so badly neglect our spiritual welfare that a yearly spiritual growth ring is almost indiscernible. Sometimes we actually throw our growth instinct into reverse gear by filling our lungs with nicotine and saturating our tissues with booze. Our growth rings also lose ground when our minds are steeped in dishonesty, our mouths filled with profanity, our hearts loaded with hate, and our eyes hungry with lust. Sin causes our crime waves to mount and our delinquency graph to shoot upward and our growth rings to disappear. Our guilt complexes cause us to lose confidence in ourselves; sin weakens our faith and enfeebles our courage. When we sell ourselves short by withdrawing our industry and abandoning ourselves, our eternal score begins a fatal drop.

Recently I had an unpleasant experience of sensing a negative, miserable attitude in a former acquaintance who was now at the extreme end of his seven poor years. He had just been released from a Church assignment, which he had held for ten years. When he was asked to say a few words to the assembled congregation, he began by saying, "I am just as frightened to stand before you today as I was when I stood up here to accept this position ten years ago." Then for the next fifteen minutes he breathed out over 2,000 people the most negative, belittling, pitiful, self-depreciating kind of ideas. In substance he said, "I am just as frightened and just as ignorant and just as weak and just as sinful and just as no-account as I was ten years ago," and it was clearly evident that he was not exaggerating. We have no business being as frightened or as sinful or as worthless as we were ten years ago. God will hold us responsible for the abuse of this growth instinct that he has entrusted us with. Certainly he did not give it to us to mock him.

So far as our talents are concerned, disuse is as mortal a sin as abuse, and just as destructive. The most bitter denunciation that Jesus ever poured out upon the head of anyone was upon the unprofitable servant who hid his talent in the ground. Jesus was kind to the repentant adulteress; he had a sympathetic interest with the thief on the cross who wanted to do better; but to the poor unfortunate who said, "I was afraid so I hid my talent in the ground," Jesus said, "Thou wicked and slothful servant." Then he said, "Take the talent from him and give it to him that has ten talents, and cast the unprofitable servant into outer darkness, where there will be weeping and wailing and gnashing of teeth." Jesus meant for us to put talents to work, and he meant for us to get the maximum benefit from our growth instincts.

Sometime ago a chief justice of a state supreme court made an interesting speech entitled, "What I Would Do If I Were 21 Again." Among other things he said, "I would take as good care of myself as

I do my automobile," and as part of himself he included his health, his appearance, his spirit, his mental attitude, and his eternal soul.

One of the tragedies of life is that frequently we have a greater appreciation of the values in our automobiles than we do of those in our eternal lives. Yet what an exciting thought it ought to be to understand that the greatest values in the universe are those eternal gifts inside of us, and that we ourselves may determine what their increases will be for eternity. Every human being is also a human becoming, and this important science of improving ourselves and becoming like God will always be the most important work of the world. In fact, this is the work in which God himself spends his entire time, as he has said, "This is my work and my glory, to bring to pass the immortality and eternal life of man." But as we make the religion of Christ an important part of our lives, it also becomes our work and our glory to bring to pass the immortality and eternal life of man. And may we pray that God will help us to perfect our timetable for putting some good yearly growth rings on our lives.

Happiness

I T IS A VERY INTERESTING FACT THAT THE MOST OUTSTANDING THING about the religion of Christ is its happiness. The purpose of the gospel is to prepare us for that highest standard of living which God himself enjoys. The divine desire is that all human beings might eventually become like God, their eternal Heavenly Father. God himself has a glorified celestial body, a celestial spirit, a celestial personality, and lives in celestial glory.

Many of our greatest satisfactions even in this life come from the way we ourselves think. Those who think negative thoughts develop negative minds. A depraved mind thinks depraved, unhappy thoughts. We can only try to imagine what it would be like to have a damned mind. Then, on the other hand, what will our situation be like to become like God and have a celestial mind that thinks only happy celestial thoughts. Our life here is an indication of our life hereafter. You will be yourself and I will be myself throughout eternity with quickened senses, amplified powers of perception, and vastly increased capacity for love, understanding, and happiness. In the great spiritual creation before this earth was formed, God created man in his own image. In the image of God created he him; male and female created he them. We were men and women in our antemortal existence, and the deserving sons and daughters of God will be men and women throughout eternity. We will have our families. We will have interesting and constructive work to do, and our lives will be characterized by a state of supreme happiness and joy. Christmas is the anniversary of the birth of Christ. It is also a time for great rejoicing and happiness. The term "gospel" itself means "the good news." The delegation of angels that came to Bethlehem on that first Christmas night said, "We bring unto you glad tidings of great joy, which shall be unto all people." Later on Jesus went around among people saying, "Rejoice, and be exceedingly glad." Peter spoke of some rejoicing with a joy unspeakable that was full of glory. (I Peter 1:8.) Paul says, "Rejoice forevermore." (I Thess. 5:16.)

It will help us to be happy in heaven if we learn to merit being happy here. Satan is miserable, as are all of those who follow him.

Every evil thought or act tends to make us unhappy, and every righteous deed tends to develop joy in our lives. To the extent that we learn to live the gospel, repent of our sins, and behave ourselves, we are happy. Criminals are not happy. Failures are not happy. Depraved minds are not happy minds. And while our greatest single ability should be to develop happiness in our lives, yet from some points of view there are not very many people who ever feel this emotion at its best very many times.

I thought about this situation the other day while in the barbershop. As I was having my hair cut I watched a television program on which some valuable presents were being given away to those taking part. I had an interesting experience of seeing a fine young woman win a brand new automobile. Judging from her reaction, I imagined she had wanted a new automobile more than about anything else in the world, and when the good fortune of winning had finally dawned upon her, her face lighted up with a glow that I had seldom seen before. She literally danced up and down on the platform with sheer delight, almost unable to contain herself. She reminded me of a bottle of Seven-up being shaken while someone held his thumb over the top of the bottle. You could almost feel the pressure building up inside of her, tending toward some kind of an explosion. Her person almost seemed incapable of containing this powerful feeling of happiness and elation that had her in its possession. Besides making her jump for joy, there was a radiance shining from her face that could be felt across 2,000 miles of television ether. With her eyes she picked her husband out of the audience and gave him the most glowing, victorious, joyous look. I found myself wishing that I had won the automobile—not for the automobile itself, but for the experience of feeling this delightful surge of joy that was overflowing her personality and pouring out into the airwaves. Then I tried to feel as happy as she seemed, and I thought what a great idea it would be if we could produce and maintain at will such a wonderful emotion of joy in ourselves. Everyone wants to be happy, and inasmuch as this joyous emotion is worth far more than any automobile or other things that can cause it, we should more effectively learn how to develop it in ourselves.

In researching this idea, I have undertaken a limited survey, seeking to discover what causes the most joy in people's lives. The most exalted moment in the life of one person might be his feeling of being deeply and madly in love. Under some circumstances this feeling may be almost overpowering. The two greatest commandments given by Jesus had to do with building up this emotion of happiness in ourselves by loving God and our fellowmen. If these commandments are lived effectively, they always produce a kind of Seven-up pressure of joy in us. Yet there are far too few people who ever have this wonderful experience very intensely or very long. I talk with a great many people about their marital and business problems and find that many lives are characterized by the opposite passions of envy, scorn, distrust, disrespect, and hate. The most exalted moment in the life of some athlete might be the occasion when he hits the winning home run in a championship baseball game, and yet even these moments following outstanding excellence are very few and far between in most lives.

I recently asked a friend of mine what he would do if he were trying to produce the most pleasant feeling in himself. I said to him, "Bill, if you just wanted to have fun, with no other factors to be considered, what would you do?" He said, "I would go fishing." I have never been a very enthusiastic fisherman, so this is a little difficult for me to understand. However, I tried as hard as I could to imagine how he felt about fishing.

Some people can raise themselves to their highest spiritual or emotional point by the inspiration of a good book, or by the thrilling strains of some stimulating music, or by the color and beauty of an outstanding painting. Some people get their greatest satisfaction from a good meal, some from smoking a cigarette, and some from getting drunk. There are those who reach their highest and most pleasurable state when some substantial honor comes to their children. With some particular good financial fortune, this internal pressure builds up inside of some people until they have to relieve themselves by expression. They sometimes describe the effects of this emotion by saying that they feel like shouting or dancing for joy. Then, thinking back to my friend winning the automobile, I wondered what heights of feeling one could reach if he won a million dollars, or saved someone's life, or wrote some great music, or was elected President of the United States. Some people know their greatest joy and highest satisfaction while rendering a constructive service. All of these causes of happiness center in the excellence of our own lives. And I thought what joy might come to us if someday we felt God's hand on our shoulder and heard him say, "Well done, thou good and faithful servant: thou hast been faithful over a few things, I will make thee ruler over many things: enter thou into the *joy* of the Lord." (Matt. 25:21.) The scriptures are clear that in heaven happiness is the highest emotion, and there is great joy there when a soul repents and turns his life upward. The Lord has said, "In me your joy shall be full." (D&C 101:36.) In a great modern-day scripture the Lord has said, "And if it so be that you should labor all your days in crying repentance unto this people, and bring, save it be one soul unto me, how great shall be your joy with him in the kingdom of my Father." (D&C 18:15.) We ought to try to understand what that means. I am sure Jesus intended that we should do and think those things that, according to his law, would make this feeling possible. Then I have thought about those thrilling gospel principles that, if followed, will someday enable us to stand before God on the most favorable basis.

Napoleon once said the greatest possible happiness came in the maximum development of oneself. We know there is extreme joy in the warmth of satisfying friendships, and in building our own character and personality traits up to their fullest potential. But what would it be like to make ourselves sufficiently worthy to actually live in the presence of God? Not as a beggar nor as a criminal with a guilty conscience and a tormented soul, but with a mind void of offense toward God and all men. What a wonderful sensation to feel that we ourselves are genuine and worthy of the love and respect of our eternal Heavenly Father. Actually, happiness is the purpose of life, and without it life loses its meaning.

Through an ancient American prophet, the Lord said, "Men are, that they might have joy." Of course, this is only possible on the condition of righteousness. Righteousness is by far our most profitable, joy-producing occupation. In a great latter-day revelation the Lord has made it known that happiness can only reach its ultimate state after we have been cleansed, resurrected, and prepared for eternal life in the highest glory. He said, "For man is spirit, the elements are eternal, and the spirit and elements inseparably connected receive a fullness of joy." But in spite of the fact that happiness is the purpose of existence and that righteousness is the process by which we qualify, yet the awful fact remains that most people are still traveling that broad road that leads toward death. In the very face of this reward we so frequently turn away from God. We break his laws and indulge in evil, and thereby we bring a pall of dark, miserable gloom upon ourselves. Jesus said, "If ye love me, keep my commandments." He also said, "If ye loved me, ye would rejoice." (John 14:28.) Even if we really loved ourselves, we would also keep his commandments with joy as a natural consequence.

Every part of the gospel with its glad tidings of great joy, was intended to make our lives happier, whereas bitterness, sin, hate, and all of the evil emotions produce poisons in the body and help to cause all kinds of physical and mental disorders. Not only is happiness one of our greatest abilities, but it is also one of our greatest responsibilities to produce this joy and satisfaction in our own and other lives. It doesn't take very much skill to be glum, disagreeable, moody, sinful, and cause others to be unhappy. However, if we are going to be happy in heaven, we should practice that process a little more while we are here.

In trying to describe this quality of joy that gets into people's hearts and shines out through their eyes and faces, we sometimes say that they have a light in their eyes, or their faces beam, or their personality is aglow, and yet I suppose that none of these things is true actually. There isn't really any light there at all. The eyes are the same size, the same color, the same shape as they were before. And yet there is something shining our from their faces that we can recognize but can't describe. In thinking about this, I thought of the description given of the resurrected Jesus as he appeared to John the Revelator on the Isle of Patmos. John tells us that he was in the spirit on the Lord's day when he heard behind him a great voice, as of the voice of a trumpet. When he turned to see who was speaking he said, he saw one like unto the Son of Man, clothed in a garment down to the foot, and he was girt about with a golden girdle. He said, "His head and his hairs were white like wool, as white as snow; and his eyes were as a flame of fire, And his feet like unto fine brass, as if they burned in a furnace; and his voice as the sound of many waters." (Rev. 1:13-15.)

Apparently the eyes of this great being were not just twinkling or beaming as were those of my friend who won the automobile. This radiant quality was probably magnified a few million times to make John say that "his eyes were a flame of fire." I suppose, however, that there wasn't actually any real flame there at all. John was trying to describe a consequence of this great quality of happiness that is indescribable. When Joseph Smith tried to describe the appearance of the Father and the Son, he said, "Their brightness and glory defy all description." We are told in the scripture that God is such a glorious personage that no man in his natural state can abide in his presence. The scripture says that no man has seen God at any time in the flesh, except quickened by the spirit of God." (D&C 67:11-13.) But if we live the gospel's glad tidings of great joy, we may someday qualify for that celestial order of which God himself is a member. Then we may understand the meaning of such phrases as "eternal happiness" and a "fullness of joy." In the meantime, may God help us to enlarge our hopes of eternal happiness by doing those things that he has specified.

He Lives

ONE OF THE MOST IMPORTANT EVENTS IN THE HISTORY OF OUR earth took place some 1,900 years ago in a garden tomb on the outskirts of Jerusalem. Matthew records this central fact in our history by saying, "In the end of the sabbath, as it began to dawn toward the first day of the week, came Mary Magdalene and the other Mary to see the sepulchre. And, behold, there was a great earthquake: for the angel of the Lord descended from heaven, and came and rolled back the stone from the door, and sat upon it. His countenance was like lightning, and his raiment white as snow: And for fear of him the keepers did shake, and became as dead men. And the angel answered and said unto the women, Fear not ye: for I know that ye seek Jesus, which was crucified. He is not here: for he is risen, as he said. Come, see the place where the Lord lay. And go quickly, and tell his disciples that he is risen from the dead; and, behold, he goeth before you into Galilee; there shall ye see him: lo, I have told you." (Matt. 28:1-7.)

We are all more or less familiar with the circumstances surrounding this all-important event, but this is the season of the year° when we try to get its importance a little more securely into our lives by reliving it in our minds. To begin with, Jesus is the Son of God, begotten by his eternal Father in heaven, long before our earth was formed. For a long period before his mortal birth in Bethlehem, he ruled and reigned with God. He came to the earth as our example of how life at its best should be lived. Then, by giving his life, he worked out an infinite atonement for our sins on condition of our repentance and our obedience to the eternal laws of life. At his death his body was laid in the tomb provided by Joseph of Arimathea. As his enemies recalled that he had foretold his own resurrection, they said to Pilate, "Sir, we remember that the deceiver said, while he was yet alive, After three days I will rise again. Command therefore that the sepulchre be made sure until the third day, lest his disciples come by night, and steal him away, and say unto the people, He is risen from the dead: so the last error shall be worse than the first. Pilate said unto them, Ye have a watch:

°given on Easter Sunday.

go your way, make it as sure as ye can. So they went, and made the sepulchre sure, sealing the stone, and setting a watch." (Matt. 27: 63-66.) Then for three days his body rested in the tomb. But his great spirit was not at rest.

Upon the cross he had announced the end of his mortal ministry by saying. "It is finished," And yet another ministry remained to be completed by him before he returned to his Heavenly Father. To the penitent transgressor who had been crucified upon the cross by his side he had said, "Verily I say unto thee, today shalt thou be with me in paradise." However, three days later the resurrected Savior said to the weeping Mary Magdalene, "I am not yet ascended to my Father." He had not gone to heaven but to paradise, which is a place where righteous and repentant spirits dwell between their bodily death and resurrection. There is also another division of this great world of spirits that is reserved for those disembodied beings who have lived lives of wickedness and who have remained impenitent even after death.

About this world of departed spirits an ancient American prophet said, "Now, concerning the state of the soul between death and the resurrection—Behold, it has been made known unto me, by an angel, that the spirits of all men, as they are departed from this mortal body, yea, the spirits of all men, whether they be good or evil, are taken home to that God who gave them life.

"And then shall it come to pass, that the spirits of those who are righteous are received into a state of happiness, which is called para-dise, a state of rest, a state of peace, where they shall rest from all their trouble and from all care and sorrow.

"And then shall it come to pass, that the spirits of the wicked, yea, who are evil for behold, they have no part nor portion of the Spirit of the Lord; for behold, they choose evil works rather than good; therefore the spirit of the devil did enter into them, and take possession of their house and these shall be cast out into outer dark-ness; there shall be weeping, and wailing, and gnashing of teeth, and this because of their own iniquity, being led captive by the will of the devil.

"Now this is the state of the souls of the wicked, yea, in darkness and a state of awful, fearful looking for the fiery indignation of the wrath of God upon them; thus they remain in this state, as well as the righteous in paradise, until the time of their resurrection." (Alma 40:11-14)

There are many passages of scripture that make clear to us that while his body lay in the tomb, Christ was ministering among departed spirits both in paradise and in the prison realm, where dwelt the spirits of the disobedient. Peter, the chief Apostle, was testifying about this fact when he said, "For Christ also hath once suffered for sins, the just for the unjust, that he might bring us to God, being put to death in the flesh, but quickened by the Spirit: By which also he went and preached unto the spirits in prison; Which sometime were disobedient, when once the long-suffering of God waited in the days of Noah, while the ark was a preparing, wherein few that is eight souls were saved by water. (I Peter 3:18-20.)

Peter also explains why this was necessary. God is also the God and the judge of the dead, and Peter says, "For this cause was the gospel preached also to them that are dead, that they might be judged according to men in the flesh, but live according to God in the spirit." (I Peter 4:6)

Jesus went into the spirit world and organized his forces, preparing the people for the preaching of the gospel as he had already done upon the earth. His ministry among the departed had been foretold and discussed by peoples as a part of the plan of salvation for a long time. Isaiah was permitted to foresee the postmortal fate of the ungodly, and he said, "And they shall be gathered together, as prisoners are gathered in the pit, and shall be shut up in the prison, and after many days they shall be visited." (Isa. 24:22) Then Isaiah told of the time when the Lord would go "to open the blind eyes, to bring out the prisoners from the prison." (Isa. 42:7.)

During his lifetime Jesus himself had said, "Verily, verily, I say unto you, The hour is coming, and now is, when the dead shall hear the voice of the Son of God: and they that hear shall live. For as the father hath life in himself; so hath he given to the Son to have life in himself; And hath given him authority to execute judgment

After three days he had finished this important responsibility of organizing the work for the departed, and the long talked of resurrection was about to take place. At the proper time the angel of the Lord descended in glory, broke the Roman seal, rolled back the massive stone from the portal of the tomb, and sat upon it. His countenance was as brilliant as the lightning, and his raiment was as the driven snow for whiteness. The soldiers stationed there to maintain the security of the tomb, paralyzed with fear, fell to the earth as dead men. When they had partially recovered from their fright, they deserted their posts and fled from the scene in terror. Yet these were not timid, easily frightened men; they were hard, bold, courageous, seasoned soldiers of Rome, who had been taught to stand in the presence of death without a quiver of emotion. But when they stood in the presence of a glorified resurrected life, they became as dead men. Then the spirit and the body of Jesus were inseparably joined together in a glorious union called resurrection, where they were no longer subject to separation. But this was just the beginning of the resurrection, as the scripture says: "And the graves were opened; and many bodies of the saints which slept arose, and came out of the graves after his resurrection, and went into the holy city, and appeared unto many." (Matt. 27:52-53). This great event taking place in the lives of so many people was not any mere idle display. This was the beginning of an eternal life.

We have a record that Jesus personally appeared to people eleven times in the forty days between his resurrection and ascension. The first appearance was to Mary Magdalene near the sepulchre. (Mark 16:9-10; John 20:14) Next he appeared to some other women somewhere between the sepulchre and Jerusalem. (Matt. 28:9.) In his third recorded appearance, he walked with two disciples along the road to Emmaus and explained the resurrection to them. (Mark 16:14; John 20:26), and to the apostles at the Sea of Tiberias in Galilee. (Matt. 28:16.) Then he appeared to five hundred brethren at once. The locality of this appearance is not specified, but it was probably in Galilee. Then he appeared to James (I Cor. 15:7) and finally to the eleven apostles on the Mount of Olives near Bethany at the time of his ascension into heaven.

During this postmortal ministry of forty days, he walked and talked with his followers. He cooked breakfast for the apostles on the beach of the Sea of Tiberias; he walked with them to Emmaus. In a meeting with the eleven apostles, he showed them his hands and his feet and said, "It is I myself: handle me, and see; for a spirit hath not flesh and bones, as ye see me have. . . . and while they yet believed not for joy, and wondered, he said unto them, Have ye here any meat? And they gave him a piece of a broiled fish, and of an honeycomb. And he took it, and did ead before them." (Luke 24:39-43.) He invited Thomas to put his finger into the nail holes and thrust his hand into his side.

After his resurrection he also appeared to the people who then lived upon the western continent in fulfillment of the words recorded in the gospel of John, when he said, "And other sheep I have, which are not of this fold: them also I must bring, and they shall hear my voice; and there shall be one fold, and one shepherd." (John 10:16) While upon the western continent he organized his Church among the people. The fact is fully recorded in the sacred writings kept by the highly intellectual people who lived here at that time. This record is available to us in III Nephi, and this section of the Book of Mormon has been called the fifth Gospel.

A reference to this appearance is also found among the traditions of the descendants of those early-day Americans and in the hieroglyphics of their ancient ruins. But he has not slighted our own dispensation. In the early spring of 1820, the resurrected Jesus again appeared upon the earth, this time to the Prophet Joseph Smith, through whom he has for the last time organized his Church upon the earth in preparation of his glorious second coming. Just before his crucifixion Jesus said, "And this gospel of the kingdom shall be preached in all the world as a witness unto all nations, and then shall the end come." Those who half believe that God is dead will have their greatest surprise when, in fulfillment of many scriptures, he will in the very near future come in great glory to cleanse the earth in preparation for his millennial reign upon it. But certainly the greatest message of the ages centers in Easter. It has to do with several facts, including that of the ministry of angels, that God lives, that the bonds of death have been broken for all mankind, that the tomb of Jesus is empty, and that all men may share the joy of a glorious resurrection. For as in Adam all die, even so in Christ shall all be made alive.

Many years after that first Easter morning the resurrected Jesus appeared to John the Revelator on the Isle of Patmos and said, "I am he that liveth and was dead, and behold, I am alive for ever more." But because God lives, and because death has been conquered, we may also live. On this special day I would like to share with you the words of a great hymn by Lewis D. Edwards, by which we may sing our Easter testimony:

> I know that my Redeemer lives;
> What comfort this sweet sentence gives.
> He lives, he lives who once was dead;
> He lives my ever-living head.

> He lives to bless me with his love;
> He lives to plead for me above;
> He lives my hungry soul to feed;
> He lives to bless in time of need.

He lives to grant me rich supply;
He lives to guide me with his eye;
He lives to comfort me when faint;
He lives to hear my soul's complaint.

He lives to silence all my fears;
He lives to wipe away my tears;
He lives to calm my troubled heart;
He lives all blessings to impart.

He lives, my kind, wise, heavenly friend;
He lives and loves me to the end:
He lives, and while he lives, I'll sing,
He lives, my Prophet, Priest, and King.

He lives and grants me daily breath;
He lives, and I shall conquer death;
He lives, my mansions to prepare;
He lives to bring me safely there.

He lives, all glory to his name;
He lives, my Savior, still the same;
O sweet the joy this sentence gives:
I know that my Redeemer lives.

May God grant that the Easter message may quicken our souls in righteousness.

Hooked

W E HAVE SOME VERY INTERESTING WORDS TO REPRESENT PAR-
ticular ideas and activities. These words have a way of
increasing in meaning as their influence in our lives becomes
stronger. There is one term that has a special significance for those
who are users of narcotics. Narcotics are powerful drugs with many
uses. They are given by medical men in moderate doses to relieve
pain, allay sensibility, or induce a state of profound sleep. In larger
doses they can cause convulsions, stupor, coma, or death. Certain
kinds of dope are sometimes illegally given to race horses to temporarily increase their speed. Another kind of dope is sometimes
given to a competitor's horse to produce a kind of lethargy or stupor
and thereby destroy his power to win.

But probably the outstanding characteristic for which narcotics
are noted is their habit-forming ability, and when one lets himself
get too much under their permanent influence, we say that he is
hooked. Many thousands of people annually have their lives ruined
because they are enslaved by dope. When drugs are taken into one's
system, the body makes an adjustment so that an increased physical
and mental demand for them is created. As the tolerance is built
up, a corresponding increase takes place in the body thirst so that a
kind of vicious cycle is set in motion, which eventually becomes so
strong that it cannot be denied by the human will.

Thus drugs probably produce the most irresistible urges known
in human life. In its advanced stages it takes precedence over fear,
conscience, sex, physical hunger, or even self-preservation. Dope
addicts have committed every crime in the fields of robbery, pros-
titution, and murder in order to get the money to satisfy the demands
of this satanic appetite. The victim suffers unbearable tortures unless this unreasonable craving is immediately satisfied. When dope
cannot be obtained, hundreds have committed suicide to relieve
themselves of their pain. Sometimes people contract this habit
while being medically treated. Some begin using dope out of curiosity. Others do it for kicks. Some are attempting to forget some
sorrow. Some allow this terrible habit to get dominion over them
because they like the temporary feeling of elation that it gives. To
get this "high" feeling, some young people become glue sniffers or

marijuana smokers, or they take shots of heroin or cocaine. While they are on this big-time drunk, they feel like they are on top of the world; but a few hours later, when the charge is gone, they must commit more crimes to get more money to buy more dope to be able to live with themselves.

The dictionary says that "a hook" is a piece of curved metal designed for catching fish or for holding or pulling something. I suppose that to be adequately impressed with the terrors of a fish hook, one would have to have it imbedded in his throat or heart or brain. It has the sharpest steel point with which to penetrate its victim, and it has the most wicked barb pointed in the other direction to prevent the victim's release. But narcotics also have some vicious reverse barbs, and so does alcohol, and so does nicotine, and so does sin. And all sins, like all narcotics, are habit forming. The thirst effectively stimulates the senses to take the hook, and then the barbs produce the greatest pain in preventing the victim from any escape. Jesus said, "Whoever committeth sin is the servant of sin." (John 8:34.) When we sufficiently obey any unrighteous or unfair idea, we become its servant; that is, we are hooked by it.

The dictionary says that the term "addict" indicates one who has surrendered. He is one who has given himself up to sin, or he has given himself over to the continual indulgence of his evil. However, the barbs of each new indulgence make the slave more helpless, and the addict is bound with stronger and stronger hooks to the thing or person that is to be his master. In their addiction some people have given themselves over to dope, but others have given themselves over to immorality or to degeneracy, and one can become a permanent addict of evil in a very short time. That does not mean that the addict enjoys being hooked any more than a fish enjoys that piercing steel point tearing through the top of its head. But the natural consequence of one nibbling at the bait is that he may find himself caught by the hook. Then frequently the more the fish struggles, the deeper the bite that is taken by the hook and the more the flesh is torn by the barbs.

Recently I talked with a young mother who, when she was a child, had been hooked by the immorality of an evil stepfather. He had contaminated her soul with his exhibitionism and evil-mindedness. As she had grown old enough to understand his degeneracy, a dreadful hate for him began to grow and fester in her mind. At age twenty she married, partly to get away from her unhappiness at home. But the hate generated by his dishonor, unfairness, and evil was still drugging and tearing the delicate cells of her mind and nervous system. After her marriage it was discovered that the poison was more potent than had been expected, and her mental and emotional life had been seriously damaged. It was as though some great hooks or some white-hot searing irons had been dragged through her mind, so that instead of normal mental and emotional equipment, she had piles of unnatural scar tissue that could not function normally. The injury done by her repulsion had also been transferred from the one committing the evil to everyone else. She married a fine man and had two healthy children, but she has a feeling for them that may be comparable to the feeling she might have for pieces of furniture.

Sometimes when people are brought up in homes where love, honesty, security, virtue, and happiness do not exist, no fertilizing cross-pollenization takes place and those virtues may not be born. Elbert Hubbard had something like this in mind when he said, "I am looking out through the library window into the apple orchard, and I see millions of blossoms that will never materialize or become fruit for lack of vitalization." The natural destiny of an apple blossom is that it should become an apple, and the destiny of every human soul is that it should be filled with those qualities of love, success, and happiness to make it resemble God. But sometimes neither of these functions takes place because the bee doesn't get there with the fertilizing pollen, or the scar tissue already formed prevents even the finest things from growing there.

When people become hooked with hate, distrust and shame, they may easily grow to be deformed or their best feelings can easily be destroyed. These people never know the devotion, light, and beauty that is their natural right. This fine lady just mentioned has been seeing a psychiatrist each week for two years, and the husband has been spending a great deal of his earnings trying to clean out the scar tissue and get her healed of her disease, but no discernible progress has been made. The wife herself would give anything to have a healthy mind, just as a one-legged man would like to be whole physically, or as every dope addict would like to be freed from his bondage. In his thoughtful moments every degenerate would like to be decent, and every drunkard wishes that he did not drink, and every smoker is sorry that he cannot free himself from that awful curse of nicotine. Everyone who is emotionally scarred and unhappy wishes he could withdraw that awful hook that lies buried in his flesh. But when one is hooked, either with his own or someone else's evil, it is pretty difficult to free himself.

We may be generally aware of the enormous waste that takes place because of crime and delinquency. But frequently we are unable to translate these statistics into terms of human degradation or suffering. Tennyson says, "Things seen are mightier than things heard." And if we could go on a tour of the great cities of our land and visit the dens of vice that are dispensing perversion, liquor, lust, dope, immorality, violence, and creating all variety of scar tissue, we would have a greater appreciation of the problems that destroy the lives of so many people.

In some dimly lit, evil-smelling places, some groups of young people are training themselves in the catalog of sin. Dope and booze are being dispensed and many personal evils are being generated. The bodies of human beings formed in God's image are being used to bait the hooks of lust, so that a substantial financial reward may go into the pockets of depraved promoters. We might try to imagine the amount of scar tissue that can be formed in one single night. Shakespeare wrote a line in which he said, "Each new morn new widows howl, new orphans cry, new sorrows strike heaven in the face." How many guilt complexes can be formed, how many minds can become a little more depraved in 24 hours? How many young lives give themselves over to evil, in a week or a month, and how many others are hooked by sensual appetites or have their passions perverted to evil that were intended to serve a much more noble purpose? Some of these young people have been led to think that they are merely gaining experience, or getting acquainted with life. They are not yet aware that vicious steel hooks are quietly and painlessly being set into their bodies, their minds, and their spirits.

The newspapers give us a daily report of the distorted lives that crowd our jails, mental hospitals, and reform schools. It is too bad that we can't look into our own souls and feel in advance the awful pain and devastation that will be caused by the scar tissue of our own sins. Many who are never confined to an institution have poisonous hooks of evil festering in their flesh, causing all kinds of mental, emotional, social, and nervous problems. What a pity that we don't make greater use of this important principle called prevention. Sometimes it is pretty difficult for a dope addict or a sex pervert or one with a distorted outlook on life to repent, just as it is pretty difficult for a fish to repent of his appetite when he is dangling on the end of a fisherman's line with a cruel hook tearing out his insides.

Even if our problems have not assumed major proportions yet, hooks with small barbs can be very painful, and sensitive spirits can be damaged very easily. Many people remain mentally and spiritually ill long after the evil itself is no longer present. And even then it is sometimes impossible for the doctors or the psychiatrists or ourselves or our prayers to get the disease out of our lives. Part of the torment of hell itself comes because we are hooked by evil memories.

Of course, every sick person is not totally ill. Some are only ninety percent sick, some are sick fifty percent, and some have a ten percent illness. But the scriptures say that God can not look upon sin with the least degree of allowance. Even in the smallest doses, sin is still sin, and every acceptance of evil carries with it the germs of that disease. Because Jesus kept himself completely free from sin, he had no scar tissue to bother him. What a great idea if we could pattern our lives after his and always keep them clean and healthy! Then we could free ourselves of being servants of lust or guilt or appetite or hate. Whether our hooks are great or small, we had better count on the barbs causing some scar tissue. One man recently complained that he didn't love his wife. But he also explained that he didn't love his children, or his parents, or his friends. He said he didn't love anyone and that he never had loved anyone. Because of the lack of the right kind of pollen, the proper fertilization had not taken place. By some error during his early formative years, this wonderful ability to love people and believe in them had been killed in him. Now, because his heart was filled with scar tissue, these emotions and abilities were unable to get started in his life. The injury may have been caused by antagonism in his parents, or some severe emotional block in him may have caused the injury. But whatever the cause may have been, he is now hooked by a terrible apathy that cancels out his natural ability to participate in that great experience of love.

Jesus set up this commandment to love as our most important law. And one of the wonderful things about religion is that every day we may build the opposite of slavery by developing those qualities of godliness into our lives. We can form the most thrilling habits of honesty, morality, cleanliness, fairness, righteousness, happiness, obedience, and love. These will prevent us from being hooked by any evil, and I pray that God will bless us to this end.

Hydrology

HYDROLOGY IS THE SCIENCE OF WATER. THIS SCIENCE CONCERNS itself with the supply, sources, distribution, physical properties, purification, and use of water. It is also interested in the effects that water has upon its environment as well as upon the various forms of human activity. Because water is the central material problem of mankind, the nations of the world have banded together and have set aside the decade of the 1960's to study it. They have called the 1960's the "International Hydrologic Decade." To launch this ten year project, some international discussions were held in Helsinki in 1960 to make plans and to learn everything possible about this great natural resource, which ranks second in importance only to air. A year later this ten-year study was endorsed by the educational, scientific, and cultural organizations of the United Nations and the International Association of Scientific Hydrology. Another preparatory meeting was held in 1963 in Paris, where forty-eight nations were represented to help launch one of the greatest international ventures in scientific cooperation.

The Hydrologic Decade is not primarily a time to build great waterworks, but rather to get the facts on which sound future building can be done in order to keep our earth a fit place to live. Up to now our water problems have been handled in municipal, county, or national spheres of authority. But water is no respecter of man-made boundaries, and a worldwide assault with simultaneous observations and study is needed, covering the entire surface of the earth. One individual arrived at his own conclusion that inasmuch as the earth's surface was three-fourths water and one-fourth land, that was his cue that he should spend three times as much time fishing as plowing.

There is more water on the earth than we can use, but most of it is salty and unfit for agriculture or culinary uses. The amount of fresh water that is available varies greatly from time to time and from place to place. More often than not, what is available is so badly polluted that it requires extensive treatment even before it can be used for industrial purposes. The waters of our rivers and lakes, if left untouched by men, would be self-perpetuating and would go on renewing and cleansing themselves eternally. But by contamination and unlimited demands for industrial uses, man now threatens the stability of his own existence. Our lives are maintained each year in the United States by the 1,500 cubic miles of rainfall, which amounts to over seven trillion tons of water. If for some reason this cycle were to be stopped, all of the water would finally come to rest in the oceans and life could continue only in the marine element. Of course, our rainfall is uneven, and much of it is lost, so that we sometimes have difficulty in supplying the sbustantial amount of water that each human being needs every day. We need water to drink, water to wash our faces in, water to bathe in, and some to wash the dishes. We use water to cook our food, run our air-conditioning systems, cool the engines of our automobiles, and keep our landscaping beautiful. A great additional, though less personal, need is to provide our pro-rata share of that great volume of water used in manufacturing, irrigation, beautification, etc. Some more intimate uses for this important substance are found in the fact that water is the medium by which food is carried to the various parts of the body and the waste is removed. Water cools the body by its evaporation from the sweat glands. Without a good operation of this water process, neither life nor health would be possible. In fact, it is said that we ourselves are approximately seventy percent water.

Our great store of water in the oceans, which we are sometimes inclined to take for granted, is 3,000 times greater than the amount of water in the rivers of the world at any given moment in time. The oceans contain over a million cubic miles of water, but it is unsuited for agriculture, manufacturing, or human consumption, and we have polluted much of the water in our streams by using them as dumping places for our filth and waste. We also have some vast underground deposits of water, which some estimates say were placed there ages ago. But for this decade of study the United States Geological Survey has brought forward a list of thirty ground-water problems that need to be researched. As water is the key of our success and prosperity, there are some oceans that need to be desalted; some rivers need to be purified, and new sources of water need to be made available in places of shortage. Pure water will also be one of the secrets of the regeneration of the earth in preparation for its millennium. The Lord has said, "And in the barren deserts there shall come forth pools of living water; and the parched ground shall no longer be a thirsty land." (D&C 133:29.) The rich treasures of the earth shall be brought forth when this living water is applied to those places that are now mere waste-lands.

Isaiah had this in mind many years ago when he said, " . . . for in the wilderness shall water break out, and streams in the desert. And the parched ground shall become a pool, and the thirsty land springs of water." (Isa. 35:6-7.)

We could presently use a lot of extra water in our deserts and in feeding and otherwise caring for our world's population explosion. There are many other problems that need to be researched during this International Hydrologic Decade. We don't know much about our underground water. It is not a fully renewable natural resource, as in some places it has to be mined like ores or oil. We presently do not know how much we can depend on this supply, but if it is to last and provide for our maximum benefit, the supply must be recharged.

We do not know exactly what happens in that relatively thin layer of the earth that contains this precious moisture. We do not know whether its form deep down is liquid or vapor, or what forces act upon it, or what part a forest plays in the passage of water to underground reservoirs. There are many of these problems that have to be resolved, and we hope to find many of the answers during the 1960's. We also need to find ways and means of getting a more equitable distribution of our other fresh water supplies and of keeping them from becoming contaminated. This may be more of a study of man than of water. Someone has said that "man is the only disorderly element in an otherwise orderly environment."

But water is the universal element. No life can survive without water. However, we have a great many other interesting uses for water. Jesus designated water as the element that we should be baptized in. It was also prescribed as one of the elements to be used in the sacrament.

As we cleanse our bodies by washing them with soap and water, so in a symbolic process we cleanse our souls by repenting of our sins. Then in obedience to God's command we have our sins washed away by burying our bodies in water, so that they can come forth in a newness of life. And each Sunday we keep this meaning alive as we renew our covenants by eating the bread and drinking the water as emblems of his atonement for our sins.

Jesus also taught an interesting lesson about another kind of spiritual hydrology. On one occasion, as he was going from Judea into Galilee, he stopped to rest at Jacobs well in a little Samaritan city of Sychar. When a woman came to the well to draw water, he asked her for a drink. She was a little surprised that he, being a Jew, would ask a favor of a Samaritan, with whom the Jews traditionally had no dealings. Jesus said unto her, "If thou knewest the gift of God, and who it is that saith to thee, Give me a drink, thou wouldest have asked of him, and he would have given thee living water." Jesus said, "Whosoever drinketh of this water shall thirst again: But whosoever drinketh of the water that I shall give him shall never thirst; but the water that I shall give him shall be in him a well of water springing up into everlasting life." Then the woman saith unto him, "Sir give me of this water, that I thirst not, neither come hither to draw." (John 4:5-15.)

Every living thing must have water if its life is to be sustained. This is not only true of the body, but the spirit must also be sustained by this living water. When people are caught in any desert without water, they soon die. But when we cut ourselves from the source of truth and righteousness, we also suffer a kind of spiritual death. The Lord sent Jeremiah with a message to backsliding Jerusalem and said to them, "For my people have committed two evils they have forsaken me the fountain of living waters, and hewed them out cisterns, broken cisterns, that can hold no water."

When we forsake God who is the source of truth, then like some wayfarer on a waterless desert we are in trouble, whereas we can live in our beautiful oasis even in the desert if we avail ourselves of our spiritual opportunities. In our day the Lord has said, ". . . unto him that keepeth my commandments I will give the mysteries of my kingdom, and the same shall be in him a well of living water, springing up into eternal life." (D&C 62:23.) If we keep our virtues watered and our abilities filled with life, then there will always be great growth in us. Jesus said, "For the Father hath life in himself; so hath he given the Son to have life in himself," (John 5:26) and we may be sure that he will also give us life springing up within ourselves, purifying and invigorating our lives and making them productive and happy. The best success in life comes from this inner growth. It is not like pouring water into the broken cistern mentioned by Jeremiah that will hold no water, rather it is like opening a self-perpetuating spring that supplies us with a source of our own.

Travelers tell us that there are rivers flowing beneath the streets of the ancient city of Sheckem. During the day hours you cannot hear them for the noise of the narrow streets and baazars. But when evening comes and the clamor dies away, when the dews of kindly sleep rest on the city, then quite audibly in the hush of the night you can hear the music of the buried streams. This is also the story of our lives and we may tap these sources of hidden waters that may spring up within us to eternal life. When this living water is flowing through our lives our whole spiritual landscape is beautified.

When John the Revelator describes the resurrected Jesus upon the Isle of Patmos, among other things he said, "And his voice was as the sound of many waters." (Rev. 1:15.) To the extent that we fail to make use of these waters of life, our lives begin to wither and we dry up with some fraction of death.

Many years ago Thomas Fuller was describing one form of spiritual drought by saying: "I discover an arrant laziness in my soul. For when I am to read a chapter in the Bible, before I begin I look where it endeth. And if it endeth not on the same page, I cannot keep my hands from turning over the leaf, to measure the length thereof on the other side; if it swells to many verses I begin to grudge.

"Surely my heart is not rightly affected. Were I truly hungry for heavenly food, I would not complain of meat. Scourge, Lord, this laziness from my soul; make the reading of thy words not a penance but a pleasure unto me; teach me that as amongst many heaps of gold, all being pure, that is the best which is the biggest, so I may esteem that chapter in thy word the best which is the longest."

The Lord has invited us to "come unto him and partake of the waters of life freely." (D&C 10:66.) But we should be sure that we get the right water, as all waters are not pure; some carry typhoid and other forms of deadly pollution, and sometimes we get a thirst for the wrong thing. Someone said to his friend with an appetite for alcohol, "Bill, this thirst of yours could make you great. But you are drinking the wrong stuff, and that firewater will never solve your thirst problem. You have to know what and how to drink. Now," said he, "I have a suggestion for you." Then he told his friend the thrilling story of that great last day of the Feast of the Passover, when Jesus stood up and cried, "If any man thirst, let him come unto me, and drink. He that believeth on me, as the scripture hath said, out of his belly shall flow rivers of living water. But this spoke he of the Spirit, which they that believe on him should receive. . . ." (John 7:37-39.) In one of his greatest beautitudes the Master said "Blessed are they which do hunger and thirst after righteousness for they shall be filled." (Matt. 5:6.)

Our lives would always be prosperous and happy if we would drink fully of this divine spirit and then follow the Master's instructions. But in spite of this invitation from Jesus, we frequently continue to drink the gall of evil, unhappiness, and bitterness, because of our personal disobedience. It might be a very good idea during this next ten years for us to carry on some hydrological research of our own. We might wash ourselves clean with the soap and water of repentance. We might desalt of its evil that great ocean in which we live, and learn to keep our own sources of spiritual supply uncontaminated. Then our own deserts would blossom as the rose as we unlock the great treasure house of our lives by applying the pure living waters upon our thirsty soil. We would realize a fulfillment of the sacramental prayer in which we ask God in the name of Jesus Christ to bless and sanctify the water to the souls of all of those who drink of it, that we may witness unto God, our Eternal Father, that we will always remember him, and keep his commandments, that we may always have his spirit to be with us.

May God help us to so hunger and to so thirst after righteousness that we may be effectively filled with all of those things that he has recommended.

Launch Out Into the Deep

THE PRIMARY MISSION OF JESUS WAS TO PROMOTE AS MUCH EX-
cellence as possible in our individual lives. But *our* help is
also needed, and when we lack the desire to live life at its best we
may not be very effective in making it better. Life itself is the most
valuable thing in the universe. And Jesus pointed out that of all
life, that which is called "eternal life" is the most important. Eternal life is not only everlasting; it is also lived on the highest possible
plane. Jesus challenged us to this end when he said, "Be ye therefore perfect, even as your Father in heaven is perfect." And we may
be sure that he would never have asked us to set any objective that
was impossible or unreasonable. With all of our inferiorities and
mortal weaknesses, it is sometimes difficult to remember that we are
the children of God, created in his image, endowed with his attributes, and heirs to his potentialities. Jesus was appointed as our
example, and we can learn much about ourselves by understanding
him.

The physical body that Jesus obtained in Bethlehem served as
the tabernacle of that eternal spirit known as Jehovah that had
previously lived with God. He was God's First Begotten Son, in the
spirit, and for a long period he served as a member of the Godhead.
As a part of the Presidency of heaven, he was the Creator of this
earth. Of him, the Apostle John said, "All things were made by
him; and without him was not anything made that was made. In
him was life; and the life was the light of men." (John 1:3-4.) We
get a little better picture of his heavenly importance from a statement made by God to Moses, saying, "And worlds without number
have I created; and . . . by the Son I created them, which is mine
Only Begotten." (Moses 1:33.)

Just think of the tremendous intelligence that would be involved
in creating and organizing an earth with all of its movements and
laws. God covered the earth's surface with some sixteen inches of
that miraculous substance called top soil. In a few years a good
farmer can get a pile of potatoes ten feet high out of this soil and
still have his sixteen inches of top soil left.

Every day God sends us enough energy, light, heat, and food

from the sun to make every accomplishment possible. This light, heat, and strength comes to us through millions of miles of unbelievably cold, dead space without giving up its treasures until it hits our atmosphere.

The Creator anticipated our needs and stored up all the necessary oil, gas, water, electricity, gold, silver, and uranium in the earth before we were placed upon it. God's foresight makes it possible for us to run our automobiles, light our homes, and provide the power for our atomic submarines. God has also set in order his thousands of other wonders and scientific laws. Then this magnificent personage who knew so much about so many things came to the earth to atone for our sins and redeem us from death. But *we* also lived as intelligent beings before our births. In our antemortal existence we walked by sight; we have all seen God. He is also *our* Father, and we lived with him as intellectual, responsible beings before this earth was formed. For a very good reason best known to God, a veil of forgetfulness has been temporarily drawn across our minds, and we are given the responsibility of learning to walk a little way by faith. We also have the assignment to develop within ourselves those abilities and personality qualities that will make us like God. Luke relates a kind of text event for this idea that once took place in the life of Jesus. He says,

"And it came to pass, that, as the people pressed upon him to hear the word of God, he stood by the lake of Gennesaret,

"And saw two ships standing by the lake: but the fishermen were gone out of them, and were washing their nets.

"And he entered into one of the ships, which was Simon's and prayed him that he would thrust out a little from the land. And he sat down, and taught the people out of the ship.

"Now when he had left off speaking, he said unto Simon, Launch out into the deep, and let down your nets for a draught.

"And Simon answering said unto him, Master we have toiled all the night, and have taken nothing: nevertheless at thy word, I will let down the net.

"And when they had this done, they inclosed a great multitude of fishes: and their nets brake.

"And they beckoned unto their partners, which were in the other ship, that they should come and help them. And they came, and filled both the ships, so that they began to sink." (Luke 5:1-7.)

Knowing how to catch enough fish to fill two boats must have been an easy accomplishment, compared to his task of creating worlds. And to catch the fish was probably less important than raising the sights of the fishermen. Lack of success sometimes destroys courage in people's lives. But by following the Master's direction, the fishermen had such great success that they nearly sank their boats. This miracle seems closely related to the announced purpose of the mission of Jesus to bring a more abundant life to people. This miracle of abundance has been performed over and over again. We have an abundance of sunshine, air, and fertility. As we follow God's laws, we receive an abundance of vision, freedom, opportunity, possibility, righteousness, knowledge, and faith.

Jesus said, "All things are possible to them that believe." He didn't say that just a few things are possible; he said that all things are possible. Jesus expects us to manifest this abundance in our own lives, and then we receive in proportion. He said, "Give, and it shall be given unto you; good measure, pressed down, and shaken together, and running over. . . . For with the same measure that ye mete withal it shall be measured to you again." (Luke 6:38.) There is no sign of any limitation here. Jesus improved human lives by making the blind to see, the lame to walk, and the dumb to understand. In this he was setting an example of what we might do for ourselves as he spoke about *our* eyes that didn't see, and *our* ears that didn't hear, and *our* hearts that failed to understand.

In his miracle of multiplying the loaves and the fishes, he was manifesting his abundance. And just before he performed his first miracle by turning water into wine at the marriage feast in Cana, the mother of Jesus gave an effective motto for abundance when she said to the servants, "Whatsoever he saith unto you, do it." That is about like saying to the fisherman, "Launch out into the deep and let your nets for a draught." Most of us dress in midget suits and think pigmy thoughts. We have too many reservations about things and proceed in life with our fingers crossed, so to speak. Then we cast our nets in waters that are too shallow. We frequently dream of being big fish in little puddles, and we forget that the big fish don't live in puddles at all. The big fish are out in the great ocean, and only the tadpoles live for very long in the mud puddles.

The ambition of Daisy Rhinehart was pointed toward launching out into the deep when she said:

> I'm tired of sailing my little boat
> Far inside of the harbor bar;
> I want to be out where the big ships float,
> Out in the deep where the great ones are.

And should my frail craft prove too slight
For storms that sweep those wide seas o'er,
Better go down in the stirring fight
Than to drowse to death by the sheltered shore.

When we get out into the middle of things, we are less likely to crash upon the shore rocks or get stuck in the mud puddles of the low tide. Shakespeare had something like this in mind when he said, "There is a tide in the affairs of men, which taken at its flood leads on to fortune, omitted all of the voyages of our lives are bound in shallows and in miseries. On such a full sea are we now afloat, and we must take the current when it serves or lose our ventures." In other words, Shakespeare was saying, "Launch out into the deep and let down your nets for a draught." The one business of life is to succeed. The great Creator and organizer of the universe does not desire that his children waste their lives in failure. Rather, he wants us to manifest his abundance in righteous accomplishment.

The gospel of Christ was intended to help people improve themselves. In the parable of the talents and many of his other parables Jesus kept saying in substance, "Launch out into the deep and let down your nets for a draught." His greatest commandments have to do with loving God, serving people, and in a big way making the most of our own lives. Likewise, his most serious displeasure is aroused by lack of productivity. He cursed the fig tree that bore no fruit, so that it withered and died. He was highly offended by the useless sins and evils of the chief priests and pharisees and the unprofitable servant who did not improve his talents. He has indicated that there is great joy in heaven when even one soul repents and begins trying to do better. Individual personal improvement was always one of the outstanding characteristics of those who followed Jesus. Under his direction, unlearned and ignorant men were transformed into saints and apostles. It is probable that our own most serious human fault is in selling ourselves short.

In John Bunyan's *Pilgrim's Progress*, he tells the story of the man with a muck rake who had trained himself to look in no direction but down. He had spent his life exclusively with the things of the earth. There was an angel standing over his head with a celestial crown in his hand, offering to exchange the crown for the muck rake. But because he had never learned to look up, he disregarded the offer of the angel and continued to rake unto himself the chaff and dust of the earth. When we place limitations upon ourselves we force ourselves to look downward. It has been said that the most widespread disease in the world is the inferiority complex. One of the reasons that doubt destroys so much of our faith is that we can't look up and down at the same time. When we rationalize and say, "I am just not religious or I am not cut out to be a success," we are headed in the direction of the mud puddles, for no one can *think* little and *be* big at the same time.

Paul was thinking this law of abundance when he said, "I can do all things through Jesus Christ that strengtheneth me." Doing and being are our greatest responsibilities. The gospel itself is not just an idea; it is activity. It is the greatest do-it-yourself program ever known in the world. Someone has pointed out that even the word gospel begins with the word "go." And the gospel philosophy is made up of a lot of other great words, such as work, listen, learn, pray, hear, tell, carry, come follow. These ideas all mean "launch out into the deep," break your nets, live at your best, be ye therefore perfect. As we read the challenging invitation of Jesus, saying, "Follow me," we might look up into the heavens and try to understand the wonders of his creation with its billions of galaxies, the wonders of his laws, and the beauty and harmony of his saving principles. The voice of Deity himself has declared our importance by saying, "I have said ye are gods, and all of you are children of the most high." Yet isn't it strange that we are so unwilling to live accordingly. We go on rejecting the giver of all our blessings; we insist on downgrading ourselves, disobeying his commandments, and working in direct opposition to our own best interest.

The God of heaven has promised that if we improve our talents he will make us kings and priests unto God, to rule and reign with him forever. But in order to qualify, we must launch out in our faith, in our good works, and in our righteousness. We should get rid of our fractional devotion, our marginal morals, and our minimum performances. Then, in a whole-souled effort, we should let down our nets for a draught.

There is an interesting old legend that comes out of India. It tells of a horseman riding at night over the desert. As he crossed a dry river bed, a voice out of the darkness commanded him to halt and dismount. The horseman obeyed. The voice then told him to fill his pockets with the pebbles at his feet, which he did. Then the voice commanded him to remount and ride on and that in the morning he would be both glad and sad.

As the sun came up the horseman looked at the pebbles in his pockets and discovered that they were rubies, emeralds, diamonds, pearls, and sapphires. Then he was both glad and sad. He was glad that he had taken as many as he had, and he was sad that he had not taken a great many more.

When we go beyond the boundaries of this life and find out a little more about God's magnificent program of eternal progression, we will be very glad that we have done as well as we have, and we will be very sad that we have not done a great deal better. May God help us to so successfully launch our lives that we might someday live in his glorious presence.

Let's Make a Deal

THE OTHER DAY WHILE IN THE BARBERSHOP GETTING A HAIRCUT, I watched a television show entitled "Let's Make a Deal." The sponsor gives away many valuable gifts to those invited to be on the program. Each participant is started out with some small present to be used as his working capital. Then if he makes the right choices, he may build up his fortunes in a series of exchanges. On this particular program, the first contestant was a very attractive young woman. She was given her original starting-off present, then the master of ceremonies asked her if she would like to "make a deal." She was told that she could exchange her initial gift for whatever might be hidden in a large wooden box backstage. She readily accepted the offer to make the exchange. When the box was opened, she discovered to her great delight that she was now the owner of a beautiful colored television set worth over five hundred dollars.

Her face was immediately transformed by the most wonderful expression of happiness. Apparently this was just what she had always wanted. Her good fortune seemed almost beyond her belief, and she looked as though she was having difficulty in containing her good fortune. The light in her face and the excitement in her eyes indicated that a wonderful joy was abounding in her heart. At intervals, she kept glancing out into the audience. The master of ceremonies asked her if she was looking for someone. She said her husband was out there; the pride in her eyes seemed to be saying to him, "How am I doing?" and everyone could tell that she expected his answer would be one of the greatest praise. The radiance dancing around in her features left no doubt in anyone's mind that she thought this business of "Let's Make a Deal" was a great idea.

After her first good fortune had had time to settle a little, the master of ceremonies asked her if she would like to make another deal. He told her that if she desired she could trade off her beautiful colored television set for whatever may be hidden behind the curtain. But the expression on her face advised everyone that she wasn't going to be taken in by any such proposition. She had her television set and she was not going to allow anyone to get it away from her. Accordingly, she informed the master of ceremonies that she was rejecting his proposed new deal. Then the curtain was drawn aside and revealed a shiny new automobile worth $3,500. This caused another bombshell to explode in her face.

The light went out of her eyes, her features lost their glow, and her personality temperature dropped to about 32° below zero. Again she looked out into the audience—this time with a sense of disappointment and apology. She had just passed up the greatest single financial opportunity in her lifetime. And she seemed as though she couldn't bear the thought of it. Even though she still had her television, she left the platform with an expression that would be described as something less than enthusiastic.

Then another lady came to the platform and made six wrong deals one after another. With each failure, her mental attitude also seemed to take a dip. And a look of frustration and discouragement kept growing in her face. But then, as a result of her last opportunity, $750 dollars in cash was placed in her hands, and her spirits soared like a sky rocket. I was amazed at the visible personality fluctuation range possible in human enthusiasm. Now with her countenance ablaze, and with happiness shining out of her eyes, she also began looking for her husband, with whom she apparently desired to share the happiness of her good fortune.

After watching this show, it occurred to me that life is also running a "Let's Make a Deal" program. However, in life there are several important differences. First, life's possible prizes are much more important; and second, in life we are given more accurate clues as to what the prizes are before our bid is placed. I thought of that occasion that took place thirty-four centuries ago, when the Lord came down onto the top of Mount Sinai, enveloped in fire, and in substance he said to the children of Israel, "Let's make a deal."

For over 200 years, these people had served as Egyptian slaves. After a great many difficulties with the Egyptian Pharaoh, the Lord gave them their freedom as their original capital. Then he told them that if they would give up their wickedness and idolatry, and if they would keep his commandments, he would bestow upon them the greatest gifts of prosperity and happiness. As permanent evidence of this deal, he would also enter into an everlasting covenant to make them a favored people, a chosen generation, a royal priesthood, a holy nation. He would establish them in a choice land, which was described as flowing with milk and honey. He agreed to go before them in person in a pillar of fire and to drive out their enemies. They would occupy the fertile land given to their fathers, which land had already been highly developed and put under cultivation by their enemies. On this point, the Lord said to them, "And thou shalt inhabit cities that thou didst not build, and thou shalt eat from vines which thou hast not planted, and thou shalt drink from wells which thou didst not dig."

Instead of being worth five hundred dollars, this deal was worth many millions of dollars. But even that was not the most important part of the bargain. God also promised to make their bodies immune to disease. They could have this great gift of freedom on a permanent basis. And instead of living as slaves, with a master's foot on their necks, they could have their own government. They would be permitted to rear their children in peace and righteousness. This group of former slaves could have all of these benefits by doing a few little easy simple things that were all in their own personal interests. In fact, they would be given greater blessings than had ever before been known in this world. In addition, these benefits would extend beyond the borders of this life, and they would be permitted to live eternally in God's highest glory.

The people enthusiastically accepted this proffered deal. The details were put in the form of a two-way covenant, and they were accepted by everyone. Then Moses went back up into the Mount to report that the people had accepted the Lord's offer. But even before he returned, these former slaves had relapsed into their idolatry. As the object of their worship, they built a gold calf. Then they launched out into a naked orgy of wickedness. When Moses returned and saw their falseness, he was so disgusted that he threw down and broke in pieces the tables of stone on which the Lord had written out the agreement with his own finger. Because of their broken contract and personal degeneracy, the Lord tried to teach them a lesson, and in a war among themselves over three thousand of their men were slain. At another time, their sins brought fiery, poisonous serpents among them, and many more lost their lives. A rebellion against God conducted at the very threshold of their promised land caused them to be turned back into the wilderness for forty years, until all of their adults except two had lost their lives. Because of their many bad choices, they had lost all of the valuable prizes offered them, including their own lives. But the show must go on, and the Lord has also offered to make a group as well as an individual deal with us. The stakes are still high; in fact, they are as great as we can imagine.

But like those people invited to be on the television program, we don't get the great prizes unless we make the right choices. Life still doesn't reward us very well for drunken orgies or rebellions against God. If we choose the poison of the fiery serpents, it doesn't do us any good to get discouraged at the punishment. We should understand that living is a serious business, and we also can lose everything here, as well as hereafter. The poet says:

> Life is real, life is earnest
> And the grave is not the goal;
> Dust thou art, to dust returnest,
> Was not spoken of the soul.

The greatest tragedy of our day is that so many people are making the unprofitable kind of deals with life. For example, I know of one man whose life started him out with a wonderful original capital. He was given some good parents. He had a keen mind and a sound, healthy body, and lived in an excellent home. The first few trades that he made with life were also excellent. He. acquired a good education, accumulated some high ideals, and developed an attractive personality. At that point he looked like a winner. He resembled someone on television loaded down with the most valuable gifts. But then he began making some of the wrong choices, and his gifts began to vanish. He traded off his steady hand for a bottle of rum. He exchanged his health for lungs lined with nicotine. He chose dishonesty and got a little immorality thrown in for good measure. When his friends on the sideline tried to prompt him to make better choices, he became indignant and began offending them. Because no one lives unto himself alone, my friend also made some deals for others. He traded off his wife's love for him for a broken heart for her. And he traded off his children's sense of security for some serious psychiatric problems. He lost one thing after another, including his employment. But instead of changing his ways, he became sullen and moody.

Like so many other people who have wronged themselves, he began a fight with life and with God, and that is always the wrong deal. Today he is a financial and moral bankrupt. His fine personality is now lying in ruins, and the chances are that he will be poorer when he leaves this world than when he entered it. One of the interesting things about life's deals is that the rewards of good and bad reach beyond the borders of this life.

Saul of Tarsus was a persecutor of the saints. Then one day, while he was on his way to Damascus, the Lord invited him to "make a deal" and change sides. The transaction was completed, and Saul stayed with it until he became Paul the Apostle, the greatest Christian missionary. Life is presently not only saying to us, "Let's make a deal." It is also making us a great number of different offers, and we may accept as many as we please. In deal number one, the Lord says, "How would you like to perfect your life and live forever in celestial glory?" It seems that everyone should know the right answer to this question. Yet only a few accept. So life has provided some alternatives. The Apostle Paul explains that "there is one glory of the sun, another glory of the moon, and other glories of the stars." He says, "As one star differs from another star in glory, so also is the resurrection of the dead." So far as this deal is concerned, we know the kind of reward that is awaiting behind each curtain. And we may choose the eternal exaltation of the highest kingdom, which differs from the lowest as the blaze of the noonday sun differs from the twinkle of a tiny star.

While watching the expression on the face of the young woman on television, I was impressed that a little difference in the value of the prize can make a great difference in how we feel. And I wondered what it would be like to see the curtains of eternity drawn aside and discover that we had missed the greatest of all of life's prizes. What kind of a look would be in our eyes if we discovered that by our wrong choices we had traded off the celestial kingdom for an eternity of misery and regret?

My friend on "Let's Make a Deal" was glad that she had the colored television set, but she was also sorry she didn't have the automobile that was seven times as valuable. Someday everyone of us will be very glad for the good deals that we have made with life, but we will be very sorry that we haven't made a lot more. In the meantime, life's master of ceremonies is saying to us, "Let's make a deal." Let's make a deal for honor. Let's make a deal for faith. Let's make a deal for righteousness. Let's make those deals that will give us a clear eye and an untroubled conscience.

Speaking of the reward, the scripture says of those who keep God's commandments, "Then all that my father hath, shall be given unto them." God is a very wealthy personage. What could be more exciting than to inherit from God? God has a great many things. He lives in celestial glory. God also has a glorious, celestial, resurrected body. He has a celestial mind that thinks only celestial, happy thoughts. He has a celestial spirit. He has a Godly character and a Godly personality. He lives in celestial happiness with a celestial family and with celestial friends. And he is saying to us, "Fill up your lives with the opportunities and blessings that have been made so easily available to you." Our greatest opportunity is to make that deal with life that will make us glad throughout eternity.

Life's Oughts

THE GREATEST VALUE IN THE UNIVERSE IS LIFE. AND THE GREATEST of all experiences is that of living pleasantly and successfully. Because we have so many variables, each life is not equally profitable. In an attempt to get our living on its highest level, various elements of our society have set up programs designed to get more success into human experiences. We have enacted civil laws, established social standards of etiquette, worked out better educational procedures, and discovered more effective rules of health. Our pure food and drug laws were written to make sure that the right ingredients get into the prescriptions and that these are plainly marked in the bottle. We have building codes and other recognized standards and processes to maintain quality in our buildings, bridges, highways, and machinery. Of course, the most important of all of our betterment programs has to do with man himself. Our high point was reached in the meridian of time, when the greatest intelligence of heaven, next to the Father himself, came into the world to establish a divine standard for our thinking and living.

The gospel of Jesus Christ might be compared to a kind of spiritual pure food and drug act. Its purpose is to make sure that no harmful substances are allowed to damage this valuable commodity of human life. It not only embodies the greatest health-producing ideas and practices, but it also acts as a kind of divine building code. It looks forward to getting the most favorable personal qualities into God's children in preparing them for an eternal life under the most favorable conditions. Jesus made his own statement of purpose when he said, "I came that ye might have life, and have it more abundantly." But Jesus went much further than to merely give us the principles of success. He personally served us as an example of how life at its best should be lived. At no time did he ever put any harmful thing into the formula, nor did he ever do anything that could be classified as mean or wrong. All of his teachings as well as his examples were ennobling and uplifting. The difference between his life and those less successful was that he lived all of the laws of success. His philosophy of life was, "Father, not my will, but thine be done." Our large number of failures is because we live our lives on the lower levels of feeling or expediency or temptation or thoughtlessness, rather than on that level of right. There are a thousand ways of doing a thing, but only one way to do it right, and probably more than anything else our success both here and hereafter depends on the use we make of this little five letter "O-U-G-H-T."

Hazlitt once said that "man is the only part of creation that understands the difference between things as they are and things as they *ought* to be." The animal creation is governed by some natural controls called instincts, from which they are not allowed to deviate. Only to man did God say, "Thou mayest choose for thyself." But God has also given to man a corresponding responsibility and a set of success laws to go by, and to the extent to which these laws are kept we succeed, and to the extent they are violated we fail. In addition, God has given us the priceless gifts of conscience, judgment, will, and reason. All of these tell us that there are certain things that we *ought* to do.

The dictionary says that the word "ought" was once used to designate an obligation or an indebtedness. It still does. The Apostle Paul had something like this in mind when he said, "Know ye not that your body is the temple of the Holy Ghost which is in you, which ye have of God, and ye are not your own? For ye are bought with a price: therefore glorify God in your body, and in your spirit, which are God's." (I Cor. 6:19-20.) Another reason why we ought to serve God is that his ways are always the best. They are always the most wise, and their results are the most pleasant and the most profitable. "Ought" also means to be bound by a duty and a moral responsibility. Certainly we are bound to do what we ought to do by our own good judgment, our conscience, and our reason. The science of medicine was designed to keep us well physically. Psychology, psychiatry, and the other studies of the mind are to keep us well mentally. Sociology helps us live together agreeably. Agriculture is the science of how we feed ourselves, and business teaches us to deal with each other agreeably.

Then we have the great science of religion, the purpose of which is to keep us well spiritually. And everything that is proper and right in religion we ought to do. Our violations of these important regulations made for our benefit are responsible for our present unfavorable situation. Among many people our nation is noted as a nation of lawbreakers. We disregard our own civil laws; we violate the laws of health; we cheat in business; and we disregard the laws of God.

Think how strangely the people reacted to the mission of Jesus. Instead of wholeheartedly accepting him and adopting his message, they hung him on a cross and then tried to destroy as much of his doctrine as possible. Isaiah had foretold the conduct of the people when he said they would transgress the laws, change the ordinances, and break the everlasting covenant. But our own reactions are very similar. It is completely unreasonable to have the worst crime wave running simultaneously with our highest educational attainment and our greatest religious programs.

I know a young man who *ought* to be more ambitious. He married a fine young woman and has two wonderful children. He had a job through which he was providing the money to support his family. But over the years, he has largely allowed his whims to replace his "oughts." Because he didn't take sufficient interest in his job, friction developed between himself and his employer. Then, following an unreasonable impulse, he quit his job and for six months remained unemployed. He borrowed money from his friends and relatives without any means of paying it back. He bought things that he could not afford and wrote checks without funds in the bank. The bill collectors began beating a path to his door and made his wife extremely unhappy. She couldn't help much because he wouldn't keep his promises either to his creditors or to her. It will now probably take a bankruptcy or a divorce or a complete nervous breakdown or a death on her part to get her out of this hell of torment that he has brought upon her. Unless he makes some substantial changes, even the bankruptcy and the nervous breakdown will only solve the problem temporarily. This man could avoid all of these difficulties and make the lives of many people pleasant and profitable merely by placing a greater reverence on a few simple little "oughts."

This powerful little word has a great many important mental, social, occupational, and religious applications. It points out our daily and our personal and moral obligations. No one can live by himself or for himself alone. Paul said we are not our own. Our parents, wives, children, and friends have a substantial interest in our lives. We must also bear our share of the responsibility for the general success of the world in which we live. We are responsible to employers, customers, neighbors, and friends. We also have a great obligation to God, who created us. Certainly we have no right to mortgage our lives to sin when we are not our own. We must also be responsible for those obligations that we have to ourselves.

The quality of our own personality, virtue, worthwhileness, fitness, ability, and eternal destiny all depend upon our "oughts."

The story is told of a salesman who was having occupational difficulties. He asked his sales manager to help him. The sales manager said, "If you will follow two simple rules, I will guarantee that you will double your sales in less than six months." Naturally the salesman was very anxious to know what they were. The sales manager said, "The first rule is, don't do any of those things you know that you ought *not* to do." The face of the young man fell. He had not expected any sales rule so difficult to follow. Then the sales manager said, "I am willing to go still further and guarantee that you will quadruple your sales in one year if you will follow a second rule, which is, do all of the things that you know that you ought to do." It is a significant fact that every salesman knows enough to double his success. And just as surely we too can double our general success in life by practicing these simple rules.

It was to help us to overcome the dismal unpleasantness of our repetitious failures that the Lord came down onto the top of Mount Sinai 3400 years ago and gave us his important list of "Thou Shalt Not's." During this memorable event he hung the red light of "don't" on such obvious causes of difficulty as:

1. False religions
2. False gods
3. Profanity
4. Sabbath day violations
5. Dishonoring parents
6. Murder
7. Immorality
8. Dishonesty
9. False witness
10. Covetousness.

But he also intends that we should make up our own list of "thou shalt not's." We ourselves should hang some red lights on unkindness, selfishness, unreasonableness, idleness, negative thinking, alcohol, and nicotine. It is only when we have definitely made up our minds about those things that we *ought not* to do that we are in a position to devote ourselves without reservation to those things that we ought to do. This important word "ought" is mentioned 92 times in the Bible. The Lord said, "Woe unto you, scribes and Pharisees, hypocrites! For ye pay tithe of mint and anise and cummin, and have omitted the weightier matters of the law, judgment, mercy, and faith: these ought ye to have done, and not to leave the others undone." (Matt. 23:23-24.) On another occasion he said, "For the Holy Ghost shall teach you in the same hour what ye ought to say." (Luke 12:12.) Jesus said unto the people, "Men ought always to pray." (Luke 18:1.) He said, "So ought men to love their wives." (Eph. 5:28.) And we should all get this word "ought" firmly established in our hearts and minds once and for all. The only way to do anything is the way it ought to be done.

After the resurrection Jesus appeared to a group of people upon the western continent. His crucifixion had been manifest on this hemisphere by some great disturbances in nature. Earthquakes, tempests, and other destructive forces had changed the entire face of the land, and the more wicked part of the people had been destroyed. Jesus was trying to help those who remained to make a new start toward a happier and more successful life. He taught them obedience to the gospel, as he had done to those on the eastern continent. At the very center of the discussion, he asked his listeners, "What manner of men ought ye to be?" Then he answered this important question with a great answer, saying, "Verily I say unto you, even as I am." (III Nephi 27:27.)

What an upgrading our lives would receive if we always lived on the "ought" level. To help us in this direction, life has erected a very sharp, straight line running all the way between good and evil. We should never cross over the line for any reason, nor should we shift it to one side to accommodate our convenience or our expedience. When we start tampering with this yellow line, we are headed for trouble. To do what we *like* is never a very good substitute for doing what we *ought,* and if we want to be the people we ought to be, then we must do those things that we ought to do. We are violating a divine law when we tell ourselves that a little poison in our medicine won't hurt us. And when we move the yellow line back and forth enough times, we soon lose track of where it ought to be.

Socrates had an interesting way of getting himself onto the "ought" level. After his service in the Athenian army, he came to think of himself as two people. One was General Socrates and the other was Private Socrates. His "General" self took great pride in seeing to it that his "private" self always did everything as it ought to be done. When we develop the authority and the will to command of a successful general, then we will not only do things right but we will do them when they ought to be done. Then we have a great advantage over those people who are governed by whims and whose accomplishments have to wait on their moods and circumstances. Life is easy when we can build up strong desires for the right oughts, and it can be a lot of fun to boss oneself effectively. There are few satisfactions equal to those that come from self-discipline. Effective generalship can train oneself to enjoy doing those things which ordinarily are difficult to do. We ourselves can answer the important prayer of the great philosopher, who said:

> Oh, that it were my chief delight
> to do the things I ought.
> Then let me try with all my might
> to mind that I am taught.

I would like to close with the "ought philosophy" of Abraham Lincoln, who said: "I am not bound to win, but I am bound to be true. I am not bound to succeed, but I am bound to live according to the best light that I have. I must stand with anyone as long as he is right, and part with him whenever he is wrong." May God help us to stand for righteousness and to live all of our "oughts" effectively.

The Light of the World

M ANY YEARS AGO THE FAMOUS ENGLISH PAINTER, HOLMAN HUNT, painted a great religious masterpiece entitled "The Light of the World." The painting is a visualization of that interesting scripture in which Jesus says, "Behold, I stand at the door, and knock: if any man hear my voice, and open the door, I will come in to him, and will sup with him, and he with me." (Rev. 3:20.)

In this painting, Jesus is shown standing outside a firmly shut door in the half light of the evening. He has his right hand upon the door knocker. At his feet weeds have grown tall and rank, indicating that the door had not been opened for a long time. But Jesus stands patiently awaiting a response. His head is haloed like the corona of the harvest moon; his kingly crown is entwined with that other crown of thorns. In his left hand he holds a lantern, which casts a flickering light upon the weeds surrounding the door and also reveals the nail prints in his wounded hands.

When the original of this picture was first exhibited in London, the critics immediately seized the opportunity to say that Mr. Hunt had made an omission in his painting. On the door a knocker was plainly shown; but a handle or doorknob by which the door could be opened had been forgotten. But Mr. Hunt explained that many of the doors with which Jesus was familiar had the latch only on the inside and could not be opened from without. By knocking on the outside, one could only make his presence known. His knock could do nothing more than to indicate his desire to be admitted; but the door itself had to be opened from inside.

Even today we have many doors where the one-way locking device is so set that it can only be opened from the inside. Turning the doorknob on the inside readily opens the door. But the outside doorknob is completely useless as a means of gaining admittance, unless the lock is released from the inside. With this device there is created an important religious symbol. It is a well-known fact that the door to one's heart can also be opened most readily from within. I suppose that no one has ever yet forced his way into the affections

---

°Given on Christmas.

or love of another person. And above almost everything else, God himself is committed to free agency and love as the governing principles of his program for his children. God never forces us to do right, and Satan has no power to force us to do wrong. Each one only knocks on the outside of the door, and we open it to whomsoever we will.

The motivation of this great scripture and picture is particularly timely at Christmas. This is when we delight most in recounting the thrilling stories connected with the birth of Jesus Christ, who was ordained to be the Savior of the world. In our minds at Christmas time, we again see the new star arising in the east, leading the wise men across the desert to lay their treasures at the feet of the new-born king. We also decorate our homes and give Christmas presents to each other. But one of the most important objectives to be accomplished during the commemoration of his birth is to get the spirit of his life reborn into our own hearts. To be directed by his spirit is the most important of all of the secrets of human success.

It was Jesus himself who said to his followers, "I am the light of the world: he that followeth me shall not walk in darkness, but shall have the light of life." (John 8:12.) John gave this idea in a little different form when he said, "In him was life, and the life was the light of men." It is wonderful to see our homes and Christmas trees beautifully lighted with electricity, but it is even more wonderful and much more important to have human lives illuminated and motivated by him who was ordained to be "The Light of the World" and to help us get his attitudes into our lives.

We might go back in imagination onto those Judean hills and sing Phillip Brooks' Christmas poem, in which he said:

O little town of Bethlehem, How still we see thee lie.
Above thy deep and dreamless sleep The silent stars go by;
Yet in the dark streets shineth The everlasting light.
The hopes and fears of all the years Are met in thee tonight.

For Christ is born of Mary; And gathered all above,
While mortals sleep, the angels keep Their watch of wondrous love.
O morning stars, together Proclaim the holy birth;
And praises sing to God the King, And Peace to men on earth.

How silently, how silently, The wondrous gift is given!
So God imparts to human hearts The blessings of his heaven.
No ear may hear his coming; But in this world of sin,
Where meek souls will receive him still, The dear Christ enters in.

Certainly one of our greatest individual Christmas pictures might well be our own visualization of "The Light of the World," knocking a little louder at Christmas time at the doors of our hearts. On the night of his birth, there was no room found for him in the inn. But his birth was not the only time during his life that he was excluded by men. For his entire 33 years on earth, this cry of "no room" almost became a theme song for his life. Herod sent soldiers to Bethlehem to kill the children, and because there was no room for Jesus in the domain of Herod, Mary and Joseph fled with him into Egypt. But even after the death of Herod many others arose to keep the antagonism alive. With many people there was no room for his teaching. There was no room for his miracles, no room for his doctrines, no room for his faith. Jesus himself said, "The foxes have holes, and the birds of the air have nests; but the Son of Man hath not where to lay his head." (Matt. 8:20.)

Even in our own day, with the judgment of time shining upon his life, we are still reenacting the ancient scene of Bethlehem by crying, "No room, no room." We make room for the gifts, but often we have no room for the giver. We have room for our own commercialism of Christmas and our pleasure seeking on the Sabbath day, but too often we have no room for worship. No room for service, no room for righteousness. The reason there was no room in the inn was because all of the available space was already occupied. And we are only following the ancients when we fill our lives so full of other things that we have no time or space left for "The Light and Life of the World."

One of the most stimulating experiences in life is that which we sometimes have of entertaining some famous person. It is a great delight when some individual of great consequence becomes our guest and honors us by coming into our home to be with us and to share with us his wisdom and friendship. We might just suppose that the mayor, or the governor, or even the president was a very close friend of ours, and that occasionally we were permitted to share in the benefits of his greatness by a close intimate association with him. How we would listen for that knock on the door that would announce his arrival. What a delightful experience it can be to enjoy a good meal with those for whom we have great love and respect. There are some people whose presence makes us glad, and we are wonderfully stimulated by their love and uplifted by their wisdom and encouragement.

While in the presence of some famous person, we listen eagerly to every word that he says. And when he is gone, we talk to our other friends about the experience. We quote him to them, in order that they might also share with us the benefits of his abilities. Merely to read about some famous individual or to receive a letter from him is never quite as stimulating as an actual face-to-face visit. It has been said that no one has ever succeeded in putting a great man down on paper. You may get his ideas, his illustrations, and his words on paper, but you can't get the man. That is, you can't get the smile on his face, or the light in his eye, or the warmth of his handshake, or the love in his voice on the paper. The best way to get the spirit of a great man is by coming into close contact with him personally.

Certainly one of the greatest needs of our personal lives is to get closer individually to the Savior of the world, and this is also one of the primary reasons that we commemorate Christmas. This is also why we set apart one day out of each seven as a Sabbath day. The Sabbath is a holy day; it is a kind of secondary Christmas on which we invite our Redeemer into our lives. On this day we lay aside the cares that usually concern us on the other six days; then we go to the House of Prayer and through our worship let our hearts reach up to God. This is also the day for which we usually reserve the best meal of the week. Frequently our family focus is centered in the Sunday dinner. We get out our best linen and make use of our finest silver and our most sparkling crystal. We obtain the finest roast, supported by all of the other things most desirable for a pleasant family dinner. Then we sit around the table, bow our heads, and say a prayer of gratitude and appreciation for our food, for each other, and for the friendship of those who enjoy the dinner with us. Even the finest dinner would not be very good if we had to eat it alone. Therefore, at our Sunday dinner we usually invite our family or some particular friend or some of those who qualify as special loved ones. But what about him who is standing outside with our door knocker in his hand? He is the "Light of the World." He is the one who said, "If any man hear my voice, and open the door, I will come unto him, and will sup with him, and he with me."

As the sun is the center of our solar system, so is the Messiah the center of our lives and our families. Without the sun, our solar system would fly apart. Without the Savior's righteousness in our lives and his faith in our hearts, our families and our lives would also fly apart. And as we come to the end of each year, we commemorate a kind of yearly Sabbath that we call Christmas. The

Christmas week is a kind of holy week. This is the best time of the year. This is when we beautify our homes, light the yule log, retell the stories, and relive the traditions of the greatest life that was ever lived. As we remember and honor him, his righteousness and his virtues are reborn in us.

Who can think of a more challenging idea than this—that the King of Kings is now knocking at our door? He is seeking to bring us the greatest blessings of eternal life. This is also our greatest opportunity that is knocking at our door. For only with his spirit in our hearts can we reach our greatest goals. With his spirit we can also partially reflect his light into some dark corners of our own smaller worlds. Jesus said to his apostles, "Ye are the light of the world. A city that is set on an hill cannot be hid. Neither do men light a candle, and put it under a bushel, but on a candlestick; and it giveth light unto all that are in the house. Let your light so shine before men that they may see your good works, and glorify your Father which is in heaven." (Matt. 5:14-16.) Nazareth itself was built high up on the mountainside. It might well be that Jesus had a night scene of his home town in mind, when he mentioned "a city set upon a hill." And similarly our fellowmen should see the light of faith coming from our lives.

George M. Docherty has pointed out that "the sound of knocking upon a door invariably arouses our immediate interest, and sometimes even a fearful curiosity. In the theatre, the audience is held in expectant silence as a heavy hand pounds upon the door upstage. This is also the case when it happens in our homes, especially if one is alone on a winter's evening. Outside a high wind may be howling and hurling cascades of rain against the black window panes. Then suddenly, in a lull of the wind's moaning, a knock is heard at the door."

Even in the uncertain turmoil of our lives, Christ knocks at our bruised and anxious hearts to bring them strength and peace. Of his gift, Mr. Docherty says, "This is a free offer of the gospel of Christ. It comes without money and without price. We should open the doors of our hearts. Rise up from your chairs of ease. Push aside the newspapers and literature of this world that are filling up so much of our lives. Then we should take off the coats of habit that are stifling our outlook. Break away from the routine of spending our days with our cozy, comfortable, contented selves. And by an act of our own free will, go to the doors of our hearts, and throw them open wide that Christ might enter into our lives."

Then when we come to the end of this existence, we may find our eternal home with God. Then may we hear repeated the Charles Dickens' Christmas prayer of Tiny Tim, who said, "God bless us, every one!"

Magna Cum Laude

I N THE DICTIONARY WE FIND THE INTERESTING PHRASE, *magna cum
laude*, which is frequently used in diplomas at commencement
time. These words have a Latin origin and are used to designate
those who do work of superior quality. *Magna* means "great," *cum*
means "with," and *laude* means "laudatory" or "praiseworthy."
Therefore, the term *cum laude* means "with praise," and *magna cum
laude* means "great with praise." Higher degrees of merit are
described in even more laudatory terms. *Insigne cum laude* means
"with notable praise," and *summa cum laude* means "with the
highest praise."

It is a very worthwhile accomplishment when people do praiseworthy work in any field. As this requires that significant values
must first be established in the people concerned, and the honor
described in the diploma merely represents the honor already existing in the student. To obtain a good education is of itself a notable
achievement. But to get it in a praiseworthy way sets the holder
apart with a kind of special significance.

Any great accomplishment is important for itself alone, but it is
often even more important for what it stands for or is a sign of and
for what it predicts for the future. When praiseworthy traits are
established in peoples' lives, they usually continue to grow and bear
the fruits of merit to enrich the future. The time of college graduation is not primarily a time of finishing. It is called "commencement" because it marks the beginning of that greatest of all
experiences called life. Commencement is usually the time when
we take up our share of the work of the world. It is also about
that time that our individual family is organized and we make a new
beginning in our religious activities. And what could give greater
promise than to begin these important activities on a *magna cum
laude* basis!

Certainly the most worthwhile part of the work of the world is
the improvement that takes place in the lives of the workers. All
education is merely about ourselves. Through psychology, psychiatry,
and the other studies of the mind, we learn how to keep ourselves
well mentally. We study medicine to keep us well physically.

Agriculture is how we feed ourselves. Law and sociology help us to live together agreeably. Business is how we deal with each other in material things. And then we have this great science of religion in which we learn how to keep ourselves well spiritually. More than anything else, excellence in this field will help us to keep our errors or foolishness and our sins as near zero as possible. But no matter which area of life is concerned, the world's most important business has to do with the development of excellence and the installation of greatness in our individual lives. We cause ourselves difficulties when our lives are aimed too low or when we lack quality in our personal performance.

We remember the poor unfortunate who attracted the disapproval of Jesus by burying his talent in the ground. If we were asked to specify our most serious world tragedy of the past, it could probably best be done by retelling the Master's story of the unprofitable servant. We are also seeing this ancient scene being presently reenacted on every hand. Some unprofitable servants take the course of educational "dropouts"; some become spiritually immature; some work half-heartedly at that part of the work of the world that life has given them to do.

There are thousands in every field who are content with an ordinary performance for their lives. When one does less than his best, he misses not only the thrill that attaches to excellence, but he is also deprived of the constructive good he could do for others. And he himself must suffer the unpleasantness of living in some measure of mediocrity. One of the disadvantages of an unpraiseworthy life is that it bears an inferior fruit; and when its stunting effects get established in one's program, it makes one's existence miserable and unprofitable. The plague also spreads to others, and our world has far too many influences leading us away from excellence. What a tragedy it would be to finish at the bottom of the class in the school of life.

Man is the only part of creation to whom has been given this Godly instinct to improve himself. He is the only one to whom excellence has any real meaning. Yet, in spite of the importance of excellence, far too many of us live on the "must" level of life, where we work largely from compulsion. We allow ourselves to be pushed from behind and get many of our motivations from the fear of unpleasant consequences. The *Magna cum laude* life does things because they "ought to be done." Excellence keeps everyone ahead of life's minimum requirements. This is a praiseworthy activity; as the Lord himself has said, "He that doeth not anything until he is commanded, and keepeth the commandments with slothfulness, the same is damned."

Excellence is more concerned with the prizes that lie ahead than with the penalties threatening us from behind. *Magna cum laude* lives rise to the top by developing the virtues and abilities that make life a joy. And when a student develops the habit of doing more than is expected, he not only wins commendation from the university, but from life as well. He also brings distinction to his classmates and honor to his school. The attitudes, virtues, skills, and habits that he develops incarnate themselves in him to set him apart both here and hereafter as *magna cum laude*.

One of the greatest concepts of the religion of Christ is its law of eternal progression. The greatest goal of life is that the offspring of God may hope to eventually become like the eternal parent. But the work of God is endless, and there is no time or place when our journey will be over or when we will have nothing else to do or nothing else to strive for. Nor is there just one point in the journey at which we can stop and enjoy the reward. God has provided that the entire journey should be a happy one. We may always have constructive and rewarding experiences if we keep our standards high and our lives fully focused and dedicated to a magna cum laude objective.

It has always been while man has been reaching upward and striving vigorously and restlessly for excellence that he has composed the finest music, created the most wonderful works of art, achieved the greatest religious insights, and had the largest amount of happiness. These have been the periods when he has unlocked the secret of the universe and set the standards that have given meaning to the phrase, "The dignity of man." But it was not intended that we should live by bread alone, and the moment we fail to live by every word of truth or cease our struggle for excellence, we begin losing our dignity as well as our destiny; and we also miss the joy the Creator intended for all of his children. Man cannot long keep his eyes fixed upon the ground without becoming morally blind like the beast and losing the significance intended for his life.

An increased interest in the exaltation of our souls with a magna cum laude spirit in our hearts moves us nearer and nearer to heaven. The principle of excellence has far more than ordinary significance in the field of religion, as most of the really important values of life are located in this area. And we should devote our efforts in proportion. Righteous men must also be competent men, and it is the elementary duty of every individual to do effectively whatever job is his to do. Because God's life is worthy of the greatest praise, we should follow him, for neither freedom nor wealth nor education can save us without righteousness. Certainly we should not call God our Father and then act as though we were orphans.

Today when we make reference to the weaknesses of our society we are usually thinking in terms of our vexing international rivalries. But our problems are far more serious than that indicated by our position in the missile race or our ability to obtain the sympathy of other nations. Long before our present national rivalries began, we were children of God, committed to building a great society upon this planet. This can never be accomplished by military or economic factors alone. Even the strongest society will fail unless it is also a righteous society, and we must learn always to ally ourselves on God's side of the argument. Our greatest assignment is to learn to live eternally on a basis of excellence. Our greatest accomplishment in life will be when our covenants, our faith, our scholarship, our industry, and our accomplishment entitle us to graduate from life with a magna cum laude written by God's hand into our diploma.

Merit Badges

A N IMPORTANT PART OF THE PROGRAM OF THE GREAT SCOUT OR-
ganizations is the custom of awarding merit badges to their
deserving members. When an approved Scout passes a specified test
given by a qualified examiner in a selected subject, he or she is
given a merit badge as an appropriate recognition of the work accomplished. A merit badge is a visual emblem signifying that the
requirements in that particular field have been satisfactorily fulfilled.

When a First Class Boy Scout gets five designated merit badges,
he becomes a Star Scout. Ten merit badges qualify him for Life
rank, and upon receipt of the twenty-one necessary badges, he becomes an Eagle. These indicators of merit are officially worn on the
uniform of the receiver.

The army and many other organizations also follow this practice
of visually recognizing merit. Every soldier is invested with the
insignia of his rank to be worn on his sleeve his chest or his shoulder
or his collar. This insignia stands for his training, ability, and authority. His various fields of experience, his fitness to command, and the
kind of service he has given to his country are all represented on
his person. Particular heroism or any manifestation of devotion
beyond the call of duty is visually attested to by the ribbons and
medals displayed on his uniform. Universities also practice this
custom by giving degrees, citations, academic robes, and doctor's
hoods to deserving people. Life itself also has a system of recognizing merit, and every time any member of the great human order
does some worthwhile thing, life awards him a badge of merit. However, this award is not worn on a uniform, but in the actual person
of the individual himself. It may be shown in the form of a clear
eye or a dependable conscience. Badges for honor, righteousness,
and intelligence are often displayed in the face and person of the
recipient.

Life also has merit badges for reason, good judgment, honesty,
fairness, kindness, and friendliness. These are displayed in a winning
smile, an eye sparkling with honor, and a wonderfully charged radio-
active spirit. However, life goes far beyond the Scout organization
and also gives badges for demerits. Some teachers and some business

organizations also operate with a system of merits on the one hand and demerits on the other. As someone has pointed out a very significant fact that we don't just live under "a profit system"; we live under a profit and loss system and we must keep this in mind. A sufficient number of merits usually entitles one to advancement in rank, pay increases, and greater prestige, while demerits lead in exactly the opposite direction. Enough demerits may cause a dishonorable discharge, life imprisonment, or even death. When Cain committed the first murder, he immediately suffered a lessening in honor, and God placed the permanent mark of a murderer upon him. But like Cain, we are all responsible for the particular marks that we wear on our persons.

A group of the ancients had an interesting system for punishing crime. When one of their number committed a murder, his punishment was to be chained to the corpse of his victim. Then wherever he went forever more, he must drag with him the result of his sin. If at a later date he should decide to kill again, another dead body would be added to his dreadful burden. He could not possibly disentangle himself from the result of his evil act. Such a punishment seems severe, and yet life has a plan of retribution that works in exactly the same way. The laws governing the awarding of demerits say that we must always be chained to whatever wrongs we commit. That is, if one violates the laws of temperance, a ruinous, driving thirst attaches itself to push him further and further down the road to despair. Everyone has seen the pitiful struggles of some poor alcoholic trying to free himself from the monstrous thing that has fastened itself upon him. His own acts not only sentence him to endure the unimaginable terrors of alcoholism, but the horrible marks of the drunkard are also stamped into his person.

The punishment of one who doesn't study is that he is chained to his ignorance. Then wherever he goes, he must drag this oppressive burden with him. He cannot lay it aside even for one hour. The sentence of one who tells lies is that the marks of the liar will be engraved into his soul. The moment that any sin is indulged, it incarnates itself and begins etching a deadly depth tattoo into its victim. Suppose that you get someone to snap your picture when your face is distorted by a violent rage or some dreadful hate. The camera will record upon the paper the hideous distortion that exists in your face at the time. After the passion has passed, your face tends to resume its natural appearance, and yet the change back is never quite complete. No evil passion can run through the human personality without doing some measure of permanent damage. For a long time it has been known that when a thought passes through the mind, it cuts a groove or engram to mark its track. This is made deeper and more permanent each time it is repeated, and it can never be erased completely. When you overstretch an elastic band or overstrain a piece of steel, it never quite returns to its original dimension or condition. It is just as certain that no one can run an evil emotion through his soul without changing his own future. Each evil makes its mark; and however imperceptible it may be, no one's mind or face ever quite returns to its original state. A depraved mind is one that has entertained enough depraved thoughts that it cannot easily think any other kind. Then the demerits manifest themselves in a hard, sinful face to match the accumulated sins in his heart.

The Apostle Paul probably had this ancient law of retribution in mind as he cried out, "O wretched man that I am! who shall deliver me from the body of this death?" (Rom. 7:24.) And our own lives might echo that cry and say "Who indeed?"

The other evening after work, while waiting for the bus, I saw a fellow human being struggling with the putrifying corpse of alcoholism. The poison of alcohol had gone all through his tissues, although at the time he was only moderately intoxicated. However he was decorated from head to foot with the badges of booze. It was perfectly evident that he had lived with his evil for a long time. His bleary eyes, bloated, discolored face, shaky hands, and unsteady legs proclaimed him a veteran drunkard. His filthy clothing served as a symbol of the hopelessness in his soul. If anyone's life could be an open book, his was. He was one of those who appeared to have passed the point of no return. Certainly no one reading the story pictured in his face would have dared trust him with any important responsibility. I wondered how he obtained the expensive liquor necessary to feed this hellish thirst.

I tried to picture what kind of a home he had, if any, and if there was anyone there who loved him and was willing to share his dreadful misery. And yet this man was a child of God, formed in his image and endowed with his attributes, even though the lines now become blurred and indistinct through the corrosion and attrition of sin. Like Paul, I thought, "who could free him from the body of this cancerous loathsome sickness that he had brought upon himself and which was now eating away his soul?"

The scriptures make it clear enough that this custom of wearing badges of both merit and demerit will be continued throughout eternity. To Abraham the Lord said, "And they who keep their first estate shall be added upon; and they who keep not their first estate shall not have glory in the same kingdom with those who keep their first estate; and they who keep their second estate shall have glory added upon their heads forever and ever." (Abr. 3:26) When Lucifer, the light bearer, the brilliant Son of the Morning, rebelled against God in the council of heaven, he chained himself to his crime and became the devil, with the marks of hell upon him.

Then in the other extreme, in speaking of those brilliant marks of merit that will be given in the resurrection, the Apostle Paul said, "There are also celestial bodies and bodies terrestrial: but the glory of the celestial is one, and the glory of the terrestial is another. There is one glory of the sun, and another glory of the moon, and another glory of the stars; for one star differeth from another star in glory. So also is the resurrection of the dead." (I Cor. 15:40-42). God operates these three degrees of glory on a merit basis. Our bodies are given to us only temporarily until we determine what they will be like permanently. Anyone who becomes a celestial spirit will be able to resurrect a celestial body.

In speaking to the Corinthians, the Apostle Paul said, "Ye are not your own For ye are bought with a price: therefore glorify God in your body, and in your spirit, which are Gods." (I Cor. 6:19-20) God wants us to make our bodies and our spirits like his. And we can make our bodies beautiful by holding in our minds and hearts beautifying thoughts. We have all seen plain people who have become beautiful by the working of a radiant spirituality. A godly spirit will make the plainest body beautiful. Great mental and spiritual qualities transform our bodies into their likeness. This is one of the miracles of the resurrection. The Scouts may receive a merit badge for remembering how many things there are in a store window. But God will give exaltation to those who remember to keep his commandments.

Our total merits and demerits will be calculated in order to arrive at our particular degrees of glory. Then our spirits and our bodies will be inseparably joined together, and those most deserving will receive a fullness of the glory of God. When Moses came down from visiting with God on Mount Sinai, the glory of God was upon him; this made his face shine with such brilliance that the people put a veil over him so that they could stand in his presence. But God's badges of beauty—light and intelligence—will make everyone's face glow, and those who are valiant and keep the commandments of

God on a maximum basis will attain that glory represented by the noonday sun. This will surpass the lower orders of merit as the brilliance of the sun exceeds the pale light of the moon or the twinkle of a tiny star. The glory of the sun will be the mark of God, and those so marked will be a part of that order to which God himself belongs.

A Boy Scout in uniform or a soldier on duty or a doctor in an academic parade each displays on his person the emblems of his worthiness and achievement. But in the more important business of life, these emblems are etched into the person of the individual himself. The old Indians used to follow the custom of giving a baby a temporary name until he could make a name for himself; then he was known by the name that indicated his accomplishment. Once when one of Napoleon's soldiers was lying upon the operating table about to undergo some chest surgery for the removal of shrapnel, he said to the surgeon, "If you'll cut a little deeper, you'll find the emperor." This soldier was carrying the emperor in his heart. The spirit of the emperor on his inside made him a good soldier. When we carry the spirit of God in our hearts, we will also become good soldiers; and when we love righteousness and fairness as God loves righteousness and fairness, then we will become like God, and our righteousness will shine from our faces, as everyone is a self-recording instrument of his own deeds.

No one will need a recording angel to look over his shoulder and jot down his deeds in a book, as a far more readable and more permanent record for good or for evil is being made in us. The Lord told Ezekiel that all of those who lived unrighteously should have a mark set in their foreheads. Sometimes we see someone's features distorted by a terrible disfiguring birthmark. But what will the mark of Satan be like? The scriptures refer to "the mark of the beast." This might well be the sum total of the marks of our alcoholism, immorality, failure, misery, and shame, which we ourselves have written there.

Life is made up of contrasts, and we may acquire the merit badges of God. When we wear the emblems of sound judgment, a stable conscience, and a righteous heart, then there will be an eternal light in our eyes, a beautiful song in our hearts, and eternal glory lighting up our souls indicating that we are first class Scouts.

The Mothers of the Bible

O N MOTHER'S DAY WE HONOR THAT IMPORTANT PERSON WHO stands next to God in benefiting our lives. She served as the mold in which our physical form was cast, but she also shapes our mental, spiritual, and moral lives. The word "mother" also has some symbolic and metaphorical meanings. Cicero once pointed out that gratitude was the mother of virtues. A genuine gratitude is a kind of matrix from which godliness, faith, and ambition may be born. It is very helpful when we also understand that character traits, ideals, and abilities also have mothers, and it is a good idea to go behind the result occasionally and get acquainted with the power that gave it its life.

It is an interesting fact that even the Son of God needed a mother. And once each year, we recount the story of that long ago night in Bethlehem when Mary started Jesus toward his destiny. The New Testament refers to 89 occasions when Jesus quoted from the Old Testament; we might wonder how many times he quoted from his mother.

The Bible is usually thought of as our greatest earthly possession. It contains the directions by which our lives may become eternal and glorious. And how greatly the Bible itself must have been enriched by those wonderful women who mothered the prophets and helped to form the culture in which we live.

I suppose that a good place to begin a study of Bible mothers is where God himself began. All of our lives started out in heaven. Paul said, "We have had fathers of our flesh which corrected us, and we gave them reverence: shall we not much rather be in subjection unto the Father of spirits and live?" (Heb. 12:9.) And certainly no one has ever had a father in heaven or anywhere else without also having a mother. Heaven would not be heaven without women. In his wisdom God also created a mortal body to house man's magnificent immortal spirit. Then God said to Adam, "It is not good for man to be alone." So a female tabernacle was prepared for the great woman who had been chosen to be the wife of Adam. It is interesting that women were created with more physical beauty than men. They also have more gentle dispositions. They are more loving

---
Given on Mother's Day.

and more spiritual in their natures. They were prepared to be the mothers of that great concourse of spirits who are awaiting the privileges of mortality. However, the scriptures do not tell us much about our maternal ancestors. In the ante-mortal existence Adam had been known as Michael the Archangel, and undoubtedly Eve was a good match for her great husband. As it was their ante-mortal excellence that had won for them the privilege of being the pro-genitors of the human family.

After their eyes were opened, the Lord explained to Adam the need to work and to earn his bread by the sweat of his brow. The divine record points out that "Eve, his wife, did labor with him." The sacred record says that the Holy Ghost fell upon Adam, and Adam and Eve were given many revelations from God; and Adam blessed God, saying, "Because of my transgression my eyes are opened, and in this life I shall have joy, and again in the flesh I shall see God." And the record says that when Eve heard all of these things, she was glad and said, "Were it not for our transgression we never should have known good and evil, and the joy of our redemp-tion, and the eternal life which God giveth unto all the obedient." And Adam and Eve made known unto their sons and daughters the great truths of God. (Moses 5.) They must also have taken great delight in teaching their children. When Cain was born Eve was delighted and she said, "I have gotten a man from the Lord." (Gen. 4:1.)

Later Abel was born, and for over nine hundred years it was the job of our first parents to effectively establish the human race upon the earth. They also knew the tragedy of having some of their chil-dren go wrong. What a shock they must have received when Cain killed his brother and brought a dreadful curse upon himself. But the Prophet Daniel tells of the time when Adam, whom he calls the "ancient of days" or the oldest man, will sit to judge his people. Then Daniel says a thousand thousands will minister unto him, and ten thousand times ten thousand will stand before him; and certainly when that day arrives, our faithful mother, Eve, will be there by his side.

There is another Bible woman who in some ways resembles Eve. Sarah was the wife of Abraham, and the Lord also called her the "mother of nations" and said that many kings would be among her posterity. She and her husband were selected to leave the sinful society of their homeland and help God establish a great new nation of righteous people. Sarah was very beautiful, and she was also one of the first women to get an extensive write-up in the Bible. Her personality qualities and great character traits still shine out brightly from the pages of sacred history. She was very intelligent, patient, and charming. Apparently she was very happy and at home in the nomadic tent life that she and Abraham lived together. Sarah brought forth Isaac, her first born son, after she was ninety years old. She helped to pass on to Isaac the love that she and Abraham had always had for Jehovah. Following her death, Isaac paid his mother the supreme compliment of those days in leaving her tent unoccupied until Rebekah entered it as his wife.

Another of the great women of the Bible was Rachel (which means "serene and meek".) She was the wife acquired by Jacob after fourteen years of toil. But Rachel was also barren. God's first command had been to "multiply and replenish the earth," and this natural instinct had been securely planted in Rachel's heart. Eventually on the verge of despair, Rachel gave out an anguished cry to God in which she said, "Give me children or I die." Finally Rachel gave birth to Joseph, a baby who was well worth waiting for. But the life of this wonderful woman came to an untimely end while she was giving birth to her second son, Benjamin. Rachel was beautiful in countenance, soft spoken in manner, and loving in disposition. And we feel that Jacob's love for her will live throughout eternity. The stone pillar that still marks her burial place outside Bethlehem also recalled to our minds one of history's most delightful love stories.

Jochebed was the mother of three famous children, Moses, Miriam, and Aaron. She was a woman of towering faith and resourcefulness and erected an everlasting monument to this important mother function. When she was faced with a government edict to destroy her newborn son Moses, she made him a boat of reeds, lined it with pitch, and hid him among the bulrushes of the river, where Pharoah's daughter found him when she came to bathe. Then Moses' faithful little guardian sister, Miriam, ran to the princess and volunteered the services of his mother as the nursemaid and teacher of her future great son.

Ruth is another inspiring Bible woman. She is celebrated primarily for her loyalty to her mother-in-law, Naomi. Naomi's husband and her two sons had died. When Naomi was left alone, she decided to return to her old home in Bethlehem. However, she reasoned with her widowed daughters-in-law that their best interests would be served by finding new husbands and remaining among their own people in Moab. But Ruth loved her mother-in-law and wanted to be with her. She shows us at its best the beautiful attachment that sometimes exists between an older and a young woman. Ruth said to her mother-in-law, "Entreat me not to leave thee, or to return from following after thee, for whither thou goest, I will go; and where thou lodgest I will lodge: thy people shall be my people, and thy God my God: Where thou diest, will I die, and there will I be buried: the Lord do so to me, and more also, if ought but death part thee and me." (Ruth 1:16)

So Ruth also returned to Bethlehem, where she gleaned in the wheatfields of Boaz. Then, under the expert coaching of Naomi, a tender romance developed between Ruth and Boaz, who later became the great-grandparents of King David.

Another of the noble women of the Bible was Hannah, the mother of the great Hebrew prophet, Samuel. Hannah is an example of dedication to God that has seldom, if ever, been excelled. Much of Hannah's time was spent in weeping and bitterness of spirit because she had no children. She offered a prayer in the temple at Shiloh in which she vowed that if God would give her a son, she would dedicate his life to divine service. God granted Hannah's prayer, and Hannah kept her promise to God. When her little boy was only three years old, the courageous Hannah took him to the temple and obediently handed her little boy over to the Lord. He began his priestly duties under the direction of Eli, and eventually Samuel himself became the temple priest, and finally the Lord's Prophet. And one of Samuel's great privileges was to anoint David King of Israel.

Then we have Mary, the virgin mother of Jesus. She is not only the *first* mother of the Bible, but she is also the *first* lady of the world. It is very interesting to contemplate the kind of young woman that Mary must have been, to have been chosen by God to be the mother of this particular son. She herself was pure in heart and beautiful in character. She made a full commitment of her life to God, and she was given the greatest role that any woman has ever been called upon to play. She became a mother when she was very young, according to our customs. But she possessed supreme humility, limitless devotion, and unquestioning obedience to God's will. In confiding to her cousin Elizabeth that she was to be the mother of the Son of God, she said, "My soul doth magnify the Lord, and my spirit hath rejoiced in God my Saviour. For he hath regarded the low estate of his handmaiden, for, behold, from henceforth all generations shall call me blessed. For he that is mighty hath done to me great things; and holy is his name." (Luke 1:46-49.) Undoubtedly, Mary shed many tears of joy and gratitude when she first held the Christ Child to her breast in Bethlehem. She must have shed other tears as she watched his splendid manhood develop. But then the hostility of the people turned upon him, and Mary was finally left to wait out those long, sad hours at the foot of the cross. But even in his death, she was highly blessed among women.

We sometimes learn a great deal about an idea by also thinking about it on its negative side. A number of years ago a stimulating Mother's Day story was written by Lillieth Schell under the title of "The Other Woman." It is a part of the story of the Crucifixion. It pictures the agony and suffering that took place upon the cross. It tells of the thirst, the parched lips, and the vinegar. Then came the bitterness of that last outcry, followed by the earthquake, the darkness, and the dreadful fear. As Jesus had indicated his beloved apostle from the cross, he had said to his mother, "Woman, behold thy son." Then to John he said, "Son, behold thy mother."

After the end had come, John took Mary and Salome and the other woman to his own home. Later that night in the midst of their weeping, a knock came at the door. John opened the door to see a strange woman standing before him. He said to her, "Whom seekest thou?" The other woman said, "The mother of him who was crucified." John said, "She is within, but I cannot suffer thee to disturb her now." The woman said, "Thou must," and she pushed by John and made her way to the lighted doorway beyond which sat this little group of sorrowing women. She paused momentarily while her eyes became accustomed to the light. Then, after identifying the woman she sought, she made her way to Mary and said to her, "I bring thee compassion."

Mary replied, "I give thee my gratitude, O woman; whoever thou art, I give thee my thanks." Then the other woman said, "O thou happy one!"

Stirred by the strangeness of these words, Mary, the mother of Jesus, lifted her sodden eyes and looked sharply into the face of the stranger. What she saw there made her forget the bitterness of her own grief. "My sister," she said, "rather would I give thee compassion. Thy loss, thy sorrow, how great it must be. Wilt thou tell me of it? Wilt thou tell me who thou art?"

"My name is Judith" answered the other woman. "I am come out of Kerioth of Judea." Mary said, "My friend, canst thou not tell me of thy sorrow? Perchance I might help thee. I will gladly share it with thee." "My sorrow," said Judith, "is such that thou canst never know." Her hand stole up to her forehead and brushed aside a lock of iron gray hair. Then, clutching her throat as if to relieve the terrible choking there, she said in a shrill whisper, "I am the mother of Judas Iscariot!"

I close with an honorable mention for just one more great woman, and that is our own mother. And may God help us to always be worthy of her.

A Motto

IN EVERYONE'S OCCUPATION AS WELL AS IN HIS SOCIAL, RELIGIOUS, and personal life there are certain standards and methods of procedure that will tend to crown his efforts with success. One very important accomplishment technique is to have a good motto or an effective slogan by which our lives may be guided and motivated.

The dictionary says that a "motto" is a short suggestive expression of guiding principles. It may be a word, a phrase, or a sentence that identifies the purpose or emphasizes the function of some particular enterprise. Certainly among some of the most prominent influences in determining the success of any undertaking is to know where we want to go and how we are going to get there. A good motto is a kind of symbol that holds the focus of our attention solidly upon the objective. In the control tower of life we need some good maxims to guide us and to quicken our progress. A motto not only indicates what our goal is, but it often helps to generate the power to bring it about.

In some music we have a recurring phrase that is referred to as a theme or a motto. As this particular strain is repeated over and over in our ears, it tends to become permanently written in our hearts. In about the same way it is thought that we might enrich the quality of our personal experience by having some strong central idea or ideal to serve us as the focal point around which to rally the forces of our accomplishment. While James A. Garfield was President of the United States, a certain statement so frequently reappeared in his speech that it came to be regarded as the personal motto of his life. He said, "There are many things that I am afraid of. One is, I am afraid to do a mean thing." As this motto became firmly established in his heart, it largely eliminated the probability that any unworthy thing would become a part of his life. A strong fear of evil or a strong fear of weakness or a strong fear of unfairness can become like a powerful anti-toxin building up bodily resistance to the disease against which it is directed. By the use of a good motto or a motivating slogan, we can build fortifications against any undesirable influence. We can, therefore, greatly reduce the possibility of any weakness or error developing.

In writing the book of Ecclesiastes, Solomon gave us a most productive motto. He said, "Fear God and keep his commandments, for this is the whole duty of man." If this motto is sufficiently established as our governing principle, it can easily solve most of our problems. If adequately strengthened with conviction and love, such a motto can be given power to make our lives invulnerable to such dreaded diseases as failure and sin.

The motto of the United States, which is printed on its coins, is "In God We Trust." This is an excellent motto with great power. It is closely related to the one Solomon wrote in Ecclesiastes. However, our problem comes from the fact that as individual citizens we do not always subscribe to it wholeheartedly. This motto is often more a part of our coins than it is of us. Actually, it should be just the other way around. A motto is something that should be a part of people. America is a great Christian nation. It was founded by God-fearing men and established on basic Christian principles. To continue American success, we who carry on its traditions must be fully dedicated to God, the author of our blessings. We must devotedly honor those eternal principles of truth, righteousness, freedom, equal opportunity, and fairness for which our motto stands. If we actually and fully trust in God, then we will have no unanswered problems. It is only as we depart from our motto that we begin having difficulties. Our national anthem itself has a glorious motto woven into its fabric. Out of the depths of our hearts we sing,

> Then conquer we must when our cause it is just,
> Let this be our motto, In God is our Trust.
> And the star-spangled banner in triumph shall wave
> O'er the land of the free and the home of the brave.

Just suppose that every individual citizen were thoroughly dedicated to the Great Christian ideals of absolute honesty, unwavering righteousness, and wholehearted love of truth on which our nation was established. What a country we would have, and what a people we would be! What privileges we would enjoy! With the proper procedures we can build ideas and ideals so solidly into our lives that they cannot be moved, changed, or disregarded. When Abraham Lincoln was just a young man, he witnessed a colored slave girl being sold at auction. The evils of slavery were so indelibly impressed in his mind that he wholeheartedly determined that he would do everything in his power to destroy it. When we are motivated by that kind of determination, the chance to do something about it usually comes very quickly.

Of course, we should make certain that our mottos are good ones. It is very easy to get our minds filled with the wrong things, and then it is pretty difficult to get them out. In America we pay hundreds of millions of dollars each year to get psychiatrists and other social workers to dig down into the dark regions of our minds and try to eliminate the distorted attitudes that are causing our problems. Sometimes we allow an unfavorable personal experience to lodge in our minds and ruin the mental balance in our lives. But even our psychiatric difficulties demonstrate the power that a dominent idea can hold over us. Whether good or bad, one single lesson or one personal experience that gets a foothold in our lives often influences us forever after. Of course, our righteous standards should be solidly built. Apostle James says there should be "nothing wavering. For he that wavereth is like the wave of the sea, driven by the wind, and tossed."

We have an interesting fairy tale in our literature entitled "The Three Little Pigs." These three little pigs, representing us, went out into the world to seek their fortunes. Like us, they had different ambitions and different attitudes about life. The first little pig built his house of straw, the second one built his house of sticks, but the third little pig built his house of bricks. It was not very long before each received a visit from his natural enemy, the wolf. With his huffs and his puffs, the wolf soon blew down the houses made of sticks and straw, and he ate up the little pigs who lived in them. But the little pig who had built his house of bricks had a different experience. He was saved because he lived by a better set of guiding principles.

This story is a small scale version of the contrast pointed out by Jesus between the foolish man who built his house upon the sand and the wise man who established his house upon the rock. Those houses that are built on the sand may be just as good as the ones built on the rock as long as the good weather lasts. But Jesus devoted his life in trying to get people to build their lives on strong, solid, permanent foundations that would weather the roughest storms. The walls, ceilings, and roofs should also be adequate to keep the occupants safe from the harmful huffs and puffs of life's evil pressures. More than about anything else, we need to follow the regulations of that divine building code given for our benefit.

Many years ago I knew two fine young men rather intimately. One of these built his house of bricks; the other one lived in a house of straw. At the beginning both were about as equal as possible in mental ability, physical appearance, and spiritual power. But one had had a vicarious experience that had established a hard core of moral strength in his life that permitted no deviation. A friend of his older brother had made a serious moral mistake, and the havoc it caused had been effectively discussed within their family circle. Under the counsel of a wise father, this young man had definitely decided that no such harmful experience would ever be permitted in his life. From this vicarious experience he had decided to build his own house of bricks. Then when the winds of temptation began to blow upon his life, they had little effect. His mind was made up, and it could not easily be changed.

However, the other young man had not been so fortunate. In his case no impressive advance lesson had built such solid fortifications in his mind. Consequently, his house of straw fell quickly before the hot, rude breath of the wolf. But during the following few years he was struck by several other major moral tragedies. His many problems did not come about because of any natural inferiority in him; the inferiority had been caused by his lack of preparation. He had not built a strong enough moral philosophy to give him sufficient protection. Tragedies always come when there is no firmly established fortification to prevent them from coming. No little pig should ever depend on his wishful thinking that the wolf may not be hungry when he arrives.

One of the most important elements of defeat is surprise. When temptations come, we always have trouble unless protection against them has previously been provided. It is pretty difficult to effectively prepare for the battle after the attack has begun. One usually doesn't mix much mortar or lay many bricks while the wolf is in the process of blowing down your house of straw. Many military as well as moral forces have been overcome from an ambush that could not have been destroyed by any frontal attack. Temptation usually does not wait for one to think things over, or hold a planning meeting, or consult his wiser advisers. The attacks of temptations frequently come from ambush, and they strike us in the place where we are least prepared. The best program for moral or spiritual security is to build with good bricks on a solid foundation and have the roof in place before the rainy season begins.

Many people made fun of Noah because he spent the dry summer months building an ark. And it always seems a little bit ridiculous to be building any arks for protection against the flood during a period of drought. It is just as difficult to understand why a house should be made of bricks when there are no wolves anywhere in sight. Yet we remember the proverb that says, "Where there is no vision, the people perish." (Proverbs 29:18.) And a few good, well-tested firmly held mottos or some wise proverbs to which we have thoroughly committed ourselves will help us to walk into the future with much greater assurance of success. Some good standards will also save us a lot of unpleasantness along the way. They act as lighthouses from which we may periodically take our bearings.

Some time ago Harleigh M. Rosenberger wrote an article telling of a fishing experience. He said, "We had drifted for hours with the changing currents of the lake. Fishing had been exciting that afternoon. And when, finally, we pulled our lines into the boat, we knew we had gone far beyond all familiar landmarks. But as our eyes anxiously searched the shoreline, we finally located the tall spruce tree on the horizon which had the funny top that we had previously noted from our campsite. From that moment on we knew where we were. We had a point of reference."

Without some good points of reference to tie to and live by, we are much more likely to get lost or become so confused that we drift aimlessly. The mariner increases both his safety and his success factors when he steers his ship by the unchanging direction from the North Star.

For us, God is the greatest and safest of our points of reference. He has established his lighthouses of truth all along the shoreline. His guiding principles do not change even in our changing world. What God has previously set up to guide us will always be up to date. His moral laws are always dependable patterns by which we can live successfully.

More especially this is true in our day when many of the old landmarks are being swept away, and we need our sure point of reference with God. Without a solid faith in God, no one can hope to live very successfully.

Winston Churchill was a great phrase maker. During World War II he lived by his "V" sign of victory. He also made the fires of faith burn brighter in the lives of others by his effective mottos and powerful slogans. But Jesus was a far greater phrase maker. He said, "Be ye therefore perfect, even as your Father which is in heaven is perfect. He said, "Man shall not live by bread alone, but by every word that proceedeth forth out of the mouth of God."

The early clans from the highlands of Scotland used their slogans as war cries or songs of gathering. We also need some rallying calls and battle cries to help us win a victory for our eternal lives. When we are able to put great scriptural lines in force in our lives, we will really be on our way.

The Nurse of Greatness

S OMEONE ONCE SAID THAT "DIFFICULTY IS THE NURSE OF GREAT- ness." There is a great deal of evidence supporting the idea that in surmounting difficulties and in overcoming hardships we strengthen character and develop ability. Sometimes we encounter many serious disadvantages merely by having too many advantages. It seems that to make the most of any situation, one needs some problems to solve.

Many men and women have developed a greater power to rise by struggling with adversity. Some of those reared amid poverty, ignorance, and lack of opportunity have climbed to success on those very disadvantages that have held others down. However, this does not mean that we should consciously promote these negative influences. Very frequently unfavorable conditions cost us much and teach us little. Neither does this idea mean that we should stop helping people and force them to sink or swim by themselves. Under no circumstances should we relax in our efforts to extend the benefits of our free and abundant society to as many other people as possible.

We should give every young person the fullest opportunity to realize his potentialities and to continue to eliminate those social conditions that create destructive hardships. As nearly as possible we should do away with disease, poverty, ignorance, prejudice, and all other human enemies as fast as we can. It is wrong to say that abundance is bad or that poverty is good. By itself abundance is not a curse, nor is poverty a blessing. While some have used their disadvantages as stepping stones, yet these same disadvantages have served others as stumbling blocks.

For every talent that poverty has stimulated, it has blighted a hundred. Abundance may dull the efforts of some potentially gifted people, but it also makes possible the nourishing of talent on a scale that would be impossible otherwise. We could sight examples of many famous men whose sons have not followed in their fathers' footsteps. But, on the other hand, countless sons of great men have equalled or surpassed their fathers. The son of a successful father may have less hardship to stimulate him, but he has many compensating advantages, including a model to emulate. There are many other advantages to growing up in an atmosphere pervaded by high standards of performance, where great expectations are held for the future. Weakness is not always born in the midst of advantages, and some entire families have created a tradition of high performance that has remained intact for generations. We might conclude, therefore, that it is not "difficulty" alone that nurtures greatness, but rather it is our attitude about it. The poet has said,

> To each is given a bag of tools,
> A shapeless mass and a book of rules,
> And each must make, ere his life has flown,
> A stumbling block or a steppingstone.

Our job is to learn how to utilize the benefits of abundance without getting trapped in its disadvantages. An abundant society is not necessarily a society without challenge; neither can we expect to rise automatically merely because we are loaded down with difficulties. The Apostle Paul gave us the key to this situation when he said, "All things work together for the good of them that love God." That is, if we love God, if we think right, if we have the right attitude, then everything works in our interests. For example, night is as necessary as day; uphill is as good as downhill; struggle is as important as ease; and even sickness and death serve our eternal purposes quite as well as health and life. If we always got our own way, no one would ever be sick, no one would ever die; there would be no struggle, and there would be no strength.

If we "love God," the example of a drunken father may serve as our most potent teacher of righteousness. The old Romans personified this attitude of right thinking in one of their ancient myths. The function of building their steppingstones was identified with the Roman goddess Levana. It was her duty to perform the earliest office of enoblement for each newborn infant. Their tradition had it that at the moment of birth the baby was laid on the ground, but lest so grand a creature should grovel there for more than an instant, the parental hand, as proxy for Levana, raised him upright, set him erect, and started him toward his destiny as the king of this world. To the Romans, Levana was the nurse of greatness. She went around lifting people up. Her name itself comes from the verb *levare*, which means to raise aloft or to stand upright, and it points toward the primary accomplishment of every life.

Because the beast goes down on all fours, nature throws his

vision upon the ground, but it was intended that man should stand upright in the image of his Maker, that he might see to the stars. And whether the symbol of this function of enoblement is identified with Levana or whether it symbolizes the parental hand or our own good attitudes that act as proxy for this uplifting office, it should have our wholehearted support and encouragement. Certainly we all need a lot of help to serve us in this function of nursing greatness.

The dictionary says that a nurse is "one trained to take care of others." A nurse waits upon the patient under the direction of a physician. The dictionary says that a nurse is one who rears someone else, or looks after him, or furnishes nutriment for him, or helps him to grow straight and strong. In one of our greatest scriptures God said, "Thou mayest choose for thyself," and one of the best places to begin exercising our choices is in selecting those influences that will most effectively help us grow. A great human being is the primary creation of God and is his most important present concern. Each of us was begotten in heaven in God's own image. And following the tradition of Levana, we begin this part of our life's journey by being laid helpless upon the earth. But success in life is a process of developing those activities of enoblement that teach us to stand upright and grow into God's own likeness.

When a new corporation is organized, one of the first things that is done for it is to provide a constitution and a set of by-laws to direct its course and help to bring about its maximum success. This is also a good idea for individuals. Dr. Henry C. Link once said "That nothing does so much to put order into our lives as a good set of sound principles." And the best set of principles are the principles of the gospel of Christ. These are the divine rules by which we may become as he is. We also have other natural laws by which we might lift ourselves upward. Each of them may also serve us as a nurse of greatness, by setting us upright and propelling us forward. We ought to mark these down in our books and practice them. A good attitude in responding to difficulty and the other events of life by which we are surrounded have already been mentioned. Former President Hadley of Yale University said that mental attitude is more important than mental capacity. We hear a lot of people complain about their lack of mental attitude, but no one needs to complain about any lack of mental attitude, as that is something that he can control for himself as proxy for God.

As principle number two, we might enlist the power of knowledge in our behalf. The Lord himself has said that no one can be

saved in ignorance. A Chinese proverb says, "To be fond of learning is to be at the gate of Knowledge." A fondness for learning can
also bring us to the gates of heaven. However, when one is allergic
to learning and apathetic about his own success, his movement
usually tends to go in a different direction. Most Americans have
access to that most important knowledge found in the Holy Scriptures. The Bible is within the easy reach of every man, and no one
can afford to leave it unopened with its lessons unlearned. It has
been said that most human beings must have the great lessons of
religion thrust upon them if they are to be learned at all.

Someone once pointed out that good teachers should meet the
students halfway. But his teacher friend thought that he was under-
stating the case, and being a little more pessimistic, he gave it as
his opinion that if most students learn very much, the teachers must
block all exits and trap them into learning, whereas good students
run to meet their learning opportunities. We place a handicap upon
ourselves when we put the burden on someone else for catching and
holding our attention. Sometimes our various teachers must be end-
lessly solicitous in counseling us, encouraging us, awakening us, and
disciplining us. We lessen our own chances when we develop what
Professor Lounsbury once described as "an infinite capacity to resist
the intrusion of knowledge."

A third of these helpful nurses to serve as proxy for Levana might
be called motivation. That is the power to take action. It is our
propelling power. Motivation has been called "morale in gear."
Motive probably transcends in importance every other success factor.
It is the good seed bed as well as the good seed. It is thought that
there are no lazy people or dull people. But there are many people
who lack the right kind of motives for doing the right kind of things.
Every man who propels himself from a lowly beginning to the top
of success must be fiercely motivated. Getting places is easy when
one has an indomitable spirit. And, therefore, high motivation often
becomes a more precious commodity than talent.

There is a science of accomplishment that is the science of
crime detection in reverse. A detective takes an accomplishment
and works backward to find the motive. If the motive can be discovered, the criminal can usually be identified; whereas, a candidate
for success in life takes a motive and works forward to an accomplishment. When one becomes master of his own motivation, he
makes almost every other accomplishment easily available. We might
say about motivation what James M. Barrie once said about charm;

"If you have it, then nothing else matters very much," and he added that "if you don't have it, then nothing else matters very much either." Individuals with lesser accomplishments are usually individuals with lesser motivations.

A fourth of these assistants that we can enlist to work for our success is the drive to carry out our ambitions. Benjamin Disraeli once said that "genius is the power to make continuous effort." A persistent, constant, driving, unwavering devotion to a great cause can make us almost all-powerful. Calvin Coolidge once said, "Nothing in the world can take the place of persistence. Talent will not —nothing is more common than unsuccessful men with talent; genius will not—unrewarded genius is almost a proverb; education will not—the world is full of education derelicts. Persistence and determination alone are omnipotent."

Sometimes whole groups of people have forced their way to the top by their drive. Pioneers, conquerors, immigrants, or followers of Christ have reached important destinations powered by such precious assets as drive, a sense of purpose, and indomitability. Drive cannot be bought, inherited, or borrowed; it can only be earned and self-developed.

Another helpful trait that like Levana, has its hand in every high performance is a kind of animated confidence in one's self called "morale." Outstanding success is never the achievent of discouraged, demoralized, hopeless individuals. High morale may not always mean that one is cheerful or carefree. In fact his life may be full of suffering with moments of despair mixed in. But deep down inside there is a hard core of conviction and self-trust that makes every righteous achievement possible. We should never expect an excellent performance without an excellent morale, and with low morale, we have no excellence.

Another nurse of greatness is the ability for self-discipline. When we can manage ourselves and get the kind of control over brain, the tongue, the emotions, and the ambitions that we have over such lesser emotions, and the ambitions that we have over such lesser organs as our hands and feet, then we will be well on our way.

A Marine officer once said, "It is discipline plus morale that makes the difference in a Marine." He said, "When those kids learn what it means to be a Marine, they grow eight inches taller." And when we understand our possible destiny and what it means to be heirs of God, we will begin a growth that will make us like him.

There are other traits that can help nurse our success. Some of these are industry, faith, and preparation. Alexander the Great once said, "What Aristotle is in the world of thought, I will be in the world of action!" That made him the conqueror of the world by the time he was 26, and that will make us anything that we want to be. "God gives all things to industry," and only as we coordinate these helpful traits together are we prepared to make the most of ourselves. All life is preparation; we prepare for school, we prepare for marriage, we prepare for our life's work, we prepare for death. In our antemortal existence we prepared for this life. In this life we prepare for eternity. Failure in the preparation means failure at the destination. Sometime ago, in an orgy of irresponsibility, Richard B. Speck killed eight Chicago nurses. But we sometimes destroy those other nurses that are helping us toward nobility, greatness and eternal life. To avoid making such an error we need to know a lot about the constitution and by-laws that God has prepared for our lives in which he sets forth his objectives and procedures for our success. We also need to be able to distinguish between the important and the unimportant aims of life. The Master's great training program promises that those who carry it through to completion may become like God. There is everything in knowing our destiny and constantly reaffirming it in our lives and then to that end making the most constructive use of these wonderful nursing powers that God has placed in our hands for our benefit.

A Real Person

SOMETIME AGO I REREAD THE STIMULATING BOOK WRITTEN BY Harry Emerson Fosdick, entitled, *On Being a Real Person.* On 254 pages Dr. Fosdick discusses the many advantages of making great character and personality qualities an inherent part of our individual lives. Almost none of the real values of the world are ever found in things, but always in people, and we point out the most distinguishing differences between them by saying that people have personality.

Animals have life the same as humans do. They also have bodies and spirits. They have a very real kind of intelligence in their spheres. Frequently their senses are more highly developed than ours are. An eagle can see further than a man, a rabbit can run faster, an elephant lives longer, a dog has a more highly developed sense of smell, and a horse has a more dependable ability in determining direction. But the animals have been given some definite limits beyond which they are never permitted to pass, whereas a man has been endowed as his exclusive right with the endless possibilities of personality. These personal endowments so set man apart that God is his only fellow in the universe. It is by an evaluation of these traits that we describe a real person that we are able to understand his eternal association with God. It is also one of man's unique distinctions that he has both God and man as his dual creators. It has been said that God supplies the raw materials and the building directions, whereas man is supposed to furnish the labor and the supervision.

Recently I listened to a recount of that thrilling Bible statement wherein it is said, "And God created man in his own image." I closed my eyes on this idea and wished that I could have been there to have seen this important event take place upon this earth. Then I remembered what I have tried not to forget: that the creation of man was not something that was finished and done with in the Garden of Eden 6,000 years ago. The creation of man is still going on, and we ourselves are the creators. Each day we are creating the faith, the ambition, the attitudes, and the character traits that will determine what we will be throughout an endless eternity. We usually think of the immortality of the soul as our greatest human concept. But what would even the immortality of the soul amount to without the immortality of those personality traits that characterize real people? And what is most important, these divine attributes continue to identify us throughout eternity. Someone has improperly compared human lives to so many raindrops which at death all run back into the ocean of the universe where their individuality is eternally lost.

This is not the meaning that the Lord was trying to convey in the sixteenth chapter of Saint Luke. There he takes us behind the scenes of eternity and shows us two men who had lived upon the earth. Both men had died, and each had gone to that great world of spirits to await the resurrection. The scripture tells us of two great general divisions in the spirit world. The man who had been righteous was carried by the angels to a place of happiness, while the other found himself in a place of misery. But even though they were widely separated, they could see and recognize each other. They could also speak, think, hear, and understand. They could remember their earth life; they still felt love, pain, happiness, and regret. And every one of us has also been promised a resurrection so that his body and spirit will be restored to each other and none of those faculties, senses, or abilities, that made him a real person will be lost. Certainly Jesus did not lose his personality either in death or in the process of resurrection. Neither has he lost it since. At the ascension the angels said, "This same Jesus, which is taken up from you into heaven, shall so come in like manner as ye have seen him go into heaven." (Acts 1:11) It is one of the greatest of the divine promises that you will be yourself and I will be myself throughout eternity, with quickened senses, amplified powers of perception, and vastly increased capacity for love, understanding, and happiness.

A frequently heard statement referring to material resources says that you can't take them with you, but this does not apply to our two most valuable possessions, which are life and personality. What a tremendous premium is therefore placed upon developing in ourselves those great personal qualities that will distinguish us in eternity.

There is a sacred scripture that says, "Whatever principle of intelligence we attain unto in this life, it will rise with us in the resurrection. And if a person gains more knowledge and intelligence in this life through his diligence and obedience than another, he will have so much the advantage in the world to come." (D&C 130:18-19.)

As the most important treasures of our mortal world, we might try to think about an accumulation of all of the best in the lives of Abraham Lincoln, Winston Churchill, Mohandas K. Gandhi, Madam Curie, Moses, the Apostle Paul, Jesus and ourselves. What a tragedy it is when we underestimate our own value and thereby sell ourselves and our possibilities short. Jesus compared the wealth of the entire earth to that of one human soul. If we could find out how many trillions of dollars the earth is worth, then with an itemized statement of our own personal resources we might gain a better understanding of our own true value.

God hid up the gold, oil, uranium, and other precious things in the earth, but he put his own attributes and potentialities into his children. The earth is God's handiwork, but man is his son. In this sphere of personality traits man is unique. Ordinarily we do not think of a rabbit as having personality. No one has ever been able to train an animal to smile, nor is any animal ever permitted to give itself any assistance in developing better attitudes or participating in the delights and joys of those experiences that belong only to people.

After man had eaten from the tree of knowledge of good and evil, God said, "The man is now become as one of us, to know good and evil." And I would like to point out in passing that the right kind of knowledge still tends to have that effect upon people. To know good from evil still tends to make men become as gods.

In the Garden of Eden a flaming sword was placed to guard the tree of life, but fortunately for us there is no flaming sword guarding the tree of knowledge, and everyone may eat of it to his heart's content. One of the traits that makes a real person is a pleasant sense of humor. He also has many other valuable senses.

The scientists tell us that there are 102 elements in nature. Some of these are known as oxygen, hydrogen, nitrogen, iron and carbon. These are nature's building blocks. Out of these elements, in the right combinations and proportions, nature fashions all of the material things of the world. A bag of salt, a sack of sugar, or even an ocean can be represented by a chemical formula. We can create, change or destroy the identity of any compound by making a rearrangement of these individual elements. Then by way of comparison someone has said that in human personality there are 51 elements. There are kindness, faith, courage, industry, ambition, spirituality, and righteousness.

If we put all of these elements together in the right combinations and proportions, we have what someone has called a magnificent human being. This is what Dr. Fosdick would call "a real person." A real person is the genuine article. He is God's greatest masterpiece, created in God's image, endowed with God's attributes, and made heir to God's potentialities. Then man is permitted to add to himself those characteristics that seem to him most desirable. The primary work of God himself is that of building the greatest possible values into human lives. However, in our role as joint creators with God, it also becomes our work and our glory to bring to pass our own immortality and eternal life.

God is eternally committed to our free agency and the natural responsibility that goes with it. It is the divine purpose that we should be honest, fair, righteous, and faithful. God is a real person, and the purpose of the Ten Commandments, the Sermon on the Mount, and every other set of divine instructions and directions that have ever been given has been to help man become more like his eternal heavenly father. God has not only given us the holy scriptures to guide our judgment, but he has also installed in each of us a divine growth instinct, a natural inner striving, including a constant prompting by the conscience in directing our lives upward. This divine upward reach is intended to help us bring these great human values in their maximum. A large research organization recently studied 10,000 personnel records to try to find out the sources and causes of success. It was discovered that an average of 85 percent of all success was accounted for by the kind of use made of the personality traits.

A number of years ago the great General Electric Corporation appropriated a million dollars and alloted four years of time to research the importance of the human element in business success. This great corporation had already spent large sums of money and many years of time in improving its manufactured products.

Now it decided that it should give some attention to the improvement of the people who made, sold, and used the products. After some of their most able scientists had worked for four years, their number one pronouncement was to the effect that "all development is self-development." It is easy to make more effective household appliances and better gadgets. It is a fairly simple matter to breed a better strain of cattle or develop bigger ears of corn or faster airplanes or more efficient refrigerators, but the most effective human development comes from within the person himself.

Personality is such a tremendous idea that we even think of God in terms of it. We speak of him as a loving and eternal Heavenly Father. He is a good teacher and a wise friend. We speak of his hands, his face, and his voice. God is not only a real person, but he is the main fact in the universe. In the Garden of Gethsemane Jesus said, "And this is life eternal, that we might know thee, the only true God, and Jesus Christ, whom thou hast sent." We need to understand more about the parent before we can really comprehend ourselves. The mission of Jesus was to teach us correct principles and to show us the way back into God's presence. The first and most important commandment given from the top of Mount Sinai was against having false gods, or practicing false religions, or believing in false doctrines. And one of the biggest problems of our present world is that the personality of God has been destroyed in many minds. Many people have lost their ability to think of God as a "real person." Some people think of him merely as some mysterious essence or influence that has no reality.

But Jesus is the Son of God. He is the express image of his Father's person. He had a real Father; he had a real birth; he lived a real life; he bled real blood; and he had a real, literal, bodily resurrection. He is still a real person and lives and rules with God, his eternal Heavenly Father. The hour is rapidly approaching when he will come to the earth again, this time in great glory, to cleanse the earth of sin and reign personally upon it for a thousand-year millennium. The nail prints in his hands and his feet will still be visible, and we will know that he is a real person. One of the problems in our personal lives is that we sometimes adopt a false religion in which God is thought of as a "thing" or an "idea". In some people's minds he is an immaterial shadowy illusion that has no real substance. It is thinking of God as an "it" instead of a "thou" that has led so many theologians to teach that the heavens are sealed, or that he has lost interest in us. When God is thought of as unreal, it is then an easy step to take away his interest or ability to help us. Then we say that direct revelations from him have forever ceased. With such a belief, it would not be difficult to think in terms of the so-called "new morality," the popular philosophy where everything goes, and the feeling that what one does is not important, because no one is responsible for his acts.

In making God less than a real person, some insist upon depriving him of his body; then we take away his personality and we say that he is dead. But God is not dead! And it may not be very long before everyone in the world will know from his own personal eye-witness experience that God is not some mysterious, shapeless, sexless mass, without body, parts, or passions, who fills the immensity of space.

The greatest idea in the universe is that God is still our eternal Heavenly Father. He is still in charge in the affairs of men. He is still interested in our welfare, and he is still committed to our free agency and our privilege to build up the finest personal attributes within ourselves. Of course, the best way for us to be real persons in heaven is to be real persons here. May God prosper our efforts in this direction.

Regret

OUR WORLD IS A WORLD OF OPPOSITES, WHERE REWARDS AND penalties follow our deeds as natural consequences. The miraculous emotion of joy has been set up as life's highest reward. Napoleon once said that the greatest possible happiness came in the maximum development of one's own life. It follows naturally that the worst misery comes in the failure of our human fulfillment. The dictionary lists sadness, gloom, melancholy, and regret as the chief opposites of joy; and to the extent to which we fail in reaching joy, we automatically get its opposites. As happiness is the state most ardently to be achieved, so the misery of regret is the condition most urgently to be avoided. Most people have felt happiness in some degree. They have also known some measure of the desolation of suffering. Every individual should get as well acquainted as possible with joy in order to produce it more effectively in his own life. We should also try to understand what it would be like to live in the gloom and eternal pain of regret, as this may enable us to eliminate it. The ability to deal effectively with pain is difficult to come by, for because of our dread of suffering we don't like to think about it, and consequently we never learn to understand it.

Next to an actual experience, the easiest approach to either the mental or spiritual anguish comes in comparing it with physical pain. A couple of years ago, an automobile door slammed shut on my finger. The extremely sharp, unpleasant sensations that resulted were almost unbearable. But if I tried to describe these pains to someone who had never had a mashed finger, my finest efforts would be completely meaningless. On several occasions I have tried by sheer force of imagination to conceive the extremes of joy and misery. We may be aware of the excruciating pain suffered by a soldier as he lies wounded, bleeding and alone on the battlefield. Instead of one mashed finger, his whole body might be torn and mutilated. And in addition he may be ravished by thirst, exposure, fear, and fever. His suffering may be so severe that his earnest prayer would beg for the relief of unconsciousness or the release of death. But lacking an actual experience, the human mind is incapable of conceiving the extremes of pain in more than a small fraction.

No one can feel a toothache in his imagination with anywhere near the vividness that he gets from actually feeling it in his tooth. Because of this failure in our perception, we lose much of the motivating power that might otherwise work toward prevention. In fact, even the actual experience of physical pain has largely been eliminated from our world. The science of medicine and the miracle of wonder drugs have made it unnecessary for anyone to suffer very much for very long. Sometime ago, I was on the operating table for several hours undergoing some serious surgery. But I was completely unaware of even the slightest pain. However, we have not been this fortunate in eliminating the more serious misery that comes in various mental and spiritual forms.

Recently I saw a woman on the verge of a mental and emotional collapse. She was screaming with an unendurable mental agony that for months had been building up in her life. Her mental suffering reminded me of the condition described in the scriptures as eternal torment.

The Bible tells of "outer darkness," where there is weeping and gnashing of teeth. It compares the torments of Hell to a lake of fire whose flames ascend up forever and ever. No one knows the extent to which mental suffering can go even in this life. We do know that it can reach such an awful pitch as to derange our minds. But with this as a starting point, we might try to imagine what the gall of bitterness or the anguish of soul might be for one who was racked with the dreadful fear and awful pains of the damned. There is no point in one trying to escape merely by saying that he doesn't believe in hell, for we do know that wrong always causes suffering. How could it be any different or any less, when the greater values of eternity are involved? Therefore, if in advance we could really understand eternal joy, we would be far more resourceful in bringing it about; and if we could beforehand understand the depths and intensity of the unhappiness of eternal misery, we could much more easily eliminate the cause.

There are some religious groups who practice what they call "whipping the flesh." They cut and burn themselves to cause themselves pain. They believe that to suffer a little pain here may save them a lot of suffering hereafter. This is not a bad idea to think about. Through a good imagination we may be able to innoculate ourselves against pain, much as we might immunize ourselves against some dread disease. And what influence could be more constructive than to vaccinate ourselves against eternal unhappiness and regret?

Recently a man of very limited means told about a large residential subdivision in an exclusive part of town that had once belonged to him. However, when he had owned it, it had never occurred to him that some day it might be worth a fortune. Therefore, he allowed it to be sold for taxes. Today this land is worth over a million dollars. How bitterly he now regrets that because of his shortsightedness, he had allowed this fortune to slip through his fingers. This man is also allowing gloomy moods to eat away his personality, and he is making himself sick with this suffering of regret over his misfortune. But who can understand what it would be like to lose a million dollars? You have great ability if you approximate in your imagination the pain of such an actual experience. Or suppose that we were to try to understand what it would be like to live throughout eternity with the realization that we had lost the eternal exaltation that we might have had with our families and friends in God's highest kingdom. Even if we can't understand the tragedy of losing our celestial values, yet we ought to keep trying to understand it. For if we have to wait for an actual experience, it will then be too late. We should also be able to understand the extremes of happiness in advance.

The Apostle Paul says, "Eye hath not seen, nor ear heard, neither have entered into the heart of man, the things which God hath prepared for them that love him." (I Cor. 2:9.) We can imagine some pretty wonderful things. We can imagine luxury, elegance, beauty, and comfort costing billions of dollars. We can imagine some of the limited forms of joy and peace, but we cannot conceive the wonders and magnificence of those things which God hath prepared for us.

I don't know what it would be like to be a telestial soul throughout eternity. I do know that it would be a condition less fine, less beautiful, and less satisfying, just as the twinkle of a tiny star is less than the blaze of the noonday sun. The celestial, which Paul describes as the glory of the sun, is that order to which God himself belongs. This celestial group is composed of those who are valiant in their faith. Then far below the celestial is this telestial group; of them it was said, "Where God and Christ dwell they cannot come, worlds without end." (D&C 76:112.)

Then below these three kingdoms of glory is another kingdom that is not a kingdom of glory. This place is called Hell. It is a place of severe misery and torment. This is the permanent abode of Satan and his angels. They will be joined by those of our own number who have sinned unto death. Of this group, the Lord has said, "It had been better for them never to have been born; For they are vessels of wrath doomed to suffer the wrath of God, with the devil and his angels in eternity; concerning whom I have said there is no forgiveness in this world nor in the world to come." (D&C 76:32-34.) It is well worth a lot of reflection now to try to understand what the feelings will be then of those who actually have this awful everlasting experience.

Aristotle, the Macedonian philosopher, was appointed by King Phillip to be the adviser and tutor of young Alexander, who was later called "the Great." Aristotle told Alexander that the greatest foe that ever confronted an army was never in the ranks of the enemy, but always in one's own camp. We might test this philosophy by asking ourselves who is the greatest enemy of America. It isn't Russia or China or Cuba. That is ridiculous. Who is it that causes our strikes, fills our jails, wastes our money, makes our ridiculous mistakes, causes our crime wave, and gets us drunk? We can't blame these things onto the weather, the Communists, or our foreign debtors. Our most serious problems all originate in our own camp. Or who is the instigator of our personal problems? Who is it that keeps me *poor* and *ignorant* and unworthy? It is always the enemy in my own camp.

Someone has told a personal story illustrating this significant idea. It was New Year's night. An aged man was standing at the window. He mournfully raised his eyes toward the deep blue sky, where the stars were floating like white lilies on the surface of a clear, calm lake. Then he cast his eyes toward the earth, and he thought of the many other miserable beings like himself who were moving towards their inevitable goal—the tomb. Already he had passed his sixtieth birthday, and he seemed to have gained nothing from his life but errors and remorse. His health was failing, and his old age was almost completely devoid of any kind of comfort. His mind was unfurnished, and his heart was filled with sorrow and bitterness. Then the days of his misspent youth rose up in a vision before him. He recalled that life had placed him at the beginnings of two roads, one leading into a sunny, peaceful, fertile land producing an abundant harvest, and resounding with the soft, sweet music of success. The other road would take the wanderer into a deep dark cave, from whence there was no issue. There poison flowed instead of water, and repulsive serpents hissed and crawled.

He looked toward the sky, and cried out in his anguish: "O lost youth, return! O my father, place me once more at the crossways of life, that I may have another chance to choose the better road!" But the days of his youth had passed away, and his parents were now with the departed. He saw wandering lights float briefly over dark marshes and then disappear. "Such," he said, "were the days of my wasted life." Then he saw a star shoot through the heavens and vanish in the darkness beyond the churchyard. "Behold an emblem of myself," he cried, and the sharp arrows of unavailing remorse struck deep into his soul.

It added greatly to his pain to remember those early companions who had entered life with him, but who had chosen the more profitable paths of virtue and industry and were now happy and in their places of honor on this New Year's night. As the sound of the chiming of the bells in the high church tower fell upon his ears, he recalled the many tokens of his parents' love for him, their erring son. He thought of the lessons they had taught him and the prayers they had offered up in his behalf. Then, overwhelmed with shame and grief, he no longer dared to look towards the heavens where they now dwelt. From his darkened eyes fell the bitter tears of regret, as with one despairing effort he cried out aloud, "Come back, my early days. Come back!"

And his youth did come back, for he awoke and discovered that all this had been only an ugly dream that had visited his slumbers on New Year's night. He was still young and ambitious. His errors were only in his dream. Then, now fervently, he thanked God that time was still his own, that he had not yet entered the deep, dark, dreadful cavern of failure, nor would he ever do so. He was still free to follow the road leading to the peaceful land where sunny harvests smiled and waved.

We who still linger on the threshold of life with any doubts as to which path we should choose should anticipate that time when the years have passed and our sins have flooded our lives with vain regret. Then how bitterly we may mourn and cry out for our lost youth and the wasted opportunities of our earlier days.

The Reverse Gear

ONE OF THE IMPORTANT FORWARD MOVEMENTS IN OUR CIVILIZA-tion took place with the invention of the wheel. The wheel is the basic factor in the operation of the wagon, the automobile, the truck, the tractor, and the railroad train. Even the airplane depends upon its ground wheels for the take-off and its propellor wheels to draw it upward and forward through the air. Our modern civilization would present a rather dismal and disturbing picture if we still had to drag our burdensome loads along the ground or carry them upon our backs, as we did in pre-wheel days.

However, we have now gone far beyond the wheel itself. Our engines are now given greater effectiveness because of those modified wheels called gears that we are presently building into our machines. We actually have a number of gears. The low gear is the power gear. This is the one used to overcome the inertia of a dead stop. This is the strong gear that we use to get things going. This is the only gear that can get our big loads over the hilltops or out of difficult places. But after the low gear has done its job, then the responsibility is turned over to the high gear to give us a smooth ride down the highway at substantial speed. And it takes only about a sixth as much energy to keep us going after our momentum has been established.

There is another interesting gear that is called the reverse gear. This gear moves us in the opposite direction of the other gears. Recently I stopped my automobile at an intersection to wait for a red light. Because I was a little too close to the crosswalk, I backed the car up a bit. But after getting it in the proper position, I forgot to take the engine out of reverse. When the green light came on, I leaned forward and stepped on the gas with some impatience. Then I received the rather startling shock of finding myself going in the wrong direction with some decisiveness. If anyone had been following me closely, we may have had some difficulty. In thinking about this experience, I was impressed with the idea that many of our problems come because we use the wrong human gears. I suppose that all of our personal gears have potential dangers. If a person can't get out of low gear, he can cause a wasteful traffic jam. Many accidents can also be caused by people going too fast.

However, the biggest danger to our society center is that group of people who characteristically operate in reverse. Negative thinking is a reverse gear. Immortality is a reverse gear. Criminals, delinquents, and sinners usually have their back-up motors on; and sometimes when these folks put a heavy foot on the accelerator, other people as well as themselves are frequently injured. Because it is necessary for everyone to back up occasionally, we have all been equipped with a reverse gear. But sometimes we cause difficulty when we overdo it and go too far and too fast in the wrong direction. And when the main focus of someone's personality gets fused into his reverse gears, we call him by such names as non-conformists, rebels, or heretics. It doesn't take much reverse mindedness to make people anti-social or they become violators of the law or disobedient to God. This is contrary to the regular order of things, inasmuch as man at his best was created with his gears in a characteristic forward movement that are headed upward.

Recently, in telling about an important group to which he belonged one reverse minded man said "I am a rebel." Then he added, "I think we need more rebels." It was suggested to him that it might make some difference as to how many rebels were needed, depending on what they were rebelling against. It is wonderful when one effectively rebels against wrong, ignorance, unfairness, and slavery. The early American colonists came to these shores in search of political freedom and the right to worship God according to the dictates of their own consciences. It was natural that they should rebel when an oppressive, offensive domination was established over them to rule, tax, and judge them without representation. They felt that they must change the situation and set up a democratic form of government for the benefit of all the people.

But to be a rebel just to be a rebel or to rebel against good is another matter. There are some people presently taking advantage of American freedom who are secretly trying to undermine the government and destroy their own country from within. During the Revolutionary War, General Benedict Arnold was known as a traitor because he secretly negotiated with the enemy to turn West Point over to the British in order to make a profit for himself. We also remember Judas, who bargained to sell Jesus for thirty pieces of silver. Some of our biggest problems are caused by our many present-day traitors and betrayers. Parents sometimes betray their children, and children often stir up a serious rebellion in their own hearts against their parents. Criminals are in a continual and costly rebellion against the society in which they live. The Communists have special people trained as trouble makers to incite one group to rebel against another so that everyone concerned will be weaker. Some people habitually rebel against decency and order, some rebel against God and the Church, some rebel against righteousness, and some even rebel against themselves.

I know of one man who seems to take an unnatural pride in his frequent and regular boast that he is the "black sheep" of the family. His parents as well as his brothers and sisters are fine, honorable people who go to great lengths to be good citizens. Their gears are securely set to carry them forward and upward. But when the "black sheep" steps on the accelerator, the family reputation, as well as his own individual welfare, starts going in the wrong direction. He seems unreasonably pleased by the fact that he does not attend church. He flaunts his antagonism to spiritual things as though it were some great virtue that he was personally responsible for. The fact that he has gone against family teaching to become a chain smoker and that he is intoxicated most of the time doesn't seem to worry him very much. Or, when some of his unpleasant moral scandals rock the family foundations, he seems to get some cheap satisfaction from boasting about it. This is completely unnecessary, as he has so securely built up his "black sheep" evidence that there could be no question in anyone's mind about it. His gears have been so seriously reversed for such a long time that righteousness probably wouldn't seem natural or right to him.

On July 14, 1966, the newspapers recounted a story about how far a reverse gear can carry us backward, when 25-year-old Richard B. Speck brutally murdered eight student nurses in Chicago. He cut the throat of one and stabbed and strangled to death the other seven. When he was arrested, his captors read his philosophy of life that he had tattooed on his left arm. It said, "Born to raise hell." Apparently this motto was intended to indicate his self-appointed mission to do as much damage as he could. He had had a long previous criminal career. Police records showed that on January 29, 1965, he had been found guilty of threatening a 28-year-old woman with a butcher knife. He was also wanted in connection with the murder of a barmaid a few months before. But this attitude of anti-progress is characteristic of many people in some degree. There are a large number of groups throughout the country whose chief purpose seems to be to do evil. The members of one of these groups call themselves "Hells Angels," and apparently this title accurately represents their mission in life.

Another group call themselves the "Nothings," which is also appropriately descriptive. An unholy personal pride seems to be taken by them in making themselves as near nothing as possible. They let their hair grow and refrain from shaving or taking a bath. They seem challenged by how dirty they can be physically, mentally, morally, and socially. They have an allergy toward work, study, going to church, and decency. Their goal is to go down hill as fast and as far as possible, and to take as many people as they can with them. They ride around at night on noisy motorcycles at high speeds, disturbing the peace of many people. They smoke, drink, and seemingly do as many wrong things as possible. Their reverse gears are set on the idea of doing nothing and *being* nothing. Apparently it seems desirable to them to indulge the opposite philosophy to that which has made America great.

As Nancy Hanks lay on her death bed, she said to her nine-year-old son, Abe, "Go out there and amount to something," and that became an ideal to which Abraham Lincoln devoted his entire life. He not only wanted to make something of himself, but he also wanted to lift up everyone he could, including the slaves. Lincoln's powerful forward gear helped him to achieve a near-perfect score in doing good. But the "Nothings" are in reverse; it is their purpose to make a zero out of everyone and everything. Think what a country we would have if it were filled with "Nothings." What an idea to have a world of people whose only excuse for being born was to raise hell!

This idea of raising hell is the chief characteristic of Satan himself. Satan is our world's chief rebel. He rebels against everything good. In the ante-mortal council in heaven he rebelled against God and sought to overthrow the freedom and righteousness of all the children of God. But as strange as this philosophy may seem, it is still with us as an active force; and sometimes about the only motivation that some people need in order to want to do a thing is to know that it is wrong.

Of course, this is not a new problem, as some people have always taken pride in being evil. This destructive perversion is pointed out in one group of whom the scripture says, "They loved Satan more than God." People can train themselves to love force, murder, immorality, dope, vulgarity, dirt, profanity, and drunkenness, even when they know that by these things they will bring all kinds of misery upon themselves. It is hard to understand why people practice this kind of reverse piety when it is so unprofitable to everyone. To refuse discipline, violate standards, disobey parents, and take a Satanic pride in being evil is not as pleasant as to be faithful to God and loyal to those who love us. When a particular person once took up horseback riding, an acquaintance, knowing his perverseness, expressed his surprise, inasmuch as horseback riding would force him to go in the same direction as the horse.

The ancient Sophists who became prominent about the middle of the fifth century B.C. gained their ill repute because of their cynicism and their violations of the accepted prevailing codes. The Sophists challenged the time-honored ideals of the people and boasted of their ability to make "the worst appear the better reason." They were like those other rebels who lack any kind of a cause worth fighting for. Many people still have this attitude of wanting to be associated with wrongdoers. Some boys playing at "cops and robbers" would rather be the robbers. Some lawyers delight in fighting the battles of criminals. Some people like to discredit good and make some evil cause appear to be right.

One man recently said, "I am for the underdog." His friend said, "I'm also for the underdog, providing that the underdog is right. But suppose the underdog is wrong." His friend said, "I am for the underdog, whether he is right or wrong." This philosophy would seek to aid the criminal against the law, the sinner against God, the "black sheep" against an honorable family, the delinquent child against his parents, the heretic against the church and the traitor against the government.

On the other hand, what a thrilling experience it ought to be to align ourselves with God and righteousness. The highest kind of right is not merely to obey God, but to agree with him. We should love right for its own sake. We should love cleanliness and order and be helpful to others. We should be anxious to accept discipline and be enthusiastic in observing the highest standards because that is the Godly way of doing things.

Someone has said that the greatest invention of all time took place 2,500 years ago at Plataea, when an obscure Greek perfected the process of marching men in step. When it was discovered that the efforts of a great group of men could be organized, coordinated, and focused on a single objective, that day civilization began. The greatest day of anyone's life is when he decides to center his attention on God and march in step with him. To be one with God should be our greatest possible accomplishment. Then we will think as he thinks, live as he lives, and be as he is.

Sackcloth and Ashes

THE OTHER DAY I LOOKED UP SOME OF THE BIBLE REFERENCES about an interesting custom practiced by the ancients. Under certain conditions they dressed in sackcloth and covered themselves with ashes. We are aware of customs among various people of changing their clothing for special occasions. We put on our best clothes for Sunday. Doctors, laborers, and others sometimes have a special set of work clothes. We have a formal dress for other important occasions. We also wear graduation robes, military uniforms, athletic outfits, bathing suits; and we have special traveling clothes. A part of the purpose of our clothing is to put us in the spirit of some particular occasion, whether it be a funeral or a skiing contest.

It was with something like this in mind that the ancients had this very special set of clothing made of sackcloth. It was designed to help them produce feelings of sorrow and pain within themselves. We are aware that one of the most important virtues that anyone can acquire is the ability to repent of his sins and turn his life upward toward more worthwhile activities. How we feel has a significant influence on what we do. It seems that repentance can be carried out more effectively when one's soul is on its knees. Water doesn't boil until the temperature reaches 212 degrees Fahrenheit. And it seems that repentance can take place most effectively when we feel an extra intensity of grief, sorrow, and regret in our hearts for the evil that we have committed. There is a certain kind of humility of spirit or mental anguish that goes with physical suffering which helps to form the kind of climate where repentance can take place most readily.

The ancients encouraged this attitude by wearing sackcloth and ashes. They not only made themselves miserable on the outside but they also went without food so that they would be hungry and uncomfortable on the inside as well.

There are some religious groups who make an adaptation of this idea of promoting their humility and teachableness by doing what they call "whipping the flesh." They cut or burn or bruise or otherwise afflict their bodies and cause themselves intense pain with the thought in mind that a little suffering now may help prevent a lot of suffering later on.

The Bible gives an interesting account of how the people living in the great and wicked city of Nineveh were saved from destruction by their sackcloth and ashes repentance. The Prophet Jonah was called by the Lord to go to Nineveh and tell them that if they did not repent, the Lord would destroy their city. However, Jonah didn't want to go, and most of the book of Jonah is devoted to describing the trouble that the Lord had in getting Jonah to deliver his message; there are only about seven verses of one chapter describing the great event that took place in Nineveh. At first Jonah tried to run away from the Lord. But those on his escape ship threw him overboard into the sea. Then, after spending three days inside a big fish, he reluctantly showed up in Nineveh and gave the people just forty days to completely change their way of life. The seven verses telling about what happened in Nineveh are as follows:

"So Jonah arose, and went unto Nineveh, according to the word of the Lord. Now Nineveh was an exceeding great city of three days journey.

"And Jonah began to enter into the city a day's journey, and he cried, and said, Yet forty days, and Nineveh shall be overthrown.

"So the people of Nineveh believed God, and proclaimed a fast, and put on sackcloth, from the greatest of them even to the least of them.

"For word came unto the king of Nineveh, and he arose from his throne, and laid his robe from him, and covered him with sackcloth, and sat in ashes.

"And he caused it to be proclaimed and published through Nineveh by the decree of the king and his nobles, saying, Let neither man nor beast, herd nor flock, taste any thing: let them not feed, nor drink water:

"But let man and beast be covered with sackcloth, and cry mightily unto God: yea, let them turn every one from his evil way, and from the violence that is in their hands.

"Who can tell if God will . . . repent, and turn away his fierce anger, that we perish not." Then the record says, "And God saw their works, that they turned from their evil way; and God repented of the evil, that he had said that he would do unto them, and he did it not." (Jonah 3:3-10.)

It would be interesting to know just what happened in these people's minds to bring about such a remarkable change in so short a time. This is especially perplexing when Jonah had had such a bad attitude about going there in the first place. But judging from the results, there must have been an effective combination of speech, sackcloth, and ashes, and the right attitude on the part of the people concerned. If we knew the details, we might profitably use their formula to help the people of our own day. It is conceivable, however, that one of our own great wicked cities might need a little longer time to effect a change of such magnitude. To help them to get into the right frame of mind, the people of Nineveh dressed themselves in sackcloth and engaged in a long fast, in which everyone seems to have participated. The king himself must have been thoroughly sold on this idea as he laid off his silks, gave up his royal fare, dressed himself in sackcloth and sat in the ashes.

Sackcloth was a very coarse cloth made from goat's hair. (Isa. 50:3.) It was used for making coarse sacks. It may have been similar to the burlap that we now use for that same purpose. Clothing made of this material must have caused the people to feel very uncomfortable, especially as the sackcloth was worn next to the skin. But to make their discomfort even greater and consequently more effective, they mixed in some of the gritty, dirty substance called ashes; and when ashes were not available, they put dust on their heads so that it would fall down their necks, get into their clothing, and make their bodies uncomfortable. Then, to finish off the misery, they would go without eating or drinking.

As I read about the sackcloth and ashes treatment that the ancients subjected themselves to, I thought of an experience that I had many years ago on the farm. For one summer I worked in the lowest-ranked job on a threshing machine which was stacking the straw. In those days each threshing machine had a long blower about a foot in diameter and many feet long, and it was used to get rid of the chaff and straw. A strong blast of air blew the chaff through this blower up onto the strawstack. The one who did the stacking worked all day in the chaff and dust under the most uncomfortable circumstances, and usually he collected a lot of dirt in his clothing, on his face, and in his lungs. But what was much worse, he got a lot of prickly, uncomfortable barley beards down his neck, throughout his clothing, and even in his shoes. Then, in the sweat of some sweltering hot days, I discovered what it was like to feel uncomfortable, and I think I can understand how the people of Nineveh felt dressed in their goat's hair with ashes down their backs.

Certainly the Lord wants us to be successful and happy but sometimes with too much comfort, ease, and soft clothing, we become arrogant, proud and sinful. And so the Lord is often forced to take away our ease and peace and let us have enough affliction to make us humble and repentant.

The people of Nineveh were wiser than most people because they put on their sackcloth and ashes voluntarily before the necessary chastisement made them even more uncomfortable. But suffering frequently serves a very important purpose in all of our lives. It is frequently an aid to our emotions in bringing about our repentance. Deity himself made an important enlargement on this sackcloth and ashes idea when he provided a divine institution designed for our reformation called Hell. This is also a place of sorrow and suffering. It is a place where through pain and unhappiness we may be induced to give up our evil. There are some people who say they don't believe in a Hell, and yet our reason tells us that there has to be a Hell. We know absolutely that evil always causes pain and unhappiness, and this natural law is not changed for eternity. God himself has said that he is not the God of the dead, but of the living, for all live unto him. And merely to pass the boundaries of mortality does not relieve anyone from being subject to God's laws. Certainly this process of repentance that was adopted in Nineveh of wearing sackcloth and ashes is probably much more simple and pleasant than to have the dross burned out of our lives in Hell. I suppose that every effective refining process is always carried on under intense heat, and it seems to me that a good way to get this idea of repentance over to ourselves would be to spend a summer as a straw stacker with our clothes full of dirt, chaff, and barley beards. Or as a second choice it might be very helpful to have a good suit of sackcloth ready to wear whenever occasion may require us to feel sorry for what we have done. If neither of these can get us to repent, then God may try to get us to give up our bad habits in the suffering of Hell.

The Lord once sent Isaiah on an interesting mission to talk to a group of women about their sins. He said to them, "Rise up, ye women that are at ease; hear my voice, ye careless daughters; give ear unto my speech. . . for the vintage shall fail, the gathering shall not come. Tremble, ye women that are at ease; be troubled, ye careless ones: strip you, and make you bare, and gird sackcloth upon your loins." (Isa. 9-11.) If these women continued to be idle, their vintage would fail, and there would be no crops to gather; consequently, they would be hungry. But with some good rough sackcloth next to their delicate skins and with a few ashes sprinkled in for good measure, they may want to change their ways.

Sometime ago I heard a sales manager say that what one of his salesmen needed was a good hair shirt. He felt that a few bristles sticking into his hide might furnish him with some needed motivation. One of the most serious problems that the Lord has always had with people is in getting them to work. Nothing ever happens any place until someone does something. Even faith can't live in isolation. If you take the works away from faith, the faith always dies. There is no such thing as preserved faith; and so, in addition, to a Sunday suit, a tuxedo, some play clothes, and some party dresses, every good wardrobe should also have a suit of sackcloth with a barrel of ashes handy. More than about anything else, we need to learn how to feel sorry for our wrongs. Personally I would not like to spend eternity with even one barley beard down my neck. The Lord said to Isaiah, "Cry aloud, spare not, lift up thy voice like a trumpet, and shew my people their transgression, and the house of Jacob their sins." (Isa. 58:1.) "The wicked are like the troubled sea, . . . whose waters cast up mire and dirt." (Isa. 57:20.) And then the Lord mentioned those who, like some of us, just like to blame other people and complain about not getting their full dues. Then we sometimes go through the motions for the *Lord's* benefit instead of our own. The Lord said, "Wherefore have we fasted, say they, and thou seest not? wherefore have we afflicted our soul, and thou takest no knowledge?" (Isa. 58:3.) We do many things to be seen of men or to impress God instead of changing ourselves. Then the Lord said to them, "Behold, ye fast for strife and debate, and to smite with the fist of wickedness: ye shall not fast [only] to make your voice heard on high. Is it such a fast that I have chosen? a day for a man to afflict his soul? is it to bow down his head like a bulrush, and to spread sackcloth and ashes under him?" (Isa. 58:5.) We need to produce the humility in ourselves, not in the Lord.

Sackcloth and ashes have become the symbol of the kind of personal sorrow and suffering that leads to repentance. There are times when more than just about anything else we need to feel sincerely sorry. We need to feel and say, as did the King of Nineveh, "Let us cover ourselves with sackcloth and taste nothing. Let us turn everyone from his evil way, and cry mightily unto God, for who can tell if God . . . will turn away his fierce anger, that we perish not." Then we may also bring about the same results wherein it was said, "And God repented of the evil that he said he would do unto them, and he did it not."

Scylla and Charybdis

O NE OF THE GREATEST WRITERS OF OUR WORLD WAS THE BLIND
    Greek poet Homer, who lived in the ninth century B.C.
His primary literary works consisted of two great book-length epic
poems. The first is known as the *Iliad*. It is the story of the famous
Trojan War. Paris, a Trojan prince, eloped with Helen, the wife of
Menelaus, king of Sparta. Menelaus then enlisted the aid of his
fellow kings in the neighboring Greek states. These warriors included the brother of Menelaus, whose name was Agammemnon,
the famous Greek fighter, who was also the king of Mycenae. Then
this assembled aggregation of fighting men sailed a thousand ships
across the Aegean Sea and laid siege to Troy, a large and strongly
fortified walled city near the Hellespont, in which Paris and Helen
had taken refuge. The long war that ensued lasted for ten years,
and even then showed no signs of any let-up, until by a trick the
Greeks finally got inside the city walls. Then in a single night they
destroyed the fighting power of Troy, sacked the city, and burned it
to the ground. They then loaded their ships and sailed for home.

Homer's second book is called the *Odyssey*. The title is taken
from the name of Odysseus, sometimes called Ulysses. He was king
of Ithaca and one of the greatest of these Greek heroes. The *Odyssey*
is an account of the experiences of Odysseus and his men as they
made their way across the three hundred miles of island-dotted sea
lying between the battleground of Troy and their home island of
Ithaca, which lies off the west coast of Greece.

Odysseus was very happy as he started for home at the head of
his own fleet of ships. His men were all delighted that the war was
over, and they rejoiced at the thought that they would soon be at
their own firesides again with their own families. But in this hope
they were doomed to disappointment, for along the way they met
with one difficulty after another, many of which were far more
destructive than the war itself had been. By the time Odysseus
finally reached Ithaca, every ship had been destroyed, and the life
of every man had been lost except his own.

This great story about the journey of Odysseus is the grandfather
of all adventure stories. Homer knew every trick of getting human

interest through storytelling. The *Odyssey* tells of man-eating giants, bewitching sirens, terrible monsters, frightening ghosts, roaring whirlpools, contrary winds, hair-raising adventures, and romantic interludes, not to mention the interest added by Odysseus himself, who was one of the most courageous and ingratiating heroes in all of our literature.

The *Odyssey* has lived in such fine repute through the ages that the word itself has become a part of our language. "Odyssey" has come to mean any long, wandering, difficult journey, and, of course, the greatest of all odysseys is the journey of life itself. We have even come to speak of our strivings for success as an "odyssey," and in the old Greek adventure we find many interesting comparisons to our success in life. But Homer was not just a great storyteller; he was also a psychologist who looked with keen insight into human lives. In a very interesting way he described the courage, strategy, and super-strength with which these famous heroes tried to solve their problems. He did this in such a way that we are able to receive a substantial benefit from their experiences. Their errors in judgment are made so plain that any repetition by us can be easily avoided. And to be made aware of the moral weaknesses that were so frequently fatal to them provides us with an easy means for our personal escape. Homer's great skill in expression turns his heroes into a reflecting mirror for our own lives. He makes it possible for us to have the advantages from their experiences without suffering any of the penalties.

As Homer describes the problems, longings, and disappointments of his men, and as he tells of the suffering that they so frequently brought upon themselves, we are enabled to plan our own lives more profitably by including all that is good in their experience and leaving out all that is bad.

One of their most hazardous adventures came as they were required to pass an island inhabited by beautiful, bewitching sirens. It was known that in times past the song of these sirens had lured many sailors off their course to their deaths. Odysseus had been warned about the hazard of listening to the enchanting music of these fascinating, dangerous creatures. As he came near their islands, he feared that his men would not be able to withstand their temptations, and therefore he had all of the members of his crew fill their ears with wax so that they would not be able to hear the sirens' songs. Overcome with curiosity, Odysseus himself did not put wax in his own ears. But because he did not quite trust his own strength to resist, he protected himself against any possible weakness by having his men bind him to the mast. He gave them strict orders that no matter what might happen, they must not release him until they had passed the island and were out of range of any temptation. When they areached the area where they could hear the hypnotic song of the sirens, Odysseus weakened and ordered his men to pull their ship into shore. But their ears were full of wax, and they could not hear his orders. Therefore, this caution of Odysseus saved the day, and they rowed out of range of the temptation with no harm being done.

This ten-year odyssey involved many different kinds of problems. After passing the danger of the sirens, Ulysses was required to run the gauntlet down the narrow Strait of Messina. He must guide his ship between the vast whirlpool of Charybdis on the one hand and a death-dealing monster called Scylla on the other. It is one thing to fight a problem or evade a danger that is all in one place. That is when one is so afraid of the sirens he can merely either put wax in his ears or give the island such a wide berth that all danger is eliminated. Some difficulties can be averted merely by putting blinders on our eyes. But the problems presented by Scylla and Charybdis cannot be escaped by any such simple means. The narrow Messina Strait made it impossible for the sailors to get a safe distance from one danger without running directly into the other. To close their eyes or plug up their ears would greatly increase the hazard.

Scylla was a frightful female monster with six dog heads, a serpent's body, and many mighty octupus-like arms. She inhabited a rock on one side of the Messina Strait. She would have presented no problem were it not for the fact that directly opposite to Scylla was another monster, called Charybdis, which caused a giant deadly whirlpool in the sea that in the past had dragged many ships and men to their deaths. While trying to escape the danger of Scylla, some had been sucked under by the evil of Charybdis. If the warriors steered a safe distance away from the whirlpool, they put themselves within reach of the octupus-like arms of the monster. And even though every man rowed with his greatest possible skill and the ship of Ulysses barely missed the whirlpool of Charybdis, yet six of his men were snatched from the deck as their craft passed the rock of the terrible six-headed monster Scylla.

This inference also represents one of our biggest problems in the odyssey called life. Sometimes in trying to miss the evils of one problem as far as possible we run directly into the arms of what may be an even worse problem. Sometimes we resemble a grandfather's clock, the pendulum of which alternates in swinging from one extreme in one direction to an equal extreme in an opposite direction.

For example, I have a friend whose marriage failed because of an unbearable weakness in her husband. This particular problem was so impressed in her mind that she developed a loathing for it. And while to most people the importance of the problem was far out of proportion in her mine, yet the grievance had been agitated until, like a cancerous growth, it had assumed enormous proportions to her. Then when this lady began looking for another husband, the one virtue that she sought was the one that her first husband had lacked. She allowed this one quality to so greatly overshadow all other considerations that it made good judgment impossible for her. It was interesting to get acquainted with her second husband. He had the one virtue that her first husband lacked, but that was about all you could say in his favor. He was short in about every other area. He couldn't support her; he had little value as a companion, and as the head of a family he rated fairly close to zero. The reason that her second marriage failed was because she had been so badly frightened by Scylla that she had gone down in the whirlpool of Charybdis.

This is an underlying cause of failure in a great many marriages and a great many other circumstances. Some little sore spot develops in the marriage and instead of healing up the irritation by reformation and forgiveness or some other kind of settlement, we sometimes pick and scratch at the sore until it becomes so enlarged, infected, and inflamed that it dominates our lives and pushes us into all kinds of problems on the other side of the situation.

One woman recently sought a divorce from her husband after sixteen years of happy married life. They had had difficulties before, but each time the problem had been resolved and their ship of matrimony had continued to sail a straight and safe course. Then the husband did something that had seriously offended the wife. The problem had arisen at an inopportune time, when tensions were strained and the usual attitudes of give-and-take were not at their customary strengths. After a flaring of tempers, the wife decided that she would not forgive her husband until he had humbly apologized. This the husband was too stubborn to do, and therefore the apology was not forthcoming. Each held onto his part of the offense with all his heart. As they thought about their problem and picked at their sores, resentments began to grow. The poison got continually greater. The soreness increased, and the dislike became more painful. Each spouse began taking advantage of whatever sanctions were available to him against the other. Then a whole group of problems of incompatibility, frigidity, withdrawal of financial support, lack of communication, etc., followed in their wake.

The marriage was pushed off its course by a dog-headed, serpent-bodied Scylla, but their welfare and happiness was completely destroyed in the whirlpool of Charybdis. In trying to steer away from one problem, they had run head on into several others, each of which was a great deal worse than the original.

I know of one woman who is thinking of getting a divorce because her husband won't let her have her proper say in the handling of the family finances. Another woman is seeking a divorce because she has to take too much responsibility for handling the family's finances. Some wives are unhappy because their husbands are away too much of the time. Others are unhappy because their husbands are home under foot too much of the time.

Most of us resemble the story of "The Three Bears." The papa bear's soup is always too hot, and the mama bear's soup is always too cold. In trying to avoid one horn of the dilemma, we get caught on the other. In rebellion against the left hand, we sometimes go overboard on the right hand. In trying to avoid in ourselves a trait that we dislike in others, we often hurt ourselves by some opposite extreme.

One of the important lessons to be learned in life is to avoid extremes on either side. Jesus talked about the straight and narrow way that leads to the greatest of all destinations, which is eternal life. Like the Strait of Messina, this pathway is very narrow, and no room is left for any meandering or detours. For example, the pathway of honesty is a narrow one. The scriptures themselves are too narrow to accommodate any evil doctrine. The pathway to health is also a narrow one. We need only to get *one* deadly disease in order to die. The path to financial success is so narrow that we can't afford to get off the track too many times.

Those who are troubled with obesity know that the pathway leading to weight control is also a straight and narrow way. It may not be broad enough to tolerate those three pieces of pie.

Success in life is the greatest of all odysseys. And this also requires an ability to be able to effectively run the gauntlet between Scylla and Charybdis. The straight and narrow way leading to eternal life is so narrow that all evil must be left out. It will do us no good to win the greatest Trojan war if we lose our eternal lives on the way home.

We can be outstandingly successful if we remember that the straight and narrow way does not always permit us to do as we please. It is too narrow for immorality and hate and atheism and disobedience to God. There are many things in our lives that must be considered as out of bounds. This is not true of the broad road that leads to death. There anything goes, and everything can be included. It is interesting that no one ever gets off the straight and narrow path at right angles. We merely make the road a little wider so that we can include more of the things that were previously out of bounds.

Jesus indicated that we should put blinders on our eyes and look neither to the right hand nor to the left. But we should always keep our eyes focused on the objective. If we get even one foot out of bounds on the left, we may get caught by the monster Scylla; and if we get out of bounds on the other side, we may go down to destruction in the whirlpool of Charybdis.

Semantics

THERE IS A RATHER HIGH-TONED, FANCY-SOUNDING WORD CALLED "semantics" that everyone should get better acquainted with. It has to do with the meaning of words and the development of our abilities to use them effectively. The dictionary says that semantics is the science of sounds. It has to do with the evolution of our language. It involves the continual expansion in word meanings and the effectiveness of our expression.

The 140,000 words that we had in Shakespeare's day have greatly grown in number, and many changes in their usage have also taken place in recent years. It has been said that if some contemporary Rip Van Winkle should wake up today after sleeping for twenty years, he would have to go back to school before he could intelligently read the morning paper or clearly understand an ordinary conversation.

Semantics is closely related to some other fancy-sounding words called semasiology and philology. Semasiology has to do with the significance of words and the development of their meanings. Philology signifies a love of learning and a devotion to literature. When we put all of these $20 words together, we have one of the most productive of ideas, meaning a satisfying expression, a fondness for communication, and a skill in fitting into a constructive whole the best of these important instruments called words. Think what would happen to our business or to our happiness or even to our lives themselves if we lost our words. We remember the calamity of the builders of the Tower of Babel. When their words could not be understood, all building immediately ceased and confusion reigned. The human intellect itself, with all of its powers, manifests itself primarily through words. In various combinations, words make up our ideas, give form to our ambitions, inspire our wisdom, shape our emotions, direct our actions, and build our Towers of Babel.

Words are the means by which our minds are enriched and our enthusiasms are given power. They are like sacred ships that are designed to carry cargoes of meanings. Words are the chief tools of the teacher, the salesman, the parent, the lover, the preacher, and the empire builder. Without words, God is silent, justice dormant, philosophy meaningless. By the proper use of words we may increase our occupational skill, multiply our social satisfactions, establish higher standards of thinking, and even help to bring about the eternal exaltation of our souls. Words also enable us to increase the happiness and success of many other people.

Therefore, whether we are operating in the field of romance, patriotism, finance, religion, or any other area of human experience, we need a good supply of the right kind of words and the ability to use them effectively. In fact, the skill that we are able to develop in the use of words can give us greater power than any other thing, either to bless our lives or to make them wretched. Except by his own choice, no one should be handicapped for lack of words, as we have the tremendous array of 450,000 different ones in the dictionary that are all placed at our disposal free of charge. These become our property just as fast as we learn to use them.

Suppose that we make and absorb a list of great key words, such as faith, works, ambition, leadership, love, knowledge, success, and fairness, or we might profitably catalog some of the famous expressions and then capture the spirit that goes with them as one of our personal possessions.

Nathan Hale said, "I regret that I have but one life to give for my country." Patrick Henry said, "Give me liberty or give me death." Joshua said, "As for me and my house, we will serve the Lord." In speaking of God Job said, "Though he slay me, yet will I trust in him." And Jesus said, "Father, not my will, but thine be done." What tremendous possessions these would be if we had a full personal possession of the words and what they stand for. Of course, we live in a world of opposites, and we should be aware of the fact that some words bear a poison fruit. Judas Iscariot said, "What will ye give me, and I will deliver him into your hands." Richard B. Speck, who cut the throats of eight nurses in Chicago, had the words of death tattooed on his arm and impressed into his soul. They said, "Born to raise hell." Everyone's success or failure, happiness, or misery will be determined by the words and meanings that we have tattooed into our lives. It is with them that we construct our oaths of office, take our pledges of allegiance, feel the meaning of the Lord's Prayer, live our marriage vows, and make our covenants of devotion to God.

The other day a young father of three children asked me to read a letter that he had just received at his place of business from his

wife. She told him how much she loved him and how she appreciated all of the wonderful, thoughtful things that he did for her and
their children. She also expressed the great confidence she felt in
him and in his ability. These few simple, heartfelt words had
stirred up something in this man's soul that was wonderful to see.
With his wife's words of love and appreciation in his heart, he felt
that he could conquer the world. Unfortunately, there are many
cases of husbands and wives where these magic words are not to be
found in their vocabulary. Neither are the emotions that go with
them lodged very solidly in their hearts.

Sometimes our vocabulary is made up primarily of critical words
that nag, irritate, belittle, and destroy. We sometimes use great
words for profane or immoral purposes, and even some of the most
profound words don't mean very much to some people. There are
those who could read the entire Bible from beginning to end without being very greatly changed. To some people, even the most
meaningful words seem hollow and empty.

Shakespeare's Polonius said to Hamlet, "What readest thou, my
Lord?" Hamlet replied, "Words, words, words." Hamlet's state of
mind had destroyed the meaning of these great words, so that they
were now empty and meaningless. One of the big problems mentioned by Jesus was our natural inclination to separate words from
their meanings. Entire creeds become meaningless when a faith
loses its works. Quicker than about anything else, empty words can
give institutions and men split personalities and cause a life to lose
its meaning.

The Holy Bible makes use of 773,693 words to effectively tell
the story of God's plan of salvation, including the atonement of
Christ, the ugliness of sin, the possibility of eternal progression, and
the horror of eternal damnation. We commit grave sins when we
debase God's words or use them to give ourselves or others wrong
meanings. We sometimes deceive ourselves by referring to "the
new morality" in order to cover up our immorality or our lack of
morality. Sometimes by a change in word meanings we impoverish
our own character, and every place we turn we find the apostate
forces of evil twisting the finest words out of shape and depriving
them of their Christian meanings. We say, "God is dead," that
"revelations from God have ceased," and that "it doesn't matter
any more what we believe or what we do." We say that the great
Christian doctrines are mere allegories or stories for our amusement.
Therefore, one of our most serious sins is our debasement of good

words by subtracting from their real meaning. Words are also used sometimes to belittle faith and make fun of the doctrines of Christ.

We have a distortion of words, a misuse of words, and sometimes we just don't use them at all. It is probable that the most serious marital sin is lack of communication. We so severely restrict our words and meanings that understanding is destroyed and happiness breaks down. By failure in our semantics, we frequently build massive "Berlin Walls" between ourselves over which very little information or love or understanding is ever allowed to pass. We have a kind of Tower of Babel situation where wives do not understand their husbands, and husbands do not understand their wives. Many parents don't communicate well with their children, and the ideas of many children are not very well integrated with the ambitions of their parents. Our greatest success is impoverished when we fall down in the science and art of semantics. Then life itself loses much of its purpose and meaning.

Socrates once said that "a philosopher should never speak until his words had been steeped in meaning." And we can more effectively carry on the business of our lives when we learn how to fashion the most worthwhile ambitions and objectives and get them over to the right people.

Sometimes one's entire existence may turn on the use of a single word. A discouraged man once called his minister in the middle of the night and asked him to come to him at once. Later the caller said, "Had you said 'no' instead of 'yes,' I was prepared to take my own life." But far more frequently we injure ourselves when we say "no" to God, or "no" to ambition, or "no" to enthusiasm; or our lives may be lost if we say "yes" to booze or nicotine or immorality. Likewise, we can ruin the reputations of others and destroy their morale, kill their faith, and seduce them into sin with words. Many people have actually been killed physically, socially, and spiritually by words. The news of some great tragedy can sufficiently shock one's constitution as to bring about his death. Many parents have lost their health and sometimes their lives worrying over their children.

On the other hand, we can establish faith and build ambition, courage, and righteousness with words. In fact, we can almost bring people back to life with the right kind of words. The night before Robert E. Lee surrendered his army to end the Civil War, Ulysses S. Grant had been sick all night. He had been sitting up doctoring himself in preparation for the following day. But early in the morning a messenger rode up to General Grant's tent to tell him that General Lee was waiting to surrender his sword. General Grant's pains and aches immediately left him, and he never felt them again. He quickly dressed and as a completely well man mounted his horse and rode to take charge of the surrender. Words of success, praise, love, and appreciation have cured many serious aches and pains in the hearts of people. Words of bitterness, quarreling, and hate will bring sickness to the mind, the body, and the spirit, whereas those who live on words of faith, courage, happiness, and love will tend to be well and strong.

We sing a song in which we say:

> O holy words of truth and love
> We hear from day to day,
> Revealed to Saints from God above,
> To guide in heaven's way.
>
> Beautiful words of love
> Coming from God above,
> How sweet, how dear the words we hear!
> They're beautiful words of love.
>
> They're from Apostles good and true,
> Whose names we all rever,
> Who daily teach us what to do,
> In words of love and cheer.
>
> They're from the Prophets God inspires,
> In councils oft withstood,
> Reproving all our ill desires,
> Commending all that's good.
>
> As gems of wisdom, pure and bright,
> That glow in lustrous ray,
> We'll seek to gain these words of light,
> Their councils to obey.

We can greatly improve our lives by watching our words and vitalizing our semantics with the right meanings.

We frequently hear someone complain that he doesn't have the words to express how he feels. And many people have spent an entire lifetime stumbling in their speech. This fault can be corrected if we firmly connect up our words with our works. It has been said that Christianity is not just an idea; it is an activity.

Dr. P. W. Bridgeman, the noted physicist and Nobel prize winner, once said, "The true meaning of a word in a man's mind is to be found by observing what he does with it, not by what he says about it."

We can also get some idea of a word's value by what it does to us. Words that we love and that represent ideas that we believe in can quickly change our lives. Then, followed by appropriate actions, we paint a beautiful picture on our mental canvasses. Great acts help us steep our words in better meanings. And if we desire to be architects of speech, we must also be masters of emotion and feeling.

There is a very important phrase frequently used in the scriptures, called "The word of the Lord." That is the most important word. The word of the Lord is the standard by which our eternal lives and our eternal success will be determined. We should make sure that we understand his word, and why it was given. We should also make sure that we have used the right words with the right meanings in making our covenants with him; we must also be certain that *he* can depend on our word. Our constant prayer should be that God will help us effectively perfect our semantics.

Six Days Shalt Thou Labor

THIRTY-FOUR HUNDRED YEARS AGO, FROM THE TOP OF MOUNT Sinai, God gave the world that great fourth commandment. He said, "Six days shalt thou labour, and do all thy work:

"But the seventh day is the sabbath of the Lord thy God: in it thou shalt not do any work. . . .

"For in six days the Lord made the heaven and earth, the sea, and all that in them is, and he rested the seventh day: wherefore the Lord blessed the sabbath day, and hallowed it." (Exod. 20:9-11.)

We have usually thought of this commandment from the point of view of what we should *not* do on the Sabbath day. But great importance is also attached to what we *should* do on the other six days. From the very beginning God has made our every success dependent upon our own labor. To Adam, God said, "In the sweat of thy face shalt thou eat thy bread." This is not a command of punishment; it is a command of opportunity.

Work is not just the way we get our bread; it is also the way we develop our abilities, build our characters, and do almost every other worthwhile thing in the world. There can be no excellence without labor, and this double command to work six days and to worship one covers most of our greatest responsibilities.

God is much more than just "the Lord of the Sabbath" or "the Lord of rest." God is also "the Lord of labor." He is the most effective individual worker in the universe. God invented, created, organized and set to work everything in heaven and on earth to serve some useful purpose. And we should follow his example in making the most of those very important six days of labor, as well as that wonderful seventh day of rest and worship.

God himself still holds down the most important of all jobs. Certainly we would be in the most serious trouble if *he* were to die or go out of business or lay down on the job. The kind of work God does is the main reason why he is God. The kind of work that *we* do also determines the kind of people *we* will become. Demosthenes said no one can have a high and noble calling while engaged in petty or mean employment, for whatever the pursuits of men are, their characters will be similar. We manifest our greatness primarily through our work. If we are not great in what we do, then we are not great.

Work is our primary means of both growth and happiness. Strength comes from struggle, whereas weakness comes from ease. If we desire to *be* more, we must *do* more. There is an old truth that says that the Lord fits the back to the burden. The way to develop a stronger back is to carry a heavier load. Through the right kind of exercises, body builders can develop chests, backs, legs, and arms to any reasonable specifications. In about the same way, this can also be done with minds, personalities, attitudes and spirits. Even our internal organs adjust to meet their particular assignments. The stomach shrinks when it is empty, and so does the mind. Both muscles and abilities deteriorate when they are not being used. Because the mole didn't use his eyes, nature took away his eyesight.

On the other hand, almost any degree of judgment, ability, and faith may be developed by use. When an extra job is given to the heart, it enlarges. When activated by the great emotions of ambition, fear, or love, the heart pumps more blood, and accordingly the pulse rate quickens to meet the extra demand. When one studies, thinks, loves, or aspires toward some greater accomplishment, the extra ability is always forthcoming. Extra motivation and extra ambition build greater capacity. As the prophet said, "God grants unto every man, according to his desire." He also grants unto every man according to his need. God gave to the acorn the miraculous ability to become a mighty oak. And he planted in man the potentiality of God.

Creation arranged to encourage our accomplishment by making every success pleasant. The members of the winning basketball team who scores 51 points have far more fun than the losers who get only 50 points. Under the stimulation of this divine "achievement instinct" we tend to repeat those experiences that give us pleasure. This is the Creator's program for enticing us on from one success to another until we arrive at God's goal of perfection.

The rapid increase in the death rate after retirement indicates that even our lives themselves frequently depend upon our work. Mothers often get sick and die when they feel that they are no longer needed. Even an automobile gets out of order more quickly when idle, and a vacant house depreciates faster than one filled with a busy, happy family.

The story is told about an old Roman aqueduct that for hundreds of years carried life-giving waters across mountains and desert with little need for repair. But as soon as the water was carried by other means so that the aqueduct was no longer needed, it immediately began falling apart, and soon it lay in ruins. Few things are as deadly either to abilities, people, or things as disuse.

In his book, *Man the Unknown*, Dr. Alexis Carroll points out that man was built for struggle. It was intended that he should fight the elements, overcome wild beasts, suffer fatigue, and earn his bread by the sweat of his brow. Man is at his best when he is lean, hungry, and overcoming hardships. He thrives on difficult toil and challenge. Doctor Carroll calls attention to the many disadvantages of a soft, easy life. When one sleeps in a heated bedroom, rides to work in a heated automobile, and avoids struggle and worry, he soon becomes fat, listless, and lazy and starts to fall to pieces.

For many years I have followed the record of a certain great salesman. Twenty years of devoted study and hard work had brought him a gradually increasing record of success. During that period he had accumulated a financial competence far beyond his possible need. After he had provided himself with an independent life income, he decided to take life easy. He gave up his work and on a full-time basis began playing golf and doing the many other things that he had previously had no time for.

But as soon as the pressures were relaxed, a deterioration began to set in. He now had nothing to fight for or to worry about. He had no production goals to meet and no financial problems to struggle with. He got up in the morning when he felt like it, and his only concern all day long was to satisfy his own pleasurable whims. This is a difficult assignment for a person to stand up under, and soon his personality itself began to slow down, and his brain lost its sharp precisiveness. His mental and spiritual powers began to lessen as well as to worsen. And he soon lost that firm, steady, stimulating, driving tempo of success that had made him great. When he let down the bars of his ambition, he soon became a different kind of person. Then, like the dried-up Roman aqueduct, he began falling to pieces mentally, socially, and spiritually. However, after a few years of doing nothing, he got very tired, and he decided that the best way for him to rest was to get back into the excitement of work.

Quite naturally he had expected to pick up his success where he had laid it down. But that is not how life's "law of fitness" works. The deteriorated aqueduct can't just start over again whenever it feels like it. After it has fallen to pieces, it can't just get up and go on acting as though nothing had happened. My friend was like an old basketball star who hadn't trained for twenty years. And when he again got out onto the playing floor of life, he had difficulty in even staying in the game. He tried to get back his former speed and vigor, but that is pretty difficult for a has-been who has lost the spirit.

There are some things in life that are very hard to relearn once they have been forgotten. When industry, ambition, righteousness, and the joy of accomplishment have once been lost, they are not easy to recover. God can resurrect a dead body, but who can resurrect a decayed enthusiasm or a spirit that has lost its fight or a personality muscle that has been destroyed by disuse? Or who can put a disintegrated character back together or revitalize a Godly way of life that has fallen apart through inactivity?

One of the most severe tragedies of life takes place when this deadly decline begins in human personality because its interest, industry, and faith have been turned off. These failures are even more serious because they largely take place unconsciously. A "success death," like a "physical death," usually takes place while the patient is in a coma. The moment of birth is an unconscious moment. While one is being born, he himself is completely unaware of the fact and doesn't discover that he has been born until long after it has happened. Most deaths are like that. And sometimes our ambitions or our courage dies unbeknown to us.

Of course, we are dimly aware of the fact that our success never stands still. Each day and each hour we are either progressing or retrogressing. And while my salesman friend was slipping downhill, his former associates who had been his inferiors were struggling upward. Then came the pitiful experience when he tried to get back into the swim.

In his mind he had expected that when he again turned on the power, his success position would be at the head of the pack the same as it had been a few years earlier. But he was now like Sampson after he had been robbed of his hair. By comparison, he was now a weakling, trailing along at the end of the procession. His power had gone, he had lost his touch, and he had also lost the spirit of success. The old skill with the exciting thrill of accomplishment was not there anymore, and instead of leading the field, he was now relegated to bring up the rear. Life that had once been so pleasant had now lost its attraction, and he soon gave up the battle. Then he again sank back into his idleness, but this time he took with him the unpleasant sense of frustration and failure.

In thinking about my friend, I remembered Aesop's story about "The Fox and the Grapes." After the fox had made a few jumps trying to get the grapes that were beyond his reach, he said, "The grapes are sour anyway." When we fail to keep ourselves disciplined organized, and motivated, we soon lose our jumping ability. Then many of life's most desirable grapes turn sour in our minds. A tolerance for sloth or an indulgence in mediocrity or too many undeclared holidays seem to make the grapes climb up a little higher on the vine. Whether we think of success in its physical, mental, spiritual, or social aspects, life at its best requires that we stay on the job and keep jumping. Every individual has something in common with the old Model T Ford. When you turned off the engine, the lights went out. But even with the most modern automobile the lights start getting dim as soon as the generator begins to slow down.

Ignace Paderewski, the famous pianist, once said, "If I fail to practice for one day, I can tell the difference in my playing. If I fail to practice for two days, my family can tell the difference. If I fail for three days, the whole world can tell the difference." That same principle applies in every field. We must either swim or sink. Even Apostle Paul, the greatest Christian missionary, was afraid of the devastation caused by idleness. He said, "I fight on, lest I myself should be a castaway." That is one of life's most important ideas, for when we stop getting better, we stop being good. When we stop getting closer to heaven, we are automatically drawing a little nearer toward hell.

Probably the greatest damage done by this process of obsolescence is in the field of religion. In youth many people are fired with some great ambition to make the most of their lives. But frequently as we grow older we begin slowing down and a weakening process sets in. We are subject to an influence resembling the dropout problem that plagues education. Life's temptations, distractions, and the love of ease to which we are so vulnerable makes us dropouts from the Church. We also frequently become dropouts from character and dropouts from righteousness. After a few years of fine effort, we often decide that we would like to take things a little easier, so we turn off the engine and the twilight sets in. To think that we will retire from Church work is a part of that unworthy ambition to get something for nothing. But when we begin by passing obedience and when our best effort becomes mediocre, then the slipping process always begins.

When our faith is abandoned by our works our faith dies. Faith like success always dies in isolation. There is no such thing as preserved faith or preserved courage or preserved righteousness. All of these are like the manna in the wilderness. What is not used immediately begins to spoil. We ourselves are often like the unprofitable servant who buried his talents in the ground, and then after a few years of disuse we try to dig them up and re-animate them.

It is a great truth that there is no growth in the grave, and we show our greatest deterioration in unrighteousness and prolonged rest. We should also remember that even all growth does not take place at the same rate. Elbert Hubbard once said that if Henry Ward Beecher had continued to grow after age 35 at the rate of growth he maintained from 25 to 35, he would have been a colossus at age 70. However, John Wesley made his greatest growth after age 50 and Walter Pitkin wrote a book entitled *Life Begins at Forty*. It is primarily a matter of how much righteous power we keep turned on.

Many people stop growing because some sin or complex blocks their progress. Then they lose their grip on life. A tombstone epitaph gave one man's history in six words, saying, "Died at 30, buried at 65." God has given us a program to insure eternal life; and to achieve our potential, we should keep our lights on and our engines running. We can solve most of our problems in life if we remember both parts of that great fourth commandment, wherein God said, "Six days shalt thou labour and do all thy work; but the seventh day is the sabbath of the Lord thy God." And may we so work and so worship that we may live at our best all of the days of our lives.

Smoke Signals

Some time ago while on an Arizona desert a friend told how the early desert Indians used to send messages to each other by smoke signals. This was the best means at their disposal of calling for help or warning friends of an enemy's approach. They were able to make puffs of smoke into a kind of dot and dash code that could be interpreted by others who were long distances away.

One story is told of two romantic young braves on distant hill-tops who sent competing declarations of love to a young princess. Each tried to outdo the enthusiasm and ardor of the other. One suitor put all of his resourcefulness together and then sent up one great impressive ball of smoke. His competitor, with a kind of inferiority complex attitude, said, "I wish I had thought to say that." We frequently hear someone say, "Just watch my smoke." He means that he is going to send a message that everyone will be impressed by. But no matter how much smoke the ancients made, it still must have been pretty dull to live when the only choices in communication lay between sending up puffs of smoke or making the long, arduous journey required to deliver the message in person.

One of the greatest wonders of our modern world is the miraculous progress we have recently made in the science of sending and receiving messages. We now have at our command the wonders of telephone, radio, and colored television. We can see and hear around the world. We may listen to the greatest orators and musicians and be uplifted by the most enlightening discussions of scientists and statesmen from all over the world. We can be entertained by professional artists in any room of the house, watch a guided missile take off for the moon, or see pictures of Mars.

Many of the greatest accomplishments of our personal lives also lie in this field of communication. The perfecting of the printing process has made available to us the greatest ideas, the most inspiring philosophies, and the most stimulating occupational aids ever produced by the minds of men. But even with these modern miracles coupled with our high standards of education, our biggest problem is still our inability to make effective use of our two-way system of communication. We may converse easily and fluently with those on the other side of the world, but frequently we can't understand the point of view of those under our own roofs or get effective messages to or from our own families. Frequently we don't even understand those important communiques that come from God.

Isn't it strange that one of our biggest businesses in this enlightened age is that of paying marriage counselors and divorce lawyers to help us to understand our spouses, our children, and even ourselves. Children often say, "My parents don't understand me." Many wives feel that they aren't appreciated, and frequently husbands are not at ease with their wives. Even our self-communication doesn't work very well as we continue to pay psychiatrists and personality doctors millions of dollars to dig down into the dark regions of our own lives to try to eliminate the quirks and complexes that cause our moods, failure, heart attacks, and nervous breakdowns. Our scrambled domestic messages are largely misunderstood by by those for whom they were intended, and often we ourselves never even discover the purpose or meaning of our own lives. It is important to make a fine impression on strangers in foreign lands, but we must also learn how to make our wives happy and inspire our children to righteousness and learn to live happily with ourselves.

A wife recently said that her husband always hit the ceiling when she approached the subject of family finances. To mention money was like stepping on a hidden land mine out in no man's land. The straw that breaks the back of most marriages is simply our inability to get along with each other. And the lack of effective communication is often the primary cause of the miserable existence of so many families. This poor interchange also frequently places out-of-bounds signs on such important matters as religion, politics, and personality differences. Many people spend a substantial percentage of their lives in the grip of ugly moods, nourishing the bitterness and resentment that make communication impossible.

Some time ago I heard a daughter complain that her father was not very pleasant with the boy friends that she brought to their home, and so she met them at other places. I know that almost more than anything else this particular father longs to be congenial with his daughter's friends. The trouble is that he just doesn't know how to communicate effectively. Most of us frequently have the experience of wanting to please someone or to make a good impression upon them, but our attempts are misunderstood and misinterpreted. Even with the best of intentions, we often seem to fall flat on our faces by always saying and doing the wrong things and thereby actually increasing the problem.

A husband recently said about his wife, "She burns me up," and that is exactly what was happening. We burn *up* our love, and then we burn *out* our nervous systems. We incinerate our mutual respect, and then we make dust and ashes out of the pleasure we should get from each other. We have set our personal progress and happiness back a thousand years because we have not kept pace in sending and receiving messages. We spend millions of dollars to maintain courts, policemen, and lawyers to help us understand and obey the law. The professional specialty of salesmen, teachers, parents, and business leaders is communication. And yet much of our effort is wasted because someone's sending or receiving station is loaded with static.

The Apostle Peter said that Paul taught some things hard to be understood, which the unlearned and the unstable wrested to their own destruction. (II Peter 3:16.) We have many more words in our dictionaries now than we have ever had before, and yet our messages sometimes don't get through any better than did the smoke signals of the ancients. Recently as a husband put his wife into her grave, he expressed his greatest lament that he had never let her know how much he loved her. This is just one of our problems. Good communication should have good words, but it should also have a spirit of warmth, joy, and light.

There have been several occasions in history when an unusual darkness was known upon the earth. We remember "the plague of darkness" that covered the Egyptians when Pharoah refused to release the children of Israel from their bondage. The Lord said to Moses, "Stretch out thine hand toward heaven, that there may be darkness over the land of Egypt, even a darkness which may be felt." Then the scripture says, "And there was a thick darkness in all the land of Egypt three days. They saw not one another, neither rose any from his place." (Exod. 10:12-23.)

Referring to a similar darkness that covered the western continent at the time of the crucifixion on Calvary, an ancient American prophet said that they could feel the vapor of darkness. He said, "And there could be no light, because of the darkness, neither candles, neither torches, neither could there be any fire kindled with their fine and exceedingly dry wood." (III Nephi 8:21.) Sometimes that kind of darkness gets into our minds, our marriages, and our work; then our communication smoke signals lose what little significance they may have had.

The Bible also mentions some other varieties of darkness that are even more serious. In foretelling the dark ages and the apostasy from God that preceded them, Isaiah said, "And darkness shall cover the earth, and gross darkness the people." The scripture refers to some *people* as "children of darkness." In public relations and in religion, some people demonstrate that they love darkness more than light. How unpleasant it is to feel the presence of this oppressive darkness inside ourselves! Sometimes this antagonism between darkness becomes so great in us that even the smallest light cannot live.

On the other hand, what a great delight to watch the sunrise and feel the abundance of warmth, light, strength, and vitality that God sends us from the sun. We don't like darkness in our eyes, but it is even more devastating to have that blackness known as ignorance in our minds, or to feel the thick darkness of sin in our souls.

The most serious part of this conflict between light and darkness comes in spiritual things. When darkness gains the ascendency, then God's light of peace and love and hope is cut off. The most severe eternal punishment mentioned in the scripture is meted out to those who are cast out into "outer darkness, where there will be weeping, wailing, and gnashing of teeth." (Matt. 8:12.) But those who love darkness may cut off their own light and destroy their ability to receive God's messages.

Certainly one of our most important abilities includes the arts and skills that enables us to get the meaning from written communications about those God-given principles involving our eternal salvation. When the Lord appeared to John the Revelator upon the isle of Patmos, he said, "I am alpha and omega, the first and the last." Then both before and after he gave his great message he said to John, "What thou seest write in a book." (Rev. l:ll.) He said, "Write the things which thou has seen, and the things which are, and the things which shall be hereafter." (Rev. 1:19.)

In the great scriptures every necessary direction has been clearly written down for our benefit. And Jesus mentioned our inability in communication when he talked of eyes that didn't see, and ears that didn't hear, and hearts that failed to understand. He also mentioned lips that didn't pray and voices that didn't honor God.

Everyone has been endowed with the ability to send and receive messages, but the Lord has said, "What doth it profit a man, if a gift is bestowed upon him and receives not the gift? Behold, he rejoices not in that which is given unto him, neither rejoices in him who is the giver of the gift." (D&C 88:33.) What doth it profit if the greatest messages are available but we are not tuned in or can't understand or don't believe?

Sometimes we don't even desire. I know of a man who has been notoriously unable to solve his problems. Whenever any good-sized difficulty arises, he takes the telephone off the hook and then he just takes off and gets drunk. He deliberately removes his mental glasses, turns off his spiritual hearing aids, and disconnects his reasoning abilities. He intentionally puts his receiving equipment out of use in order to make sure that no messages will get through. His personality, overloaded as it is with sin, can only send out its smoke signals of degradation and failure.

Below the deck of each British man-of-war is a compartment called the communications room. It is equipped with facilities enabling its commanding officer to be in constant contact with all of the ship's battle stations. From *this* room the navy's fight for victory is carried forward. It is unlikely that any successful battle of life can be carried on without an equally well-equipped, effectively operated communications room. Our communications room should have in it a set of the holy scriptures, giving us every detail of those of life's battle plans, that have been prepared by Deity himself.

God has also equipped us with a great brain with which to reinforce the importance of this message. He has also given us a will to put the program into operation. But if these communications from God are never opened, understood, accepted, or executed, then naturally we can get no profit from them.

But besides God, we also have parents, teachers, doctors, social workers, and religious leaders who are anxious to share their wisdom with us. Our communications room should also be equipped with a receiving set for the still, small voice, but if we leave the phone off the hook, what does it profit? If properly cared for our conscience has the ability to successfully direct our lives. However, our judgment is no better than our information, and if lives remain uninformed, then they may likely remain unsuccessful.

We have also been equipped with great sending abilities, and our every act sends out a message. In addition to our example, we have voices, testimonies, and emotions with which we may share our information and inspiration with our families and our friends. And one of the most important functions of our communications room is to receive messages from God. All good things come from him, and an adequate receiving ability will assure us every victory.

Sometime ago a great radio commentator and broadcaster was discussing the large amount of money spent by people to send their messages out across the major radio networks. We often use these wonderful facilities to try to get people to buy merchandise, smoke cigarettes, drink liquor, vote for some particular political candidate. Someone asked this noted radio man to identify the most important message that he had ever had a part in broadcasting, or, they said, what was the greatest message that he could conceive to be broadcast to the people of the world? He said that the greatest message that he could conceive would be that God had again spoken to his people upon the earth.

The Church of Jesus Christ of Latter-day Saints testifies to all that God *has* again opened official and personal communication with men. Not only has he spoken, but he has come in person. He not only delivered a message, but he caused it to be written down in three great volumes of new scripture outlining in every detail the simple principles of the gospel of Christ. Once again every important point of doctrine has an official statement attached saying, "Thus saith the Lord." In addition to making many obscure passages clear, this new revelation also supplements, reaffirms, and reinforces the ancient scriptures in every detail, this becomes all-important, as our eternal lives depend upon what we do about them. But first we must get the message; we must study and pray and live worthily. Jesus himself has said, "If ye shall do my will, ye shall know of the doctrine." I would like to bear my personal witness that God lives, that we are his children, created in his image, and that great things are about to take place upon this earth. If we can effectively receive his messages, then the greatest benefits of eternal life may be ours while there is yet time.

Solomon's Temple

ALTHOUGH WE LIVE AMID THE GREATEST OF THE SCIENTIFIC MAR-vels and miracles of all time, yet we may also draw inspiration from the ages past. We still talk about the seven wonders of the ancient world. A "wonder" is something that is wonderful and that may produce some favorable reaction in us. Wonder is also an emotion that builds our faith, challenges our enthusiasm, and arouses our industry.

Among the ancient wonders of the world, we think of the Hanging Gardens of Babylon. These were imitation mountains built by King Nebuchadnezzar in trying to cure the longing of his homesick wife for her native mountains of Edom. Another ancient wonder was the Colossus of Rhodes. This was a giant statue to the sun god Helios. It stood astride the Mediterranean harbor at the island of Rhodes, and it was said that ships sailed between the statue's giant legs. Behind the open eye sockets of the Colossus gleamed great beacon fires shining out into the ocean at night.

The city of Alexandria in Egypt was the rival of Athens as the seat of power in the Mediterranean area; and as a symbol of its superior strength, Alexandria built the Pharos Lighthouse in its harbor. It was 400 feet tall. Great fires were built on its summit, backed by a huge mirror that cast a great beam of light for many miles out across the sea. This lighthouse was the tallest man-made structure of its time, and brush fires on its top were fed by a caravan of donkeys climbing the spiral roadway running to its summit. This giant lighthouse safely guided ancient mariners into the Egyptian harbor for more than a thousand years.

Another ancient wonder was built five thousand years ago on the edge of the Egyptian desert. The famous King Cheops constructed a great pyramid, covering thirteen acres. It is the oldest man-made object known in the world. Another of the wonders of the world is the Taj Mahal, a magnificent and costly tomb built of white marble by the Indian ruler Shah Johan in memory of his wife Mumtaz Mahal.

But from more than one point of view, the greatest wonder of the ancient world was the Temple of Solomon. It was one of the few edifices in our world that was built under the direct command of God. God himself drew the plans and provided the specifications.

Some 480 years before the building of the temple began, the Israelites had been released from Egyptian bondage and in their third month were encamped before Mount Sinai. Then God called Moses up to meet him in the mount; and among other things during his forty-day visit, God gave Moses the details for building the famous tabernacle that would be a small-scale pattern of Solomon's Temple. It was also designed to serve as the center of worship for the children of Israel. God has always required some special place where certain sacred religious ordinances could be performed that are not otherwise acceptable. The tabernacle had a special place for the Ark of the Covenant, which contained the tables of stone on which God had written the Ten Commandments with his own finger. The books of the law given to Moses were also kept in the Ark of the Covenant.

The temple was covered by a cloud, which was the token of God's presence, and the glory of God filled the tabernacle. (Exod. 40:34.) The lifting of the cloud from the tabernacle was God's signal to the Israelites that they were to take up their march. When the cloud rested upon the tabernacle, they were to encamp in the wilderness. (Num. 9:17-18.) This tabernacle was taken down and carried from place to place by the children of Israel during all of their wanderings in the desert and in their subsequent conquests of their promised land. When this conquest was completed, the tabernacle was more permanently established at Shiloh, some twenty miles north of Jerusalem.

By the time Solomon ascended the throne, the Israelites had become very numerous. They needed a larger place to serve them as the house of the Lord. The Lord wanted them to have a temple, and Solomon's father, David, had had a consuming desire to build the temple. It was during David's reign that the Lord had designated that the temple should be built on Mount Moriah in Jerusalem. The temple site had once served as the threshing floor of Ornan. (II Chron. 3:1.) This site David had purchased at the command of an angel as a place to build an altar on which to offer sacrifice.

Much of the gold, silver, and other materials had been collected by David. (I Chron. 22:14.) Under God's direction, he had also planned the building and its furniture in detail. (I Chron. 28:11-23.)

He had also collected a number of skilled workmen (I Chron. 22:15), and had bound the people to a zealous cooperation. However, David was a man of war, and the Lord had told him that the building of the temple must wait until after his death. But he promised the great old warrior king that his son, Solomon, would fulfill his father's great desire. And to Solomon belongs most of the credit of the actual accomplishment.

In the beginning of the fourth year of his reign, construction began. Solomon made many advantageous alliances. One was with Hiram, King of Tyre, who furnished him with men skillful at working in gold and silver. Hiram also sent Solomon the expensive cedar and algum trees out of Lebanon.

Hiram used his great fleet of ships to bring gold and precious stones from Ophir and many other parts of the world. Solomon appointed seventy thousand of his own men "to bear burdens" and eighty thousand "to hue in the mountains of Lebanon." They were directed by thirty-six hundred overseers. (II Chron. 2:1-2.)

No expense was spared in making the temple as magnificent as possible. It was made of the finest wood, much of which was overlaid with pure gold and ornamented with precious gems, and richly furnished with fine twined linen. The linen had been prepared with special embroidery in various colors of blue, purple, and scarlet. Even with their fleets and the huge labor force of skilled workmen, it required seven years to build the temple. Some idea of the amount of wealth that went into it may be had from the scripture, which says, "Now the weight of gold that came to Solomon in one year was six hundred and three score and six talents of gold." (II Chron. 9:13.)

This would mean that in that one year alone there came into Solomon's hands some twenty-one million dollars worth of gold to be put into the temple. Then the record says, "Beside that which chapmen and merchants brought. And all the kings of Arabia and governors of the country brought gold and silver to Solomon." (II Chron. 9:14) In fact, the record says that Solomon "made silver and gold in Jerusalem as plenteous as stones, and cedar trees made he as the sycamore trees that are in the vale for abundance." (II Chron. 1:15.)

The government leaders of our own day who worry about our gold leaving the country would have envied Solomon, as the scripture says that His "ships went to Tarshish with the servants of Huram . . . [and broght back] gold, and silver, ivory, and apes, and peacocks." It says, "And King Solomon passed all of the kings of the earth in riches and in wisdom. And all the kings of the earth sought the presence of Solomon, to hear his wisdom, that God hath put in his heart. And they brought every man his present, vessels of silver, and vessels of gold, and raiment, harness, and spices, horses, and mules." (II Chron. 9:21-24.)

As one example of the lavishness of the temple, the record points out that the porch that was in front of the house was some 180 feet tall and was overlaid with pure gold. It says, "And the greater house he ceiled with fir tree, which he overlaid with fine gold, and set thereon palm trees and chains. And he garnished the house with precious stones for beauty;. . . . He overlaid also the beams, the posts, and the walls thereof, and the doors thereof, with gold. . . And he overlaid the upper chambers with gold. . . And he made the vail of blue, and purple, and crimson, and fine linen, and wrought cherubims thereon." (II Chron. 3.) And King Solomon made two hundred targets of beaten gold: and six hundred shekels of gold went to one target. This would amount to a total of over $6,000 worth of gold per target. "And three hundred shields made he of beaten gold: three hundred shekels of gold went to one shield." (II Chron. 9: 15-16.) That would mean about $3,000 worth of gold in each shield. "Moreover the king made a great throne of ivory, and overlaid it with the best gold . . . and all King Solomon's drinking vessels were of gold." (I Kings 10:18-21.)

Finally after seven years of work, the temple was ready for dedication. When the priests came out from setting the ark inside the Holy of Holies, the house was filled with a cloud, "So that the priests could not stand to minister by reason of the cloud: for the glory of the Lord had filled the house of God." (II Chron. 5:13-14.)

Then Solomon stood before the altar of the Lord in the presence of all the congregation of Israel. He spread forth his hands toward heaven, and he and all of the people dedicated the temple unto the Lord. He prayed that if a man should sin against his neighbor, or if the people should be smitten before their enemies because of their sins, or if because of their transgression there would be no rain, then if they should pray toward the temple and confess God's name and turn from their sins that God should hear their prayer and forgive their sin. Or if there should be famine or pestilence or blasting or mildew or trouble with military enemies, or whatever plague or sickness there may be, if they should spread forth their hands toward the temple, then said he to God, "Hear thou in heaven thy dwelling place, and forgive their sins. If they pray unto the Lord, toward this city which thou hast chosen and toward this house which I have built to thy name, then hear thou in heaven their prayer and their supplication and maintain their cause." (II Chron. 6.) When Solomon had finished his prayer, "fire came down from heaven and consumed the . . . sacrifices." (II Chron. 7:1.)

Then again by night the Lord appeared unto Solomon and said, "I have heard thy prayer, and have chosen this place to myself for an house of sacrifice. If I shut up the heaven that there be no rain, or if I command the locusts to devour the land, or if I send pestilence among my people; If my people, which are called by my name, shall humble themselves, and pray and seek my face, and turn from their wicked ways: then I will hear from heaven, and will forgive their sin, and will heal their land." (II Chron. 7:12-14.)

For many years this temple was not only one of the wonders of the world; it was also the earthly house of God and the symbol of Jehovah worship. The word "Tabernacle" literally means God's dwelling-place. (Exod. 25:9.) But the people did not always keep their covenants, and when the temple was desecrated, it was soon shorn of its magnificence. It was spoiled of its treasures by both foreign and local sinners. Some of the gold was used to buy off the attack of foreign powers. Some was used to purchase the co-operation of other nations. Finally the temple itself was burnt to the ground and utterly destroyed by Nebuchadnezzar (II Kings 25: 9) and all of value that still remained was carried to Babylon. (II Kings 25:13.)

From this chapter of history we learn many useful lessons and helpful analogies. We know that temples have always been a distinguishing characteristic of God's church. But whether in ancient or modern times, as soon as people have departed from their faithfulness, then even the most magnificent or costly things have little value so far as God is concerned. Many times God has indicated that in his sight the most magnificent treasure in the world is a great human soul, which is also God's temple. As Paul has said, "Know ye not that ye are the temple of God, and that the Spirit of God dwelleth in you? If any man defile the temple of God, him shall God destroy; for the temple of God is holy, which temple ye are." (I Cor. 3:16-17.)

Before all material things, we should build out of our lives a temple of such magnificence that the spirit of God may be pleased to dwell therein. Then God will bless our efforts, heal our land, and inspire our hearts. But everything depends upon how effectively we ourselves perform. It is interesting that even these beautiful, wonderful bodies have been given us of God only on a temporary basis. They will not be ours as a permanent possession until after the resurrection, when we will have the power to resurrect our bodies with the degrees of glory to which our lives entitle us. Then the spirit and the body will be inseparably connected, and those who are worthy will receive "a fulness of joy" as well as "a fullness of the Glory of God." The righteous children of God are actually the greatest wonders of the world, and I pray that we may effectively dedicate that life to God, and good works.

The Sorting Table

ONE OF MY EARLIEST RECOLLECTIONS OF FARM WORK HAD TO DO with the apple Harvest. The apples were brought from the orchard into a packing shed and run over a large sorting table, where they were graded according to their size, color, and freedom from defects. The sorters would put the grade "A" apples in one box; the grade "B" apples would go into another box; and the culls would be put in a third box. If an apple was smaller than a certain size or if it lacked color, it was considered to be second grade. Wormy apples and those with other defects that made them unfit for commercial use were carried away and fed to the pigs. Of course, the grade A's brought the highest price and were the most pleasant to work with. It was pretty hard to get buyers interested in small, less perfectly developed apples. And, of course, no one was interested in the culls at any price.

In the years that have passed since then, I have been impressed with some similarities between growing apples and living. If the best results are to be achieved in either case, there is a certain amount of cultivating, fertilizing, irrigating, and spraying that must be done. And through all of the growing operations one should always keep his thoughts on the harvest and the substantial premium that is paid for every grade A product. There is never a very great demand for cull apples, scrubby potatoes, runt pigs, diseased beef, knotty lumber, or inferior human beings. Spoiled food is thrown away, defective goods have no market. And human plans that are ineffective or attitudes that go sour are sometimes worse than worthless. Life itself becomes a kind of sorting table on which our abilities, virtues, attitudes, personality traits, and moral defects are placed for examination and grading. From the earliest years of our lives, a sorting process is always taking place. The occupations operate a kind of sorting procedure. Our personal behavior also places us in a particular social group according to our merits. Penitentiaries, reform schools, and mental hospitals receive those who are not acceptable in some more desirable classification.

Because the grading job is never fully completed in this life, it naturally follows that the most important part of the sorting operation reaches over into the hereafter. It is at that time that the Lord will separate the sheep from the goats. A certain quality of excellence will entitle some people to go to the celestial kingdom, and with an inferior performance others will have to be content with the telestial. In speaking of the great and final judgment, the scripture says that some will come forth in the resurrection of life and others will be a part of the resurrection of damnation. The Lord has said, "Before the earth shall pass away, Michael, mine archangel, shall sound his trump, and then shall all the dead awake, for their graves shall be opened, and they shall come forth, yea, even all. And the righteous shall be gathered on my right hand unto eternal life; and the wicked on my left hand will I be ashamed to own before the Father; Wherefore I will say unto them, Depart from me, ye cursed, into everlasting fire, prepared for the devil and his angels." (D&C 29:26-28)

Nothing in the scriptures is more plainly written than the fact that everyone will be judged according to his works. This means that there will be many gradations of merit. However, the scriptures point out that there will be four great general subdivisions. Three of these will be kingdoms of glory, and one will *not* be a kingdon of glory. The Apostle Paul compares the brightness of the three degrees of glory to that of the sun, moon and stars in the firmament.

Many of those who make up the lowest of these three kingdoms will be unrighteous people who have not sinned unto death. These will be cleansed by their own suffering in hell. And the Lord has said that after their final redemption and education they will be assigned to the telestial kingdom and the glory of even this lowest kingdom will surpass all human understanding. (D&C 76:89.)

Then below these kingdoms of glory is a fourth kingdom. Those consigned to this kingdom will be the ones who have allowed themselves to be overcome by evil. They have gone beyond the point of no return and are doomed to suffer with the devil and his angels throughout eternity. Concerning these the Lord has said that there is no forgiveness in this world nor in the world to come. (D&C 76: 31-38.) These will compare to the culls or the wormy apples, so to speak. These will be those for whom no redemption has been provided. Their terrible fate was indicated by the angel who said to John the Revelator, "He that is unjust, let him be unjust still: and he which is filthy let him be filthy still." (Rev. 22:11.)

Fortunately this kingdom will contain a relatively small number of people. All of the rest of God's family will be redeemed in one of the degrees of glory according to their individual merit. And even though all will be redeemed from death by the atonement of Christ, yet each will be rewarded or punished according to the merit of his individual works. Even our human wisdom would not think it just to sentence the murderer, the Sabbath breaker, the adulterer, and the profane with the same punishment; neither would we think it proper to bestow a one-talent reward on one who had made a ten-talent effort. No fair-minded judge would say that Jesus, Pilate, Judas, Caiaphas, and Simon the Sorcerer should all be rewarded alike.

Certainly no intelligent farmer would put his cull onions, rotten apples, wormy gooseberries, and knotty potatoes in the same package with those that were Grade A. When we go to the state fair and see all of the choicest fruits so beautifully arranged, the culls are conspicuous by their absence. Any other procedure would be very bad business from many points of view. We know what happens when even one rotten apple gets into a Grade A barrel. Preventing the contamination of evil has always been one of our world's biggest problems. We have many examples where one man with a perverted sense of truth or a distorted spirituality or a rotten attitude has sometimes destroyed an entire civilization. Lucifer, Herod, Hitler, Lenin, and Pilate might be cited as examples. Even the smallest rotten spot becomes a source of danger and damage.

The seeds of death that were allowed to grow in the lives of Laman and Lemuel finally destroyed the entire pre-Columbus civilization that flourished on the Western continent for a thousand years.

Recently we have heard a great deal of discussion about integration and segregation. There are some who think that the integration of one group with another will more or less automatically solve their problems. But some kinds of integration have not seemed to work very well in the past. Long before the earliest civil rights bill, we had had many problems with the integration of evil. One integrated carrier of contagious disease can cause an epidemic. It seems that alcoholism, dope addiction, venereal disease, and atheism all have a strong desire for integration, but frequently the Lord has instituted some severe segregation instead. The Apostle Peter tells us that during the three days when the body of Jesus lay in the tomb, his spirit went and preached to "spirits in prison" who had been disobedient in the days of Noah, some 2,500 years earlier. These people had been segregated for a long time. When the Lord spoke of separating the wheat from the tares, he was also talking about segregation. Certainly the Sons of Perdition are going to be segregated. Of them the Lord said, "These are they who shall go away into the lake of fire and brimstone with the devil and his angels- and are the only ones on whom the second death shall have any power; yea verily, the only ones who shall not be redeemed in the due time of the Lord." (D&C 76:36-38.)

It is interesting that no one is ever sent to hell by someone else. Everyone who goes to hell goes there of his own accord. However, if we are drunkards and sinners, we had better not count on being integrated with those who qualify for God's presence. God himself has said that no sin will ever be permitted in his presence. Of those who merit the lowest glory, the Lord has said, "They shall be servants of the most high, but where God and Christ dwell they cannot come, worlds without end." (D&C 76:112.)

All sinners bring about an unprofitable kind of segregation upon themselves. We limit ourselves in occupation, education, social position, and our own eternal glory, which requires some kind of segretation. This separation process began even before we were born. In the grand council of heaven Lucifer rebelled against God. Those who followed Lucifer were banished from heaven and became Satan's angels. They not only segregated themselves, but they denied themselves the privilege of further progression. On the other hand, all of those who will ever live on the earth were obedient to God in their first estate and were granted the blessings of mortality. We have not yet achieved the final objective, and so throughout our mortality this sorting process continues.

When one becomes a dropout from school, he is segregating himself from certain future benefits and privileges. Further restrictions take place when we become dropouts from our faith, and dropouts from our greatest possibilities. When unresolved problems are allowed to continue in our lives, they can soon cut us off from our blessings. This conforms to the natural selection process constantly going on in nature. The wormy apple has the weakest hold upon the tree. Nature has provided that the wormy apples are the ones that are most likely to fall. This is in order that the tree's strength may be conserved to mature the grade A apples. Some orchardists shake their trees in order to rid them of the wormy apples as early as possible. The Lord probably also had something like this in mind when he said, "Once more I shake the earth—that those things which cannot be shaken may remain." (Heb. 12:26-27.)

The Lord is always conducting some "shaking" or "testing" processes to discover which blessings we are worthy of. He has said that those who are valiant shall qualify for celestial glory. The valiant are those who cannot be moved from righteously serving God. On the other hand, those who develop serious defects or fall before every temptation will soon find themselves with the culls.

If we properly handle ourselves on life's sorting table, we may qualify as grade A human beings and enjoy the many advantages of excellence. A mail clerk sorts his mail according to its destination. And that is also about what we do for ourselves. The sort of people we will become will determine our destination; and while we may select our characteristics, yet we will not be left ungraded. If we become small, poorly colored apples, we cannot expect to be placed with those that are grade A. And if we are a little wormy and have a rotten spot here and there, we can guess what our own destination is likely to be, as God has said that no unclean thing will be permitted in his presence. He has left no doubt about the fact that life's rotten apples will not be integrated with those that are grade A.

I know of a man who violates almost all of the Ten Commandments. The question of whether or not God is dead is of no concern to him either one way or the other. His immorality has soured the lives of several other human beings. He has integrated many other people into his program of alcoholism with no sense of guilt, and yet he would be surprised and seriously offended if anyone suggested that he would need to radically change his ways to qualify for God's presence. Yet God has clearly said that liars, adulterers, covenant breakers, and other seriously unrepented sinners will be segregated for eternity.

Health authorities take those with highly contagious diseases and put them in isolation. We used to call this isolation a quarantine. And before people could get out of quarantine, they not only had to get well, but they also had to be fumigated. It may be that when we stand before God, if we show ourselves to be dirty, unworthy, disobedient, and unprepared for one of God's kingdoms of glory, we may have to go through a fumigation process that we will wish we had avoided.

We don't like to think about hell, because it is unpleasant; and yet hell is a divine institution prepared by God as a place to burn out the dross of our lives so that we may qualify for as high a kingdom as possible. We pray that God will help us toward this end, that we may entitle ourselves to receive his grade A rating.

Subtraction

It is a very interesting idea that negative motivation is usually much stronger as a success factor than positive motivation. For example, suppose you knew that tonight a burglar was planning to come through your back window and take the $5 bill that you have in your pocket. Most people would sit up all night, if it were necessary, to prevent that from happening, and yet very few people would be willing to sit up all night to make $5.

This very important fact that most people are usually willing to work much harder to prevent a loss than they are to affect a gain of a corresponding amount has many important applications in our lives. For this reason, nature uses negative motivation to stimulate our development. That is, when one fails to use the muscle in his arm, nature takes the muscle away. The mole didn't use his eyes, and so nature took away his eyesight. The Lord also uses this powerful negative motivation. If you don't appreciate your blessings, God takes them away. Anciently the people didn't honor the priesthood, and so the priesthood was taken from the earth. After the days of Jesus, they didn't live the gospel, and so they brought the great apostasy upon themselves.

As a kind of text for this idea, I would like to read to you from an ancient American scripture in which the Prophet Nephi says, "Yea, and we may see at the very time when [God] doth prosper his people, yea, in the increase of their fields, their flocks, and their herds, and in gold, and in silver, and in all manner of precious things; . . . sparing their lives, and delivering them out of the hands of their enemies; softening the hearts of their enemies that they should not declare wars against them; yea, and in fine, doing all things for the welfare and happiness of his people; yea, then is the time that they do"—what? That is, when God pours out his blessings upon us, what do we do? One would naturally suppose that we would respond in kind, that we would be obedient, grateful, and faithful. But that is not always what happens. In response to great blessings we sometimes become arrogant and proud and turn away from the Lord. For example, our present-day high standards of living have brought forth from us a sharp upturn in our crime and delinquency rate. The ancient prophet gives expression to the result of this strange phenomenon by saying, "Yea, then is the time that they do harden their hearts, and do forget the Lord their God, and do trample under their feet the Holy One [of Israel]." He said, "And thus we see that except the Lord doth chasten his people with many afflictions, yea, except he doth visit them with death and with terror, and with famine and with all manner of pestilence, they will not remember him." (Hel. 12:2-3.)

Because we sometimes turn away when he gives us his blessings, he frequently takes our blessings away that we might return to him. I would like to follow a similar procedure with you now in your imagination. That is, instead of talking to you about gaining additional benefits for your lives, in your minds I would like to take away those that you already have, this with the hope that it may so arouse your resistance, that you will not actually lose them.

I would like to begin by retelling Edward Everett Hale's great revolutionary story, entitled *A Man Without a Country*. You may remember that Philip Nolan was a fine young officer in the American army, but in a moment of thoughtlessness and anger he said, "I wish I may never hear the name of the United States again." And that became his punishment. His sentence was to be put on board an outgoing ship, and from that day until the day of his death, he never came into an American port or ever heard the name of his country spoken again until on the day of his death. Then he said to those who sat about his cot, "Bury me in the sea. It has been my home, and I love it. But won't someone erect a stone in my memory at Fort Adams or Orleans? Say on it 'In memory of Philip Nolan. He loved his country as no other man ever loved her, but no one deserved less at her hands.' " Phillip Nolan said that he loved his country more than anyone had ever loved his country and yet he had to lose his country in order to gain that appreciation.

It is a pretty big price to pay when we have to lose the things we love before we can understand their value. Because of thoughtlessness, Philip Nolan became a man without a country. For the same reason, someone else becomes a man without an education, another becomes a man without a faith, someone else becomes a man without a family, or a man without a God.

Sometime ago I attended a marriage ceremony held at a university sorority house. The young people were both college graduates. They were beautifully dressed and were fully enjoying the good wishes and love of their friends. Then amid flowers and music and happiness these two young people joined their right hands and said to each other, "Until death do us part." After the ceremony was over, the guests were visiting in little groups, enjoying the refreshments and sociability. In the group where I stood someone said, "I wonder why they weren't married in the temple?" A friend of the groom said, "I don't know, I am sure that his parents are members of the Church, but I don't think he has ever been baptized." She said, "I suppose that they have just overlooked it," and I thought what a tremendous thing to overlook.

But sometimes we overlook the most important things in our lives. We sometimes overlook God and eternal life and the welfare of our own souls. Under these circumstances no one would have overlooked a wedding ring or a particular kind of wedding dress, and yet they have overlooked each other. God has announced that marriages should be performed in his holy temples by one having authority, and that the family unit was intended to be eternal. Jesus said to Peter, "Whatsoever thou shalt bind on earth, shall be bound in heaven, and whatsoever thou shalt loose on earth shall be loosed in heaven." Marriage as God ordained it is for time and for eternity. When the first marriage was performed, death had not yet entered the world. But in our day many people adopt a kind of combination marriage and divorcement at the same time. In some of our modern ceremonies the contracting partners say to each other, "Until death do us part." I would not like to lose my wife and family here, and I can think of no reason why it would be any more pleasant to lose them hereafter. In fact, I imagine that if I were to multiply by a few million times the grief that I would feel in losing them here, I might get some kind of idea what it would be like to lose them hereafter.

To try to help you understand in advance the pain that might attend a situation of that kind where your *separation* was also provided for in your marriage ceremony, I would like to have you lose your family in your imagination. I can best assist you with this project by telling you Lord Tennyson's story about a man who lost his family.

You may remember that Enoch Arden was one of three children around whom this story revolves. The others were Philip Ray and Annie Lee. These children played together, they went to school together, they loved each other, and they grew up together. When they were old enough to think of getting married, Annie Lee was asked to choose between these two young men which one she would marry. After some hesitation she married Enoch Arden, and in the course of events four children were born to that union.

Enoch Arden made his living trading on the sea. One day an opportunity came for him to sail to a distant port and buy an expensive cargo that he might sell elsewhere at a profit. He sailed away. The cargo was purchased under very favorable circumstances, and then he turned the prow of his little craft back toward home. But the homeward journey was not so successful. Contrary winds took his ship off its course and crashed it upon some reefs. The ship was broken in two, and all was lost save only Enoch Arden, who managed to swim to a little uninhabited island in this beautiful tropical sea, and there he lived alone for the next eleven years. Tennyson said, "He had no want for sustenance"; that is, all of the material things of the world were present in ample abundance to minister to his needs. But Tennyson said, "What he feign would see, he could not see: A kindly human face or ever hear a kindly human voice." Suppose that you were to try to understand what it would be like to own all of the material things and then be denied human companionship, especially that of your own family that you loved the most.

After eleven years, another ship off its course put in at this little island, and Enoch Arden was taken aboard. A few weeks later he arrived back in his home village. Immediately he went to the place that had been his home, only to find the house deserted and the windows boarded up. During these years of living by himself, some unpleasant changes had taken place in him. His speech had degenerated, his health had been broken, and he was not recognized as the once proud and successful Enoch Arden. Without knowing who he was, someone told him a story of his family. It seems that things had gone as might have been expected during the period for which provision had been made. When he did not return, his family began to be in want. His old friend offered assistance, which his wife declined, because she thought it inappropriate. Then she tried to go into a business for which she was not prepared, and other sums were lost.

Slowly, one dreary year dragged on after another until almost eleven years had passed. And then, thinking that certainly her husband must have perished, Annie Lee married Philip Ray, and a child was born to that union. By this time Enoch Arden had returned. After learning about his family, he decided that he would not intrude himself upon their happiness. But he could not resist the temptation of wanting to see them again, and so one night after dark he crept up to the house and looked in through the window upon his wife and family.

Now for a moment, I would like to station you outside the window, looking in upon the people that you love more than anyone else in the world, but who have now been placed forever beyond your reach.

Of this experience Tennyson said, "Eleven years had passed, nor yet had perished when his lonely doom came suddenly to an end, and he was rescued by an off-course ship and began his journey homeward. Home. What home? Had he a home? In port Mariam Lane, a tavern keeper's widow, not recognizing him, told him all the story of his house, his baby's death, his wife's growing poverty, how she had finally married Philip Ray, the slighted suitor of old-times, and of the birth of Philip's child. But Enoch yearned to see her face again. He thought, 'If I might look on her sweet face and know that she is happy.' The thought haunted him and drove him forth at evening of a dull November day. 'A thousand memories of unspeakable sadness unrolled upon him until by night up by the wall behind the yew tree through the window of Philip's home, Enoch saw.

"Now when the dead-man-come-to-life beheld his wife, his wife no more, and saw the babe, hers yet not his upon the father's knee and all the warmth and peace and happiness of his own children, tall and beautiful, and him the other reigning in his place, lord of his rights and of his children's love, then he, though Miriam Lane had told him all because things seen are mightier than things heard, staggered and shook. And holding the yew tree branch he feared, lest he might send abroad a shrill and terrible cry which in an instant like the blast of doom would shatter all the happiness of that shining genial hearth.

"He, therefore, turned softly like a thief, crept to the gate and opened it, and came out upon the waste, and there he would have knelt but that his knees were feeble, so that falling prone he dug his fingers into the wet earth and prayed. Too hard to bear, why did they take me hence? Oh God, almighty, blessed Savior, thou who didst uphold me on my lonely isle, uphold me, Father, in my loneness a little longer. Aid me, give me strength not to tell her, never to let her know. No father's kiss for me. The girl so like her mother, and the boy my son.' Here speech and thought and nature failed, and he lay still. Finally he revived, he rose and paced back wearily toward his tavern rooming house, his solitary home."

True to his resolution, he kept his identity a secret until he died. Unimportant employment provided for his meager needs, but he didn't live very long after his experience, and Tennyson records his end by saying, "But since his labor was only for himself, there was no life in it and he died."

There is never very much life in labor that is performed only for one's self. Men and women were created to live together to love and serve each other. God himself said, "It is not good for man to be alone." So far as this life is concerned, Enoch Arden solved his problem by dying, but what about eternal life? Andrew Jackson once said, "Heaven would not be heaven to me without my wife," and heaven will not be heaven to you without your wife, and without your children, and without the other members of your family all sealed together in an eternal family unit.

We have the privilege of using the most powerful motivation, both positive and negative, in bringing about the excellence of our own lives, the perfection of our families, as well as the eternal salvation of our own souls.

The Switchboard

WE SOMETIMES GAIN A SUBSTANTIAL ADVANTAGE FOR OURSELVES when we compare ourselves with the things and people around us. A particular personality trait is sometimes illustrated by saying that one individual is a ball of fire, while someone else is as cold as an iceberg. A person may be as sharp as a tack, or as stubborn as a mule, or as dumb as an ox.

The human heart is the center of a marvelous pumping system. A prominent British neurophysicist recently said that no one could construct an electronic computer for three billion dollars equal to the human brain. The nervous system has been compared to a vast communication network. These various instruments of human equipment have all been divinely endowed with abilities to serve our specific needs. But one of the most important of our personalized operations is centered in a kind of telephonic switchboard. Through this human communication center thousands of messages come and go every day, and they must be sorted, interpreted, and properly acted upon by us.

Both our conscious and our subconscious minds are constantly receiving and sending messages. There are communications that come through our eyes, our ears, as well as from our feet, and our hands. Our nervous system and each of our bodily organs are also broadcasting and receiving communications. If one's stomach gets empty, it begins to send out some hunger pain impulses. The stomach tells us whether our bodies need proteins, carbohydrates, or fats, and in what amounts. In language that cannot be misunderstood, our muscles tell us when they are tired and want to rest. Even a pin prick on any part of the body is immediately picked up and relayed to the brain, which reports the exact location, significance, and the severity of any injury done. Our sex impulses, hates, prejudices, fears, and timidities, as well as our inferiority and guilt complexes all engage in a different kind of speech, but the brain has a kind of gift of tongues that hears everyone of these voices in its own language.

We are also equipped to receive communications from ourselves and from God. As long as the right messages are being received and the right action taken, our situation will remain satisfactory. But when our switchboard gets out of order, or when the automatic operator gets its wires crossed, then we get the wrong message and begin having problems. Even our reception from God can get jammed occasionally. Frequently Satan does a little wire tapping and with a voice of some authority sends his messages through on God's line. Other problems develop when messages of fear, hate, or discouragement drown out the message of our reason and good judgment. Sometimes our gluttonous instincts are over-developed so that the stomach is able to get its messages accepted over the most earnest protests of the brain. This is in spite of the fact that the brain was created and commissioned to be the presiding officer of the entire personality.

Many of our problems arise because we turn a deaf ear to the authority of the mind and listen to the deceptive voices of the body. There are some voices urging us to get drunk, and some are contending for a greater number of undeclared holidays. Some voices with great feeling behind them are inciting us to be immoral. We often listen to our own broadcast of rationalizing excuses and weakness that are working directly against our own best interests. Many people listen to those messages that destroy our positive mental attitudes, our peace of mind, our health, our spirituality and our ability to think straight.

When we don't accurately live by the facts, the ensuing conflicts can bring on a serious spiritual disorder or a nervous breakdown. Frequently when logic goes against us, we abandon our own power to reason. One chain smoker who didn't want to get lung cancer tried to solve his problem by refusing to read about it. When we are too greatly influenced by our passions or our feelings, we so seriously downgrade our logic that it becomes difficult for the messages of right, fairness, and reason to be heard.

Sometimes we are influenced by messages of hate or discouragement that do us serious harm. It is illegal to send certain kinds of messages over a public telephone network. But with our own private communication system, we frequently let down the bars so that harmful, dishonest messages have more influence than those that would be helpful. We sometimes deceive ourselves by soft-pedaling our own wrongdoings or allowing our own negative thinking to set us up in a state of neutrality midway between success and failure. Frequently we permit a type of negative propaganda that keeps our personality confused and demoralized. Sometimes our sex impulses get too much authority, or some evil habit is given such a free hand that our lives themselves get out of control.

Sometime ago I talked with a young man within whom the battling contradictory elements were almost literally tearing him to pieces. He had a natural inborn sense of right, which was trying to keep him straight. But the sex department of his life had been given such power that he was being jerked back and forth between his own right and wrong. It was as though his conscience was pulling on his right arm while his immorality had him by the left arm. These antagonistic influences were jerking him in opposite directions at the same time. For a time he would give in to his evil; then for a comparable period he would hate himself for what he had done. This seesaw had gone on until the evil Mr. Hyde within him was threatening to destroy the more worthwhile Dr. Jekyll. But his unfavorable appetites and emotions on the one side were steadily gaining power over his weakening sense of righteousness on the other. After his immorality had had its inning, his better self was tortured by shame and regret. But when he tried to do right the evil hungers that he had previously set in motion were making his life miserable, and the awareness of the damage that he was doing to others made his existence itself ugly.

A few weeks ago he committed himself to a period in the mental hospital in an effort to get hold of himself. He knows that if this conflict continues much longer, he is likely to suffer a complete mental collapse. Being so divided against himself, he cannot hope to be successful in marriage, occupation, or religion. And all of this bleak, unhappy outlook has been brought about because he has been getting his messages mixed up, with no clear-cut authority by which to operate his life.

Another young man told about how in his youth his mother and father were always fighting and yelling at each other. The main messages that had come over his family exchange were about quarreling, drinking, unpaid bills, and personal bitterness. He had been unable to endure the sins of their incompatibility, and so at age fifteen he had moved out on his own. But his condition did not improve, as he soon developed a whole new set of his own antagonisms and bitterness. By the time he was eighteen he had stomach ulcers; but he has some mental and spiritual ulcers that are causing him even greater problems. However, the confusions continue, and the conflicting messages are pouring so much evil through his switchboard that he is also in danger of losing his mental balance. Yet, like a nicotine addict, he does not now have the strength to stop his trouble, and he is getting weaker.

Some time ago a movie producer tried to convey to his audience an impression of the sounds that bombard an unbalanced mind. It was a confused conglomeration of loud, hollow noises all mixed up together. Nothing could be understood clearly, and each antagonistic voice seemed to have about as much authority as the others. Some time ago a doctor warned LSD users that they should make no important decisions for at least three months after they had used this drug, as their minds would not be back to normal. And very frequently it takes months and even years after a period of confused and wrong thinking for our minds to get back to normal and sometimes it never does, even with expert direction.

It has always irritated me a little bit when placing a telephone call to have the secretary ask, "Who is calling?" Some people may be interested in speaking only to certain people. However, I have been impressed that over our personal exchanges we should know in advance who we are talking to, and whether it is drugs or doubts or our wishful thinking that is speaking to us. Certainly we should know when we are listening to our fears and our prejudices. We should also know when we are listening to our reason, our ambition, and our courage. Important decisions should never be based on the testimony of our hates or our lusts. And before we begin taking dictation from unseen voices, we should know who is speaking. Antagonistic nations sometimes try to jam the radio reception of each other so that a given message will not go through. But we make an even bigger mistake when we allow our enemies, fears, hates, sins, and prejudices to spoil the influence of our spirituality, industry and faith.

Recently I talked with a man who "thinks" almost entirely with his emotions. Sometimes he imagines that he is having his prayers answered when his feelings are merely replaying some old record of hate and prejudice. These contrary influences can so badly jam the lines that nothing can be heard from wisdom or the sources of good. Everything this man's reason tells him is contradicted by an opposing passion. Because he is on an intimate basis with certain evil emotional responses, their voices sound more familiar to him than the still, small voice of the Spirit or even the voice of his own reason. We hear most easily and clearly those voices that we want to hear or that are nearest to us.

Some time ago I sat on the stand in church directly in front of a large choir. During one musical number, a quartet sang the verse and the entire choir sang the refrain. However, instead of the quartet members going to a central place, they remained in their regular choir positions while they sang. I have no doubt that the audience heard a quartet, but because I was sitting directly in front of one of the singers, I heard a bass solo. Sometimes we sit too close to our profane, irreverent, crooked, or alcoholic inclinations to hear the things that we are supposed to hear.

Esau sold his birthright for a mess of pottage. That kind of an exchange may seem a little bit ridiculous, but the voice of the pottage was strong because it was close by, and the voice of the birthright was weak because it was down the road a few years. We are still making this same kind of mistake every day, because voices that are a long way off sometimes lose much of their authority. When you put a magnet close to its object it has great power, but as the distance is increased, the power is lost. The closer we can keep to righteousness, the better off we are. The prophet said, "Draw nigh unto God, and he will draw nigh unto you."

Sometimes we fail because we let heaven and righteousness get too far away, whereas our success requires that we bring them up as close to us as possible. On the other hand, one of our difficulties is that we are too strongly attracted by those evils that we let get too close to us. We frequently sit in front of the wrong voices; then we can hear the loud clamor of commercial voices, the false cry of pagan voices, and the enticing whisper of evil voices. There are iconoclastic voices that seem to have great authority as they attack our old standards and trusted ideals. We are also adversely influenced by the voices of fear, hate, dishonesty, immorality, and weakness, when they are lurking in our own camp too close at hand.

Satan has a way of getting close to us, and he gets his henchmen on our private line. Because Satan knows so much about direct dialing, we have another reason we should know with whom we are doing business. Frequently people do only the things that they feel like doing without bothering to find out whether these things are reasonable or logical. God has given us the greatest power known in the universe, which is the power to think and reason. If we keep our minds in proper balance, we can effectively compare the advantages of alcoholism and sobriety. We can also understand the damage done by unkindness, idleness, and immorality. On the other hand, we can know of the many benefits of righteousness. We know that the one who goes to church and centers his mind on the right things will have greater opportunities for happiness than the one who absents himself from church and engages in evil. We might try to appraise the advantages of living in the celestial kingdom and of belonging to that great order of which God himself is a member.

Many years ago Chauncey Depew was offered a one-sixth interest in what is now the American Telephone and Telegraph Company for $10,000. He had already decided to go ahead with the deal. But he made the mistake of first asking a friend what *he* thought about it. His friend shook his head as he pointed out that the telephone was a new invention, that its patents were weak, and that it would have difficulty in competing with the telegraph. Because Mr. Depew listened to the wrong advice he turned the opportunity down. The one-sixth interest in A.T. and T. which he could have owned for $10,000 is now worth over a billion.

However, there is a better opportunity available to us right now than anything ever offered by A.T.&T. We have been placed upon this earth to work out our eternal exaltation, and when atheism says that God is dead and our birthrights are worthless, we had better know who is speaking. The Master himself said that the worth of a soul was greater than the wealth of the entire earth. Compared to this, even a one hundred percent interest in A.T.&T. would look pretty small. Our primary problem is to keep God's messages on the telephone wires of our lives. And we pray that we may have success in this all important undertaking.

The Tap Root

A T THE GRAND CANYON OF THE COLORADO, NEAR THE SPOT WHERE
the famous Bright Angel Trail begins its descent from the
rim of the canyon, there is a lone pine tree growing on the canyon's
edge with its root system exposed to view. This tree began its
interesting life's experience when a seed fell into a small crack in the
surface of the rock. It was covered with a few grains of soil blown
into the crack by the wind. Then, stimulated by the rain and the
sun, the seed sprouted. It sent a tiny shoot upward and a tiny root
downward, and through a miraculous process called growth, it soon
became a seedling and eventually a sturdy pine.

As the tree rose into the air, the roots made a corresponding
descent into the granite. Little by little it opened up a crevice and
finally split the canyon wall wide open, sending a million tons of
rock crashing into the chasm below.

As this interesting tree now stands there on the canyon's edge,
it reveals a growth made into the rock comparable to that which has
been made into the air. This tree is also a symbol of the most
extraordinary power in the world known as growth. One scientist
has figured out that the growth of an ordinary root, three feet long
and three inches in diameter, is capable of exerting fifty tons of
pressure.

And yet root power is largely unseen, and frequently we are
unaware of either its existence or its importance. We are much
more conscious of that part of the operation of nature and of life
that we see above the ground. We understand the wonders and the
benefits that come from the tree's frame, on which are produced its
foliage, flowers, fragrance, and fruit. But very frequently we fail to
appreciate the beneficial functions of that productive part of life
that operates below the level of our sight. The roots provide plants
and trees with one of their chief sources of nourishment. They also
provide the tree's primary mechanical support. A giant redwood has
been known to raise its bulky trunk over 300 feet into the air. In
one redwood, enough lumber may be manufactured to construct
many entire houses.

Isn't it interesting to try to imagine the kind of root system that such a tree needs. First, the root must hold the tree's great lever-like body firm against the millions of tons of pressure sent against it by the most fierce winds. The root of a giant redwood must also send its magic root fingers through a very large area of earth to search out the right elements in the right combinations and amounts in order to keep this tremendously important manufacturing process in operation. In the course of a normal day's work, a giant redwood sends hundreds of tons of sap flowing upward, in seeming violation of the laws of gravity. Some of this sap not only flows 300 feet into the air, but it also originates a great distance below the surface of the ground.

This growth process is not just one of the wonders of the world, it seems also to be carried on without any outside assistance or supervision. This tree has had no previous education in growing; it has no book of instructions; it gets no pay raises; it has no strikes, no absenteeism, and no morale problems. It needs no coffee breaks, makes no miscalculations in its engineering, and has no labor-management disputes. Most human businesses are usually very short-lived. Even nations often do not survive intact for very long, but some of these giant redwoods have gone on happily growing and prospering for over 3,000 years.

Of course, the roots of different plants serve different ends. The roots of carrots, sugar beets, turnips, potatoes, onions, and radishes not only perform the regular function of roots, but they also serve as storage reservoirs, where their high-quality manufactured products are accumulated for future use. This great miracle of food produc-tion is not performed for the plant's own good. Carrots and potatoes do not have their own welfare in mind when they pack sunshine, vitamins, and health into their manufactured products. To me one of the evidences of man's divinity is that all of the efforts of these plants are devoted to the good of man, who lives in a higher order of existence than the plants themselves occupy.

It is also interesting that these plants do not duplicate the work of one another. The potato, the sugar beet, and the carrot may grow side by side under the same conditions, yet the specialty of one is to produce starch, another produces sugar, and the third concentrates Vitamin A.

But no matter how we may look at it, one of the most important wonders of the world is the work performed by a simple root, which is sometimes called the tap root. It serves as the tree's central support, collector distributor, and growing agency. It is also in exclusive charge of the tree's welfare below the ground. It supplies the tree with life and helps to produce its most worthwhile products.

A great tree supplies a very interesting comparison for our own growth. Men and women also depend very largely upon a kind of operation that we might refer to as our root functions. Nothing very important ever happens in our lives until we effectively get our roots down. Like an apple tree, a human being needs the equipment necessary to absorb the sunshine and other above-the-ground elements. We also need to be able to root into the soil a little bit for ourselves. We need to be able to reach into the depths of the unseen for strength, power, and growth.

A large part of our human success also comes from an unseen and largely unknown area. We are not fully aware of the source of our potential mental and spiritual powers. God has equipped us with instincts, a conscience, a spirit, and a great resource that we refer to as the subconscious mind. Like the potato, we also have a storage department where we store up ideals, faith, and ambitions for our future use. We know that man should not live by bread alone, and like a sugar beet, we have some warehouse space where the real food supply of our lives is kept. We do not always understand the details of this great process of inspiration that so greatly enriches our lives. The mysterious abilities of our minds and spirits reach out through the universe to bring back to us all of its law, beauty, and harmony.

We have a miraculous ability to grow spiritually as well as physically. The human mind is one of the greatest known inventors. Out of the brain of Thomas A. Edison came a whole string of electric lights, phonographs, refrigerators, and hundreds of other things that no one had ever thought of before. The human personality is also a great creator. And out of the human heart we can get honor, love, ambition, and courage from a God-given supply. We might say that it was the root functions of Abraham Lincoln that lifted him from the dirt floor of a log cabin and made him stand like a giant redwood above his fellows.

One of the most provocative of the parables of Jesus also had its main focus in the root functions of life. He told of a sower who went forth to sow. Some of the seeds fell by the wayside and were eaten up by fowls. Some fell upon stony places where, because of insufficient soil, the root system failed to function. Some of the other seeds sprouted, but their roots were inadequate to keep them from being scorched by the sun, so they withered away. But the seeds that fell in good ground had no trouble, because they got their roots down into the soil and then nothing could stop them. Jesus pointed out that these plants "brought forth fruit, some an hundred-fold, and some sixtyfold and some thirtyfold." (Matthew 13:3-9.)

In this parable about the sower, three cases of failure are mentioned, as opposed to only one case of success, and the differences between them were caused by what the roots did or did not do. When the roots failed to supply sufficient water and nourishment, the plants had no success or permanence. Jesus used his parables to point out lessons for our lives. He was trying to help us to understand that we fail or succeed in about the same way as the plants. When we don't learn to get our roots down, we may be scorched by the sun, smothered by the thorns, or gobbled up by the birds. More than about anything else in our lives, we need the equivalent of a good vigorous root system grounded in righteousness.

The hardy pine at Bright Angel Point had a tap root that was sufficiently vigorous to survive and grow strong under very unfavorable conditions. It also had enough power to split the canyon. When this particular seed began to grow, it was very small. It requires five thousand of the seeds of the giant redwood tree to weigh a single ounce. But with a good root system, these tiny seeds are capable of producing the largest living things on the earth, and they are able to stand up against the most severe winds that have ever blown in the last three thousand years.

In the old days out on the farm, I used to be very impressed by the treatment given the young sugar beet plants. By the time they were thinned, the ground would usually be getting pretty dry. When the young plants began to get thirsty, they started crying for water. As the soil lost more of its moisture by evaporation, the young plants would frequently wilt and lie flat on the ground during the heat of the day, appearing as though they were dead. It seemed to me that if it was not already too late, they should be irrigated immediately. However, I learned the interesting fact that as soon as a young plant feels an urgent need for moisture, it starts sending its tap root deeper and deeper into the soil. Then, when it has just about gone its limit and its search for moisture has added as much as possible to its length, it is irrigated and it then becomes a long large beet, instead of just a little nubbin on the top of the ground.

All too frequently that also represents our own situation. We need enough depth to be able to get our own water supply. Sometimes when life makes us too many gifts, we are like the sugar beet that gets "too much too soon," and then we may think that we have no need to develop a more adequate root system of our own; consequently, we become nubbins on the surface of life. Then sometimes, when the sun scorches us a little bit, we become deadbeats and die like those mentioned in the parable. Jesus talked a great deal about our drinking of the waters of life. This requires roots, and it is only when we get them down deep that we locate some of the most important sources of strength and power. This is also the way we gather together those magic success elements that guarantee an abundant life.

Of course, our roots carry only a part of the responsibility for our success. And the scripture tells of several occasions when, in spite of good roots, the tree's branches still produced no fruit, and therefore they were pruned out and burned. Then more productive branches were grafted in to take their places. But when something goes wrong with the roots, the entire tree is in trouble. Through Isaiah, the Lord told of some people whose roots were infected with rottenness. About the only treatment for rotten roots is to use the tree as firewood and start over.

The Prophet Job tells of another problem. He speaks of people whose roots had dried up, and then their whole lives become useless. (Job 18:16.) In a disturbing prophecy now awaiting fulfillment, the Lord said through Malachi, "For, behold, the day cometh, that shall burn as an oven, and all the proud, yea, and all that do wickedly, shall be stubble: and the day that cometh shall burn them up, saith the Lord of hosts, that it shall leave them neither root nor branch." (Mal. 4:1.)

A great deal of the thinking that Jesus did about our success was in a sort of horticultural sense. He said, "I am the true vine, and my Father is the husbandman. Every branch in me that beareth not fruit he taketh away: and every branch that beareth fruit, he purgeth it, that it may bring forth more fruit." (John 15:1-2.) He also described our need for pruning and other kinds of care, that we might learn to produce. In what may have been his most fundamental statement, Jesus said, "By their fruits shall ye know them." To bring forth good fruit, we must have good branches, but we should also make sure that we have a root system capable of supporting the crop that our lives are expected to produce. And the roots largely influence all other functions.

The Apostle Paul said to the Romans, "If the roots are holy, the branches are likely to be holy also." (Rom. 11:16.) Probably the best way to develop holy roots is to make sure that we get them down deep into the fertile soil of truth and righteousness. If our lives are rooted in sin and ignorance, our chances for success are greatly reduced, and we run the risk of being thrown into the fire mentioned by Jesus. Shakespeare speaks of a "rooted sorrow," and Paul taught the Hebrews about what happened when roots are filled with bitterness. (Hebrews 12:15.) We should also make sure that we do not allow ourselves to get root-bound, because we have provided too small a space for growth; it is pretty difficult to grow a giant redwood in a flower pot.

May our root system be such that we may reach into the deep, rich soil of the gospel and produce in ourselves the fruit of an abundant eternal life.

The Temple of God

IT IS AN INTERESTING FACT THAT NO ONE HAS EVER SEEN HIS OWN spirit, and yet that is the primary part of every individual. The human spirit is the most important thing in the universe. In its absence there is no intelligence, no personality, no activity, and no life.

Isn't it strange that one of the things that we know less about than anything else in the world is our own individual selves. You can ask a man questions about science, invention, or history, and he will answer you. But if you ask him to write out an analysis of himself and tell you about his mind and soul qualities, you may not get a very good answer. Or suppose we ask ourselves why we do the things that we do when we believe the things that we believe. Or suppose we try to define the purpose of life or try to understand our own divine origin or destiny.

Significantly enough, the only subject that we know less about than ourselves is God, our Eternal Father. Because of the relationship that exists between us, man and God can best be studied together, and the most reliable information on both subjects is of divine origin.

There are many scriptures proclaiming the fact that God is "the Father of spirits," (Num. 16:22, 27:16; Hebrews 12:9), and everything that we know about the laws of heredity indicates that the offspring may eventually hope to become like the parent. What a stimulant it should give to our interest in life and how greatly it should improve our self-image to know who we are. The scripture also makes it clear that Jesus Christ is the first begotten Son of God in the spirit. (I Cor. 1:12.) Consequently, he is our elder brother. He was also the most capable of God's spirit children, and therefore in the grand council of heaven, he was ordained to be the Savior of the world and the Redeemer of men. He was also ordained to be the Only Begotten Son of God in the flesh.

It helps to answer many questions about ourselves when we understand that the human spirit is of great antiquity. Nothing is more plainly written in the scripture than the fact that the life of

Christ did not begin at Bethlehem; neither did it end at Calvary. It is just as plainly written that *our* lives did not begin when we were born; neither will they end when we die. William Wordsworth said,

> Our birth is but a sleep and a forgetting;
> The Soul that rises with us, our life's Star,
> Hath had elsewhere its setting
> And cometh from afar;
> Not in entire forgetfulness,
> And not in utter nakedness,
> But trailing clouds of glory do we come
> From God, who is our home.

Mortality is only one link in a well-integrated program of eternal progression. We had been endowed with a personality and had acquired great intelligence long before our mortal birth. In our pre-mortal existence, as in this life, we had our free agency; and we had a vote in determining the program for our own futures. We were a part of that great council at which Christ was chosen and ordained to be the Savior of the world.

In referring to this appointment, Peter says that we are redeemed "with the precious blood of Christ, as of a lamb without blemish and without spot: Who verily was foreordained before the foundation of the world." (I Pet. 1:19-20.) In fact, it was through him and by him that the earth itself was created for our benefit. John says, "All things were made by him; and without him was not any thing made that was made." (John 1:3.) But even then, he was no novice as a creator. In a revelation to Moses revealed anew in our day, God says, "Worlds without number have I created; . . . And by the Son I created them, which is mine Only Begotten." (Moses 1:33.)

Everyone had his own work to do in the spirit world, and many of God's other children also rose to great heights of accomplishment. In a revelation to Abraham, the Lord permitted him to see his own pre-existence, which Abraham describes as follows: "Now the Lord had shown unto me, Abraham, the intelligences that were organized before the world was; and among all these there were many of the noble and great ones;

"And God saw these souls that they were good, and he stood in the midst of them, and he said: These I will make my rulers; for he stood among those that were spirits, and he saw that they were good; and he said unto me: Abraham, thou art one of them; thou wast chosen before thou wast born.

"And there stood one among them one who was like unto God, and he said unto those who were with him: We will go down, for there is space there, and we will take of these materials, and we will make an earth whereupon these may dwell;

"And we will prove them herewith, to see if they will do all things whatsoever the Lord their God shall command them;

"And they who keep their first estate shall be added upon; and they who keep not their first estate shall not have glory in the same kingdom with those who keep their first estate; and they who keep their second estate shall have glory added upon their heads for ever and ever." (Abr. 3:22-26.)

The scripture tells us that all did not fulfill God's success requirements in their first estate. Lucifer the Light Bearer, the brilliant Son of the Morning, rebelled against God and led away one-third of the hosts of heaven after him. As a part of their condemnation, their progress was stopped, and they were denied the privilege of being "added upon" with the tremendous benefit of a mortal body also formed in God's image.

Of course, this was a serious tragedy for them; for as wonderful as the spirit is, it is incomplete when it is alone. Although Jesus was the most worthy, the most intelligent, and the most powerful Son of God, yet before his mortal birth he was also a spirit. A spirit body is made of finer material, but we all looked forward to the day when we could be added upon with this necessary body of flesh and bones.

Some 2200 years before he was born in Bethlehem, Jesus revealed himself to an ancient prophet known to us as the brother of Jared. The ante-mortal Christ said to him, "Seest thou that ye are created after mine own image? Yea, even all men were created in the beginning after mine own image." Then he said, "This body, which ye now behold, is the body of my spirit; and man have I created after the body of my spirit; and even as I appear unto thee to be in the spirit will I appear unto my people in the flesh." (Ether 3:15-16.)

We were so delighted at the prospect of being added upon that, as the scripture says, "All of the sons of God shouted for joy." (Job 38:1-7.) Mortality brings us one step nearer to the time when through the resurrection the spirit and body will be inseparably connected so that we can receive a fullness of joy. But in God's program this development could not all be brought about all at once. For reasons best known to God, the association of the spirit and the body in mortality was to be on a temporary basis. It was necessary that the body and the spirit should be separated by death in preparation for the final cleansing and education preceding our resurrection and final exaltation.

It is thought that we may do ourselves a severe injustice by underestimating the importance of the body. Mortality has sometimes been looked on as an imprisonment. Too often the body has been despised by the religionists. But Jesus regarded the body as a holy temple. Certainly it is absolutely necessary for our maximum eternal happiness. The Apostle Paul said to the Corinthians, "Know ye not that ye are the temple of God, and that the Spirit of God dwelleth in you? If any man defile the temple of God, him shall God destroy; for the temple of God is holy, which temple ye are." (I Cor. 3:16-17.) Again he said, "Your body is the temple of the Holy Ghost which is in you, which ye have of God, and ye are not your own." (I Cor. 6:19.) We should be very careful when we are entrusted with the use of property that is not ours.

Next only to the human spirit, the body is the most marvelous piece of equipment ever devised or imagined. Think of these tremendous instruments that we call hands. Or think of the reason, vision, imagination, and circulation system of man. When an individual is born, he may weigh seven pounds, and yet he has thousands of little blood vessels running in all directions—each one functioning perfectly, with the proper supply of fluid. All are hermetically sealed. Suppose we try to understand his construction in the period before birth. Imagine, if you can, when this circulation system began to operate, and who determined the size of the pipes, and how they were kept from being mashed shut. Who was the overseer of construction, and why do they never clog or congeal?

Or try to understand the human nervous system. It is far more mysterious than electricity, and far more wonderful. The nerves reach to every part of the body, and the slightest sensations are picked up by them and transmitted to that great central intelligence station, the brain, where they can be interpreted and acted upon. If a nerve is severed, it heals itself and resumes operations.

Then there are the eyes of man; they are perfectly located in the place giving the most advantageous view. Both are perfectly coordinated. They take thousands of photographs every day in full color and in three dimension. Their adjustment to light is automatic. They close in a flash if any harm is threatened to the eye. They sometimes last for a hundred years without lubrication, without cleaning, without adjustment, without photographic supplies. The eyes are said to be the windows of the soul, and in turn they play many characters. They twinkle with merriment, or they blaze with anger; they beam with love, or they dilate with scorn; they sparkle with hope and eagerness, or they are dull with despair; they shine with admiration, or they are clouded by a film of sadness; and sometimes they become bloodshot with sin, or dead with disease.

Then there is that master wonder, the brain. The brain of an ordinary man weighs about three pounds and is probably the size of my two hands. The brain is made up of 14 billion cells. It can contain more information than can be put in ten truckloads of books. A prominent British neurophysicist recently said that you could not construct an electronic computer the equivalent of a human brain for three billion dollars. The brain is the most wonderful problem-solver. It is the greatest inventor. It is the finest source of contentment and happiness.

Then there are the character, the personality, and the emotions of man wherein lie the greatest possible opportunities for research and development. Here is a source of wealth greater than is had in all of the diamond mines or oil fields.

Man is the only one of God's creations with the ability to smile. An electric lineman once came in contact with a live wire, which paralyzed the left half of his face. During the following trial the judge asked him to smile, and as a result the court awarded him damages of $50,000. If a half of a smile is worth $50,000, how much is a whole smile worth? We might try to imagine what our abilities for love, faith, devotion, and happiness are worth, and how their use, either here or hereafter, would be handicapped without this tremendous creation of the body. Then try to imagine what this Godly creation will be like when it is purified, resurrected, glorified, and made beautiful beyond all imagination as it vibrates with eternal life. We might say with Shakespeare:

What a piece of work is man,
How noble in reason,
How infinite in faculty,
In form and moving how express and admirable;
In action how like an angel,

In apprehension how like a god.

(Hamlet, Act II, Scene 2)

And we might add, How indeed!

This tremendous physical creation is the indispensable counterpart of the eternal spirit. The spirit is an architect that molds the body into its likeness and stature.

Only by proper care of the body and its auxiliaries of mind and personality is it possible to achieve the greatest eternal joy. And what possibilities one denies himself when he fails to realize the advantages of the sight, hearing, feeling, and other sensations that belong only to a well-educated, well-cared-for body. Without this perfection of body, it is impossible to enjoy the delicious freshness of morning, or to revel in the invigorating sunshine of noonday, or to enjoy the calm peace of the evening time. What a delight to know the pure pleasure that comes to us when our physical selves' are in perfect condition. Our minds are like search lights to pierce the clouds of doubt and to show us the glory beyond. What treasures of satisfaction await us if we keep sacred this holy temple of God!

The Trumpeter

O N THE CENTER SPIRE OF THE EAST END OF THE SALT LAKE
Temple, 210 feet above the earth, is the statue of an angel.
It faces the east with a great trumpet pressed to its lips, as though
to sound a message to all the world. The statue is covered with leaf
gold, and as the last rays of the declining sun shine across the lake
and western mountains, an impressive luster radiates from this
angelic symbol. This interesting figure is a representation of Moroni,
the last of a long line of prophets living in pre-Columbus America.
In the final battle of his people, fought in 384 A.D., Moroni was
second in command to his great father, Mormon. In this conflict the
more righteous element of a once great civilization was destroyed.
And by divine decree, Moroni alone was spared in order to prepare
their history and prophetic writings, that we who now live might
have a knowledge of God's dealings with those who occupied our
choice land before us.

This great record is called the Book of Mormon. It was written
by God's prophets in ancient America, much as the Bible was
written by those who occupied the eastern continent. The writings
were made on metallic plates, and were hidden up unto the Lord by
the Prophet Moroni in the year 421 A.D., just before his death.
Fourteen hundred and seven years later, this same Moroni, now a
resurrected, glorified being, was sent back to the earth to make
known the record's hiding place. Then, by the gift and power of
God, it was translated into English by the Prophet Joseph Smith.

Moroni fulfilled a great mission to our civilization, which had
been foreseen by John the Revelator during his lonely exile on the
Isle of Patmos. All of the other apostles chosen by Jesus had already
been put to death, and the great apostasy from God was well under
way. In describing his vision of our day, John said, "And I saw
another angel fly in the midst of heaven, having the everlasting
gospel to preach unto them that dwell upon the earth, and to every
nation, and kindred, and tongue, and people, Saying with a loud
voice, Fear God, and give glory to him, for the hour of his judgment
is come." (Rev. 14:6-7.)

The Savior himself referred to this restoration as one of those events that should precede the Lord's glorious second coming to the earth, when he said, "And this gospel of the kingdom shall be preached in all the world as a witness unto all nations, and then shall the end come." (Matt. 24:14.) This angelic messenger sounding his trumpet is a visual symbol of the message that under divine direction is presently going forth among men.

Throughout history the trumpet has been the instrument by which many great proclamations have been made. Just before the Lord gave the Ten Commandments from the top of Mount Sinai, the record says, "And it came to pass on the third day in the morning, that there were thunders and lightnings, and a thick cloud upon the mount, and the voice of the trumpet exceeding loud; so that all the people that was in the camp trembled. And Moses brought forth the people out of the camp to meet with God." Then God gave the people their law. (Exod. 19:16-17.)

There are several figurative Bible passages where the one who acts as a spokesman is called a watchman or a trumpeter. He is the one who calls people's attention to the great truths, and sounds the warning when they do wrong. On one occasion the Prophet Ezekiel said, "The word of the Lord came unto me, saying, Son of man, speak unto the children of thy people, and say unto them, set [a man up to be a] watchman: If when he seeth the sword come upon the land, he blow the trumpet, and warn the people; Then whosoever heareth the sound of the trumpet, and taketh not warning; if the sword come, and take him away, his blood shall be upon his own head. . . . But he that taketh warning shall deliver his soul. But if the watchman see the sword come, and blow not the trumpet, and the people be not warned; if the sword come, and take any person from among them, he is taken away in his iniquity; but his blood will I require at the watchman's hand."

Then the Lord said to Ezekiel, "Son of man, I set thee a watchman unto the house of Israel; therefore thou shalt hear the word at my mouth, and warn them from me. When I say unto the wicked, O wicked man, thou shalt surely die; if thou dost not speak to warn the wicked from his way, that wicked man shall die in his iniquity; but his blood will I require at thine hand. Nevertheless, if thou warn the wicked, . . . and he do not turn from his way, he shall die in his iniquity; but thou has delivered thy soul." (Ezek. 33:1-9.)

In our own day, we stand on the edge of momentous events. The greatest possible physical, as well as spiritual, dangers are all around us. More than ever before we should be aware of the warning trumpet calls from God. We might represent his message and indicate our own cooperation in the words of a sacred song, which says:

Hark! listen to the trumpeters!
They sound for volunteers.
On Zion's bright and flowery bank
Behold the officers.

Their horses white, their armor bright,
With courage bold they stand,
Enlisting soldiers for their King
To march to Zion's land.

It sets my heart all in a flame
A soldier brave to be;
I will enlist, gird on my arms,
And fight for liberty.

We want no cowards in our bands
Who will our colors fly.
We call for valiant-hearted men
Who're not afraid to die.

To see our armies on parade,
How martial they appear!
All armed and dressed in uniform
They look like men of war.

They follow their great General,
The great Eternal Lamb;
His garments stained in his own blood,
King Jesus is his name.

The trumpets sound, the armies shout,
They drive the hosts of hell,
How dreadful is our God, our King,
The great Emanuel!

Sinners, enlist with Jesus Christ,
Th'eternal Son of God,
And march with us to Zion's land,
Beyond the swelling flood.

The other day, I thought of this Bible symbolism of the trumpeter as I listened to a young man tell about his experience in the army. One of the things that impressed him about military life was the use of the bugle. Promptly at 6 a.m., the bugler sounded reveille, which was the signal for everyone to get up and dress in preparation for the work of the day. A little later the mess call was heard, which meant that everyone should present himself ready for breakfast. If there was any group instruction to be given that day, the bugler sounded assembly, which meant that the soldiers were to gather quickly at the meeting place. There were many other calls meaning other things. One bugle sound meant "forward march"; one meant to prepare for battle. Sometimes the bugler sounds a "retreat," and sometimes he trumpets a "charge." Every warrior likes to hear those thrilling bugle notes announcing that victory has been won. Then in each case, after the work of each day has been completed, the bugler plays "taps." This means that all lights should be out and all soldiers should be in their beds.

When I was very young, I attended a Boy Scout camp, and each night I liked to listen to the peaceful notes of the bugler high up on the hillside in the moonlight, sounding taps. And even now at the end of the day, I often hum the words:

> Day is done, gone the sun,
> From the lake, from the hills, from the sky.
> All is well, safely rest, God is nigh.
> Failing light dims the sight,
> And the stars in the sky say,
> "Good night."

There are some soldiers in the army and in life who don't respond very faithfully to the calls of the bugler. Some resent doing even the right things in order and on a schedule. There are soldiers who don't want to go to bed at night, and they are never quite ready to get up in the morning. Some soldiers in life never get very enthusiastic about those calls meaning "forward march." And frequently we spend too much time in "retreat and surrender." But whether our interest is military, business, or religious, if success is to be achieved, it is necessary that we understand the regulations and respond to them with an orderly obedience and timeliness.

Solomon said, "To every thing there is a season, and a time to every purpose under heaven; A time to be born, and a time to die; a time to plant, and a time to pluck up that which is planted; A time to kill, and a time to heal; A time to break down, and a time to build up; A time to weep, and a time to laugh; a time to mourn, and a time to dance; . . . A time to embrace, and a time to refrain from embracing; a time to get, and a time to lose; a time to keep, and a time to cast away; A time to rend, and a time to sew; a time to keep silence, and a time to speak; A time to love, and a time to hate; a time of war, and a time of peace." (Eccl. 3:1-8.)

There is also a time to listen to the word of the Lord and a time to repent of our sins. The warnings from God's trumpets are always made in our own interests. God communicates with us through the words of the sacred scripture and the directions of the Church that he has established upon the earth. He has also given us a kind of direct wire of conscience and the still, small voice of the Spirit. But we must not ignore the bugle calls sounded by the watchmen who are upon the walls. It would certainly not be very good military procedure if the commanding officer had to write each soldier a personal letter informing him of an assembly or to call him on the telephone to wake him up or to send a messenger to put him to bed.

Many of the teachings of Jesus were about his own glorious second coming to the earth. Just three days before his death, his disciples said, "Tell us, when shall these things be? and what shall be the sign of thy coming, and the destruction of the wicked which is the end of the world?" Jesus said to them, ". . . ye shall hear of wars and rumours of wars: see that ye be not troubled: for all these things must come to pass, but the end is not yet. For nation shall rise against nation, and kingdom against kingdom: and there shall be famines, and pestilences, and earthquakes, in divers places. . . .

"And then shall many be offended, and shall betray one another, and shall hate one another. And many false prophets shall rise, and shall deceive many. And because iniquity shall abound, the love of many shall wax cold."

Then he gave that significant proclamation in which he said, "And this gospel of the kingdom shall be preached in all the world for a witness unto all nations; and then shall the end come." (Matt. 24:3-14.) Jesus said, "When [the fig tree] putteth forth leaves, ye know that summer is nigh. So likewise ye, when ye shall see all these things, know that it is, near even at the doors." (Matt. 24:32-33.)

Certainly we have enough signs about us that we ought to be sounding a few warnings of our own. Men and nations are hating each other with great intensity, and we have wars and troubles on every hand. Many people bear a fervent personal testimony that the gospel has been restored by divine command, and that it is now going forth.

In our own day the Lord has again foretold the end of our world as we know it. These events will also be the signals for many other important happenings. The Lord has said, "For a trump shall sound both long and loud, even as upon Mount Sinai, and all the earth shall quake, and they shall come forth—yea, even the dead which died in me, to receive a crown of righteousness, and to be clothed upon, even as I am, to be with me, that we may be one." (D&C 29:13.)

Again, the Lord said, "Behold, verily I say unto you, before the earth shall pass away, Michael mine archangel, shall sound his trump, and then shall all the dead awake, for their graves shall be opened, and they shall come forth—yea, even all." (D&C 29:26.)

He said, "The day cometh that the Lord shall utter his voice out of heaven; the heavens shall shake and the earth shall tremble, and the trump of God shall sound both long and loud, and shall say to the sleeping nations: Ye saints arise and live; ye sinners stay and sleep until I shall call again." (D&C 43:18.)

The Apostle Paul spoke of this great event to the Corinthians when he said, "In a moment, in the twinkling of an eye, at the last trump: for the trumpet shall sound, and the dead shall be raised incorruptible, and we shall be changed." (I Cor. 15:52.) Again Paul said, "The Lord himself shall descend from heaven with a shout, with the voice of the archangel, and with the trump of God, and the dead in Christ shall rise first." (I Thess. 4:16.)

If we live correctly now, we will be better prepared for the trumpet sound on that great and last day. In the meantime, we might be stimulated by the words of our own great "Battle Hymn of the Republic," in which we say:

> He has sounded forth his trumpet
> That shall never call retreat;
> He is sifting out the hearts of men
> Before his judgment seat.
>
> O be swift, my soul, to answer him;
> Be jubilant, my feet,
> For God is marching on.

As our own general, each of us should remind himself of his

great opportunity to be a good soldier and obey every one of God's commands in preparation for that great trumpet call that will some-day sound in our ears. And God will bless our lives if we will study and live those great gospel principles that he has revealed.

Woman Suffrage

IT IS UNFORTUNATELY TRUE THAT MARITAL PROBLEMS CAUSE A GREAT deal of the unhappiness, heartbreak, and pain that occurs among people. This is particularly true of that part of the human family that we sometimes refer to as the weaker sex. To many women and children the crime waves, delinquency problems, and immorality that we hear so much about have some very personal meanings, as they must usually bear the brunt of the unpleasant consequences.

Each day brings into our world of men a long series of new drunkenness, unfaithfulness, and weakness. The Lord himself has been greatly concerned about this problem, and through the ancient American Prophet Jacob, he said, "I will not suffer . . . that the cries of the fair daughters of this people, . . . shall come up unto me against the men of my people, saith the Lord of Hosts. . . . for they shall not commit whoredoms, like unto them of old. . . . save I shall visit them with a sore curse, even unto destruction." He said to them,"Ye have broken the tender hearts of your wives, and lost the confidence of your children, because of your bad examples before them; and the sobbings of their hearts ascend up to God against you." (Jacob 2:32-35.)

It seems that since Jacob's day our problems have not made many changes for the better. Each new day a vast throng of heavy-hearted women must suffer the mental depression caused by the bad tempers, domineering attitudes, and other personal weaknesses of their husbands. A great Bible text refers to the spiritual creation in heaven before the earth was formed, saying: "And God created man in his own image, in the image of God created he him, male and female created he them." All men and all women first existed in heaven. Then after earth life began, God established marriage as the primary relationship between the sexes. As God blessed the union that he had established, he ordained that male and female should be as one flesh, to serve jointly as the head of the basic family unit.

It was decreed in heaven that the marriage covenant and the family organization should be eternal, as when the first marriage was performed, death had not yet entered the world. The scripture also points out that "whatsoever God doeth, it shall last forever."

Marriage also provides for each spouse to be the custodian of the happiness of the other, and yet this very relationship is frequently used by each to bring pain and misery upon his mate. The broken families, the homicides, and the extreme unhappiness within some marriages cause our most destructive problems. Because women have more tender feelings and more delicate natures, they must endure more suffering and misery when subjected to this terrible weight of oppression and unhappiness. As the head of the family, one of the first duties of every husband is to make his wife and family as happy as God desires them to be.

In a little lighter vein someone once suggested that everyone should be kind to his wife, even if it did frighten her a little bit at first. Of course, one of the most important responsibilities of the gospel itself is to make people happy. There is a great scripture that says, "Men are, that they might have joy." No husband or no wife can be happy unless his mate is also happy. And the shortest way to accomplish this is by a process of mutual love and respect. William James, the great Harvard psychologist, pointed out our greatest need when he said that the deepest hunger in human beings is the desire to be appreciated. And certainly there is no success outside the home that can compensate for failure on the inside. This is particularly true so far as women are concerned. In order for them to have the best mental, physical, and spiritual health, they must know that they are loved, admired, and needed. And one of the places where many members of the male sex fall down most is in failing to develop this happiness in their wives. Even the public treatment of our women has never been such that we could be very proud of it.

Some time ago, I read a brief history of the woman suffrage movement that was prominently discussed throughout the country a few years ago. The dictionary describes suffrage as an intercessary prayer, a petition to God, a supplication for aid or assistance. In a political sense woman suffrage referred to the request of women for equal rights with men, and particularly for the right to vote. For generations our laws have indicated that men believed that women did not have sufficient judgment to assist in choosing a political candidate. The male attitude that a woman's reason was not equal to his has frustrated this female hunger for appreciation and caused her unhappiness.

For centuries women were largely confined to taking care of household duties. Generally they were denied the advantages of education and any kind of independence, either financial or otherwise. They have been bound down by social customs and traditions and have generally submitted themselves to the authority of men. This would not be quite so bad were it not for man's unrighteousness and the unhappiness that he brings upon both sexes as a consequence. Over the ages, women have not only been forbidden to vote; they have also been denied the privilege of speaking in public or even taking part in public betterment movements.

The most determined movement for woman suffrage in the United States began at about the time the temperance movement was getting underway. And one of the first groups of women was organized to fight the liquor interests and the male proneness to alcoholism that still afflicts our society. Women were forced to endure the oppression of drunken husbands in silence and live with the general degeneracy that always accompanies the use of alcohol. Even the Bible was interpreted by many as placing women in an inferior position. To compel a woman to live within such narrow limits has tended to make her feel like something less than a real person.

Then came the Revolutionary War, based on the fundamental principle that there should be no taxation without representation. This idea aroused in these awakening women a feeling that they should have a little more voice in what went on. If women were better behaved than men and shared in all of the hardships of men, why shouldn't they stand on a par as human beings? They were working with men in the fields and in the mills, in addition to caring for the children. Women were responsible for their sons getting an education in which they themselves could not share.

While John Adams was away from home attending the Continental Congress, he received a letter from Abigail, his wife, in which she said that she longed to hear about the formation of an independent nation and hoped that its new legal code would give more rights to women. She said to her husband, "I desire that you should be more generous and more favorable to the ladies than your ancestors were. I hope that you will not put such unlimited powers into the hands of husbands. Remember that all men would be tyrants if they could." She reminded her husband that if some consideration was not given to the ladies, they were determined to foment a rebellion. Nor would they hold themselves bound to obey any laws in which they had no voice.

During some early-day periods, daughters were not even permitted to inherit property if there were any sons in the family. Under early Roman laws a husband could condemn his wife to death for certain offenses even without a public trial, but because husbands so greatly abused even this law, it had to be changed. Men have never quite been willing to give up the philosophy behind this law. And almost every day the newspapers tell of some wife or ex-wife having been killed by her husband.

Anyone who does very much marriage counseling knows that even though husbands have been deprived of the privilege of condemning their wives to death, yet they frequently condemn them to misery by tormenting them with drunkenness, immorality and various kinds of personal weakness. Not the least of these weaknesses is the one mentioned by Abigail, that all men would be tyrants if they could. One young woman recently said that she had given up any idea of marrying, because the tyranny of her father had given her such a revolting opinion of men generally. Even in comparatively recent times, the power of initiating a divorce was held exclusively by the husband. And in the present many women endure physical and mental cruelty, sex oppression, and other indignities that are almost unbearable to her.

From the time of Plato and before, there had been individual protests made against the subjugation and mistreatment of women. In recent years the champions for women's rights have become more numerous and their expressions more intense. And yet, women have done a great many wonderful things. Women carried a great deal of the burden of responsibility for winning the Revolutionary War.

They were also among the leading exponents for freeing the slaves. In 1837 the first women's anti-slavery convention was held in New York. But as these forces of women began to get organized, they also began thinking about their own general development and the extension of their own rights. A world anti-slavery convention was held in London in June 1849, attended by eight women delegates from the U.S., and they were not permitted to vote. Eight years later these same women called for a public discussion of women's rights. They prepared their own declaration, modeled after the Declaration of Independence, and set up resolutions enumerating practically every right that women presently enjoy. The convention met in New York July 19-20, 1849, and the idea of woman suffrage was officially on its way.

It is to their honor that some of the first timid attempts of women speaking in public and taking part in conventions were made in behalf of temperance, freedom for the slaves, and the emancipation of women. However, the opposition that they met in state and national legislatures was immense. The National Association for Women Suffrage presented its message before every Congress from 1869 to 1919. They also conducted 56 campaigns to amend state constitutions, and a volume could be written about their hardships and disappointments. The 19th Amendment to the Constitution of the United States was finally adopted, guaranteeing equal rights for women.

With their increased opportunities, a remarkable group of women arose during the last part of the nineteenth century. The first woman physician, Elizabeth Blackwell, was graduated in 1848, and women found their way into many important fields previously forbidden to them. Some of the great women of this period were Harriet Hosmer, Maria Mitchell, Harriet Beecher Stowe, Julia Ward Howe, Clara Barton, Frances Willard, Jane Addams, Elizabeth Stanton, Susan B. Anthony, Carrie Chapman, and many others.

Someone once asked what men would be without women. And the answer was humorously given that they would be "mighty scarce." But without women we would also lose a lot of other important advantages. All men owe their lives to women, and most men also owe their success, their comfort, their righteousness, and their happiness to the women in their lives. As a rule, women are far more spiritual than men and have greater culture. They are more gentle. God made them more beautiful than men in body and also in mind and spirit. They are more righteous and probably more industrious. But even yet, many women are still being oppressed, degraded, and having their hearts broken by the men whom God created in his own image to be the leaders, champions, and ennoblers of women.

God also endowed every man with an interesting self-improvement instinct. Certainly one purpose of this instinct is to make him worthy of his wife. As a young man prepares to enter the courting period, he gets a natural urge to wash his face, comb his hair, and clean himself up generally. What a helpful idea it would be if we would enlarge this attitude and keep it in full force throughout our lives.

There is one uplifting custom that in the presence of women

men should uncover their heads. This attitude helps to build respect for women more solidly into our lives. But the honor in which women should be held has had some setbacks because women have not always lived up to their possibilities. The story is told of one man who took off his hat when he entered an elevator with two women. But after listening to their conversation for a few minutes, he put his hat back on his head again.

Man himself is ennobled and built up as he puts good women up on pedestals as the objects of love, faith, and appreciation. This might be a good place to apply the quaint Quaker statement of John Greenleaf Whittier, who said, "Me lift thee and thee lift me, and we will both ascend together." Neither man nor woman can be exalted in the highest of God's kingdoms alone. And the higher that women are lifted up, the better off the lives of men will be.

The scriptures say that God delighteth in the chastity of women. He also delights in their general welfare and happiness. And we pray that God will help us to exalt the lives of both women and men and to give each a greater vote in the welfare of all.

The World's First Book

ALL OF OUR LIVES WE HAVE TALKED ABOUT THE SUBSTANTIAL values in that great book called the Holy Bible. The Bible is probably the world's most useful and worthwhile resource. It accounts for much of the differences found in human lives. As a measure of its meaning, we might make a comparison between the Christian attitudes of the American founding fathers and the objectives held by such Godless, atheistic men as Hitler, Stalin, and some of our present-day dictators. There are men living even in our enlightened age who, if they thought they could, would enslave the entire world without a moment's hesitation. We see a reflection of Bible values as Abraham Lincoln translated its benefits and made them serve his country's welfare. Many other great men have been able to extract these virtues and make them negotiable in individual lives.

Various surveys show that a large percentage of the people who live in the United States at least *claim* to believe in the Bible. Many accept this great book as the word of God. Of course, there is a much smaller number who effectively study it and do what it says, so that they get its fullest benefit. It is comparatively easy to believe in the Bible as a distant object of our adoration. When it sits unopened on the shelf, the effect of its doctrines is often too indefinite to cause a conflict in our minds. And when there is no pressure to put its commandments in actual operation, we are inclined to think it is a wonderful book.

But when the Bible is opened with its doctrines exposed and its philosophies inviting our practice, then we sometimes lose some of our enthusiasm and turn our backs. Therefore, even though the Bible remains our greatest possession, we are still losing much of its value as we lack a full acceptance of its theology and a full utilization of its religion. When we follow any process of *partial* enthusiasm for the Bible or *fractional* obedience to its doctrines, we are to that extent wasting one of the greatest of our national resources. This might be more than ordinarily tragic, because the benefits of the Bible are available to the most humble without the necessity of raising taxes, increasing the work week, lessening the gold reserves, or even trimming the family budget.

The Bible is not only the world's first book of religion; it is also the world's first book of philosophy. It is the world's first book of history. It is the world's first book of literature. Most of the great writers repeatedly refer to the Bible. Jesus quoted from the Old Testament 89 times. The works of Shapespeare contain 550 quotations and allusions to the Bible. The writings of Emerson are filled with Bible ideas and philosophies. The poetry of Tennyson contains 330 Bible references.

The Bible is one of the most significant miracles of all ages. Most of the textbooks on science that were written fifteen years ago are now almost entirely out of date. The success principles and methods used in agriculture, manufacturing, engineering, medicine, and business are constantly being changed and corrected. But God's great truths never need correction. And even though the Bible was written when the camel was our chief means of transportation, yet in many respects this book is even more up to date than it would have been if it had been written today, as a very large number of the events discussed in the Bible are still awaiting fulfillment. The Bible contains many inspired teachings about the relationship existing between God and ourselves. Some of its history concerns a period of time before this earth was created; on the other hand, many of its instructions were written specifically for our own day and beyond.

Some Bible prophecies are presently being fulfilled before our own eyes. And in other chapters we may look ahead to such overwhelming events as the cleansing of this earth by fire in preparation for the glorious coming of Christ with his holy angels, to reign upon the earth during its promised millennium of a thousand years of peace. The Bible also tells of such personal events as our own resurrection and the conditions surrounding our future eternal destiny. In the United States alone during the last ten years, more than two hundred novels have been written that are based on Bible events. And in the next ten years other hundreds will be written. Every week thousands of ministers, statesmen, and philosophers use Bible texts and illustrations as the basis of their most scholarly preachments and dissertations.

The Bible is also the world's first book of success. In a period of less than one year the great New York Times ran 367 editorials based on Bible passages. But the wisdom of the Bible has scarcely been touched. There are thousands of inspiring stories, commandments, and philosophies capable of molding the lives and changing the attitudes and activities of everyone who will make an effort to get on intimate terms with them. The Bible is the world's first book of drama. The great plays of Shakespeare and many others have run for years at a time in the world's greatest theaters. Half of Shakespeare's plays were tragedies, and the others were called comedies. In those days a comedy was not a funny play; it was a play that had a happy ending. But every event in the Bible was intended to contribute to a "happy ending" for human life. The Bible teaches on both the positive and negative sides of success. It tells us what we ought to do, as well as what should be avoided.

The people of Noah's day acted out the earth's greatest tragedy on a worldwide scale and made it unnecessary for us to repeat their mistakes. Other tragic performances have been built around Babel, Sodom, and Rome, as well as the great empires of Babylon, Greece, and Persia. There are the individual tragedies of Cain, Nebuchadnezzar, King Saul, and Judas that warn us against repetition. These Bible plays furnish us the cues for developing in us those wonderful qualities of courage, excellence, and righteousness that will lead us to celestial glory in God's presence.

Some time ago in admiring a great portrait, I noticed that no matter where the viewer stood, the eyes of the person in the picture always seemed to be focused upon him. This is also an interesting characteristic of the Bible. It has a kind of personal focus that always puts the reader in an individual spotlight. There are many great books of science, philosophy, and fiction that have little meaning for us personally. But the Golden Rule, the Ten Commandments, the Beatitudes, etc., seem to have been written for us individually. The doctrines of faith, repentance, baptism, spiritual excellence, eternal love, and everlasting happiness all have a personal and individual meaning. Isn't it interesting that this great book, written in ancient times in a foreign land, should belong to us in such a distinctive, personal way. It not only looks forward to our personal improvement, but a much bigger percentage of people in the United States presently read, study, and are influenced by the Bible than is true of the people of any other land, including Palestine and the other areas where so much of it was written.

A number of years ago an article was written about the Bible entitled "The Book That Has Helped Most in Business." Again we see this strange paradox of a book being written before the printing press and before the establishment of any school of business, written among a people unnoted for their business procedures, and yet having such a profound effect on modern America in developing business techniques that are among the wonders of the world. The Bible has been a material factor in raising our standards of living far above anything ever known by those who lived in Bible times.

A few years ago the Harvard Graduate School of Business gathered together over a thousand of the top business leaders of the United States. One of them was former General Lucius D. Clay, later head of the Continental Canning Corporation. He gave a talk before this large convention entitled, "The Art of Delegation." He took his text from a Bible event that occurred 1500 years B.C. Moses was given the leadership of a great group of former slaves with the objective of making them the chosen people of the Lord. But Moses was settling most of their disputes and doing much of their other work for them personally which resulted in delay, confusion, and discontent. Then Jethro said to Moses, "The thing thou doest is not good." This ancient priest then laid out a program for the delegation of the authority of Moses, which effectively solved their problems. And 3,454 years afterward, this event was used to inspire a group of America's sharpest business leaders. Most American leaders use the Bible and its philosophies in their daily work. A great American sales manager recently gave his company salesmen some instructions in salesmanship in which he also used Moses as an example.

When Moses was starting across the desert with his vast company of people, he needed someone who knew the desert to serve as their guide. There was a man living on the edge of the desert by the name of Hobab, whose services Moses desired to obtain. Moses said to him, "Hobab, come with us, and we will do thee good." But Hobab said, "I will not go." However, because Moses needed Hobab, he tried again. But this time he altered his approach and said, "Hobab, come with us, that thou mayest be as eyes to us in the wilderness." In this he used an entirely different appeal.

When Moses had tried to induce Hobab, saying, "We will do thee good," Hobab was not impressed. Most people are not greatly attracted by "do-gooder" programs. Yet we are still making this kind of appeal in many places today, frequently without great success. For example, we say to a prospective church member, "You come to church, and we will do thee good." In other words, we say we are all nice people, and it would do you good to be associated with us. That may be a great idea, but its appeal usually doesn't have very much power. But when Moses said, "Come with us, that thou mayest be as eyes to us in the wilderness," he was saying, "Hobab, come and be our leader. You know the desert better than we do, and we may get lost without you to show us the way.

Translated into our language this says, "You come and teach this class in religion or lead this cultural or recreational group. You have an ability that we don't have, and we need you to be our eyes in the wilderness." This service appeal was too strong for Hobab to resist, and he was soon on his way, guiding the children of Israel toward their promised land. Like Hobab, most people respond more readily to an invitation to serve than to one to be served. The Bible is filled with many such up-to-date business principles and is the world's first book of sales psychology. The Old Testament contains its famous Ten Commandments on religion, but the New Testament gives us ten others to guarantee our business and sales success. Here are some samples:

1. Do unto others as you would have others do unto you.
2. Be not afraid.
3. Be of good cheer.
4. All things are possible to him that believeth.
5. Let not your heart be troubled.
6. Follow me.
7. Love your enemies.
8. Blessed is he who is not offended.
9. Seek ye first the kingdom of God and his righteousness.
10. He that loseth his life shall find it.

The scripture points out that "man does not live by bread alone." We need a good dose of inspiration occasionally. We need something to wind up our faith, increase our enthusiasm and get us headed for success. This is one of the Bible's functions. The Bible is also the world's first book of self-discipline. It is the world's first book of life.

The Bible is the word of the Lord. It contains the only program ever written on the greatest of all subjects—our eternal progression. Our lives started out in heaven as the spirit children of God. Then we were added upon with these beautiful, wonderful, mortal tabernacles. We are now being tested and tried to determine to what degree of eternal success we are worthy. We have the promise that if we do certain things we will be resurrected, glorified, and become even as God is.

The Bible is the most important fact book in the universe. It says that God lives, that we are his children, formed in his image, endowed with his attributes, and heirs to his potentialities. And certainly one of our greatest opportunities is to study this tremendous wonder volume and make it a part of our lives. A survey has shown that the most popular play ever written was Shakespeare's Hamlet. This tragedy involves some very depressing events. The King of Denmark was cut down by a murderer without time for repentance. He not only lost his kingdom, but his soul was consigned to hell. His family was broken up, and everything of value was lost.

How much more exciting it ought to be to read God's great religious drama about the establishment of our families to be the basic units of life throughout eternity. It also tells us about Christ's atonement for our sins, and promises us eternal success and happiness on conditions of our righteousness. Life at its best has the greatest of all happy endings. If we effectively follow Bible directions, we will someday find our own names written in the world's first book of glory. And may God help us to this end.

The "X" Factors

IT IS A WELL-KNOWN TRUTH THAT EVERY WHOLE IS MADE UP OF ITS parts, and no whole can become greater than its parts can make of it. Probably the best way to effectively promote any success, therefore, is to give the proper attention to the individual factors from which the total accomplishment will get its value. Automobile manufacturers give careful notice to such things as the safety factor, the economy factor, the appearance factor, the utility factor, and the comfort factor. If each of these has been satisfactorily provided for, then the finished product will be a success more or less automatically. Sometimes the automobile factory has to recall certain cars to correct a particular weakness. However, it is far better if every part can be made perfect to begin with.

This principle of doing things right the first time is even more important when one is building his own success. For once a personal weakness is set in motion, no one can tell what the outcome will be or when it will be corrected.

Many years ago, Oliver Wendell Holmes wrote some verse around this interesting philosophy. His poem was entitled "The Deacon's Masterpiece." It has to do with an enterprising deacon who got a great idea for making a horse-drawn carriage to serve his personal and ministerial needs. But he planned that this vehicle should not be an ordinary conveyance. The deacon knew that everything breaks down at its weakest point; and as the central idea for his projected triumph, he decided that he would merely eliminate all of the weak spots during the chariot's construction. Instead of allowing any vulnerable places, he would make each weak part exactly as strong as the strong parts, and, therefore, the chariot would have no place in which anything could go wrong. Naturally, if it had no weak places, it couldn't break down; and because the strong places would all wear out at the same rate, he knew that his chariot would last a very long time. The deacon's masterpiece turned out to be all that he had planned for it. It lasted for exactly one hundred years and then fell to pieces all at once on the great earthquake day.

Because we now make some automobile parts so much inferior

to the others, we are forced to throw the entire car away while some of its parts are still as good as new. What a great saving there would be if automobile manufacturers could duplicate the deacon's performance and have each of an automobile's 3,375 parts last as long as every other part! Then the tires would last as long as the steering wheel, and the motor would be in tune as long as the gas tank would hold gas.

But a program for permitting no weaknesses in our personal success presents an even more desirable opportunity. Life is the most valuable commodity known in the universe, and the most constructive of all employments is to live it at its best. Each of us is his own deacon, responsible for his own chariot, and throughout our entire lives we are permitted to construct only one life conveyance. Whether we make it a masterpiece or the opposite will be entirely determined by us. If we equip this vehicle of our lives with flat tires, a sick engine, and a troublesome transmission, we may have a bumpy, unpleasant ride through life. But certainly such things as a bad attitude or a worthless industry or a touch of discouragement can make our whole journey unprofitable. Unfortunately, in building ourselves, there are not many people who are willing to make the effort to produce a masterpiece, or even to pay the price to provide those factors that we want the most. However, because this is the most important construction job that we will ever have a part in, we should see to it that, like the deacon, we become expert workmen.

A father was once explaining to his son that he, the father, was a self-made man. The son thought the result was a horrible example of unskilled labor. It is true that only a few people work effectively enough at their self-building jobs to turn out champions in themselves. And yet the greatest opportunity of our lives is to plan and study and work so effectively as expert life builders that we may make each part strong enough to endure any strain that will ever be placed upon it. By the exercise of sufficient intelligence and self-discipline we may bring our faith factor up to its greatest power. Just suppose that we imagine our improvement if our motive factors were all fully developed. A good self-motivation can become a miraculous power enabling us to reach any predetermined goal. Then suppose that in full strength we added such tremendous success factors as "courage," "industry," "dependability," and "self-control." And while each of these abilities can contribute greatly to our welfare, yet they apply differently to different people, so that each of us must be responsible for fashioning his own parts and supplying his own needs.

But some of the most important success factors are not always considered by us. Someone has called these factors the "X" factors. I remember that in a high school algebra class "X" was frequently used to represent an unknown answer. Then, with a little reasoning and a series of calculations, students were supposed to learn the identity and the value of "X."

We frequently carry some of our algebra over into life itself. There are some instances where "X" has been used to represent the divine. For example, the word Christmas came from two words meaning "Christ's Mass." These words originally referred to the Church festival held on December 25, in memory of the birth of Christ, but some people still spell Christmas "X-M-A-S." They let "X" represent the most essential but sometimes unknown part of Christmas. And the "X" might be used to represent those divine qualities in us that too often tend to remain unknown and unincluded. It is thought that the most important talent in people is the religious talent. That is the talent that we use in lifting our lives up toward the Infinite, and the most important success factors are frequently the religious factors. All other factors lose much of their value if the religious factors are absent. As someone has said: "What profits chemistry without character, or of what avail is mathematics without manhood?"

We know how to split the atom; now we need to learn something about the Ten Commandments and the Sermon on the Mount, and how, with a little more devotion to God, a little more self-analysis and a regular check-up, we could keep most of the usual problems out of our working machinery.

With real religion we can build as we go along. A good set of "X" factors will make us both successful and happy in the places where it counts the most. It has been said that "wealth is not so much what we have as what we are." We don't work merely to acquire; we work to become. Success in life isn't just what we can get out of it; it is what we can become by it. With the "X" factor of honesty, we would always tell the truth, be responsible, and do our duty so that we would have fewer moral breakdowns. Our other "X" factors could regulate our standards and our ideals and would keep us operating according to the best principles.

A good set of "X" factors puts ethics into our conduct and

insures fairness in our dealings. They guarantee dependability in our social relationships and leadership in our occupational efforts. They charge our inner motivators with power and vitalize our achievement drive. They feed the will to win and provide our enthusiasm and persuasive ability. When such foreign matters as sin or unfairness enter the personality, they can be quickly eliminated if our "X" factors are in good working condition.

In the eighteenth century, Alexander Pope wrote a provocative line, saying, "The proper study of mankind is man." An effective and frequent inventory of our "X" factors is necessary to make our lives complete. This will always keep us aware of any missing parts as it is possible for even the best men to become almost totally worthless if they lack certain abilities and virtues.

Dr. Norman Vincent Peale tells of a leathery old cowboy who spent his life working on the cattle ranches of the Northwest, where the winter storms took some terrible tolls among the herds of livestock. Freezing wintery rains would come whipping down across the prairies, and howling winds would pile up the snow into enormous drifts. The temperature would sometimes quickly drop to many degrees below zero. In this icy maelstrom, the cattle would often turn their backs to the deadly blasts and slowly drift as far as they could downwind, until they would finally come to the boundary fence that would bar their way; then they would pile up against the fence and die by the hundreds. However, the cowboy observed that those cattle of the Hereford strain often reacted differently. They would head into the wind and slowly work their way forward against it until they came to the fence at the windward end of the range. There they would stand, shoulder to shoulder, facing the storm. He said, "We found that the cattle that faced the wind usually stayed alive and well." And then he added, "That is the greatest lesson I ever learned on the prairie."

One of these character qualities teaches us to meet all difficulties head-on and master them, rather than trying to avoid the problem by drifting downwind before our problems. The kind of escapism that keeps us running from our difficulties not only costs many people their success, but it also destroys their peace of mind. For once a fearful person starts running, he usually keeps going and becomes more fear-ridden and miserable with each step that he takes.

I know of a man who some time ago accepted a responsible job as a salesman. For about eighteen months he worked effectively and well under the excitement and challenge of his new employment. He had already mastered the problems connected with his poverty, but because other necessary character qualities were missing, he fell before the temptations of his prosperity. Without giving it adequate thought, his spending began to overshoot his income. Then, after stubbing his toe a few times, the unpleasant consequences began closing in upon him. His morale broke down and he turned his back to the wind. He got an unlisted telephone number so that he could more effectively dodge his creditors. He began denying his evil even to himself and fighting those who were trying to help him. He soon reached the bottom fence, where he couldn't go any further. There his success piled up, and he succumbed in a storm that he himself had created.

A good set of "X" factors gives one a clear conscience and makes it possible for him to be at his best when his back is against the wall. Then he has to watch in only one direction. "With the right amount of righteousness and faith, one doesn't fight like a conscript, but like a patriot." High ideals and strong conviction give men great power! When men believe in themselves and have necessity urging them from behind, they can become invincible. When one has fully accepted his responsibility, then there isn't any place for him to go but straight forward toward the foe.

Someone once told a story about a cat whose life was made miserable by the neighbor's dog. The dog was always hounding the cat and took great delight in keeping her up a tree much of the time. But there was one period each year when things were different, and that was when the cat had kittens. Then the cat didn't run, but she stayed and met the problem head-on. When the cat had kittens to protect, she gave no ground to any antagonist. The dog soon learned that at kitten time, he should seek other forms of activity and that the cat should be left strictly alone! The need always gave the cat the added strength that was unknown even to her at other times.

This "X" symbol is a very interesting one in many ways. It is the twenty-fourth letter of the English alphabet, but it appears in some other identities. Among the Roman numerals it stands for the number ten. But it not only has value in itself; it also greatly effects the numbers next to it. For example, when an "X" is placed in front of some other Roman numeral, it indicates that ten points must be subtracted from that number's value; that is, the Roman numeral C represents 100 but XC stands for 90. But when the "X" is placed behind some other number, it means that ten points should be added; that is CX is 110. And when we stack a few of these religious factors up behind our immortal spirit, they add to life's meaning and give drive to our success. With our "X" factors in full operation, it takes a lot of temptation or opposition to get us up a tree and they also keep us from drifting with the wind.

To have a good set of "X" factors is like discharging a rocket from a launching pad after having tied ourselves aboard. Then we can go straight to the top of an anticipated success; and, like the "Deacon's Masterpiece," we will never break down before we wear out, nor will we waste our magnificent eternal lives because some small part of our personality has been put out of order by temptation.

God endowed us with all of his own personal traits and eternal potentialities, and if they are effectively developed and used by us, we will not only create our own masterpiece, but we will also save our souls and bring about our own eternal success and happiness.

Yes Men

PAUL TILLICH WAS ONCE ASKED TO GIVE A THUMBNAIL SUMMARY OF his new book. He pointed out that the entire philosophy expressed was that of saying "Yes" to life. And what a great idea that is. Someone has said that a man's philosophy is the most important thing about him; that is what he thinks about, and believes in, and works at, and lives by, and fights for. What a great way of life to be able to say "Yes" to the most worthwhile proposals. That would mean no negative thinking, no reservations, no hesitations, and no one dragging his feet. In some places, at some times and with some people, "Yes Men" have been discredited and given a bad name. But nothing ever looks very good when the approach is wrong.

Someone has explained that a "Yes Man" is one who says "Yes" when you ask him to do the things that ordinary men are unwilling to do. A "Yes Man" does things that seem impossible to a "No Man." "Yes Men" are those who accept the great challenges; they they are the one's who rise to great occasions, who take opposition and hardship in their stride, and who run to meet their opportunities.

In most situations it is so much easier to say "No." "No" means the end. With a "No," the issue is settled, the conversation is closed, the responsibility is passed, and no further effort is required. But a "Yes" is just the beginning; the challenge has just been accepted, and both the battle and the triumph yet lie in the future. If life asks you to do a job or to get prepared for greater responsibility or future opportunity, it is a very simple matter to begin a process of rationalizing and alibi-ing. Then we think of the work involved and the problems to be overcome. A "Yes Man" sees opportunities in his obstacles, whereas a "No Man" sees obstacles in his opportunities. It is very easy to dispose of any great enterprise merely by saying "No." "No" means don't venture, don't put your neck out, and don't assume any risks. "No" marks the course that promises the greatest ease and the most safety. But "Yes Men" are a different breed; they have broader foreheads, stronger shoulders, deeper chests, and bigger hearts. "Yes Men" will always outrank "No Men."

Some things are important for themselves alone, but most things are much more important for what they are a sign of. "No" may be a sign that there is:

1. No faith
2. No desire
3. No courage
4. No ambition
5. No go
6. No interest
7. No principle
8. No enthusiasm
9. No hurry
10. No success
11. No future.

The biggest reason for our present unwholesome world situation is that on too many occasions we have said "No" to life. We have said "No" to honesty, "No" to morality, and "no" to temperance. We have said "No" to kindness and "No" to worship. We have said "No" to God and to his teachings. In the grand council of heaven, Lucifer said "No" to free agency, and "no" to individual initiative, and "No" to the divine plan of eternal progression. Think of all of the trouble that has come because of this one example of negative thinking.

Frequently a "No" indicates that we have given no thought, or made no investigation, or done no careful planning. Just a few negative decisions on the great issues of life may wreck an eternity of accomplishment and happiness. A big "No" is usually preceded by a lot of little no's until finally we become "No Men," and support ourselves in a kind of no man's land. So many times a "No" means that we lack preparation or courage or that we are unwilling to make the required effort. One of the easiest ways to condemn an occupational enterprise is to get a few no's where our yes's ought to be. The "No" habit is the shortest route to that kind of mediocrity that knows nothing higher than itself. The negative influences behind a "No" causes us to lose money, prestige, spirituality, success, and happiness. Tragically enough, it often means that someone who could have been will never be. The poet wrote:

> Of all sad words of tongue or pen,
> The saddest are these:
> "It might have been."

The philosophy of saying, "Yes" to life means that success might even yet be. It takes ambition and courage to say "Yes," whereas without either brains or character one may say "No" to even the greatest causes. There are many ways to say "No," but just one way to say "Yes." One may say "No" merely by the use of this small two-letter word, but the same effect can be achieved by inactivity or default. By any of these simple means we can kill the greatest possibilities. To say "no," one doesn't have to do anything wrong; he can just do nothing at all. A "No Man" can be good, but it takes a "Yes Man" to be good for something.

When we answer life by saying "No," then whatever good we may have been considering goes out the window and may never return. It may be a contemplated educational course or a program of self-improvement, or it may be an idea for installing greater incentives in the mind. The very best program to overcome bad habits or to repent of our sins may be killed by a "No." The "No" response to life was the reason Jesus said, "Many are called, but few are chosen." There is little chance to be chosen when our hearts are so set on lesser things that we say "No" to our real opportunities.

In his great poem, John J. Ingles has opportunity say:

> Master of human destinies am I.
> Fame, love, and fortune on my footsteps wait,
> Cities and fields I walk; I penetrate
> Deserts and seas remote, and, passing by
> Hovel, and mart, and palace, soon or late
> I knock unbidden once at every gate!
> If sleeping, wake—if feasting, rise before
> I turn away. It is the hour of fate,
> And they who follow me reach every state
> Mortals desire, and conquer every foe
> Save death; but those who doubt or hesitate,
> Condemned to failure, penury and woe,
> Seek me in vain and uselessly implore—For
> I answer not, and I return no more.

Soon after the United States Constitution was written, it was criticized by the English historian T. J. McCaulley. He said, "This revolutionary approach to self-government is all sail and no anchor." Mr. McCaulley felt that this new free people were putting too much power behind the drive wheels and not enough in the brake. However, the subsequent history of America has indicated that this formula for a lot of sail and not so much anchor is a pretty good one.

It is also true that as individuals most of us need more things to propel us forward and fewer things to slow us down. No one moves very fast or goes very far with his brakes on. We live in an age characterized by jet propulsion and power steering, and we need vision, ambition, and character qualities to match. If we are to take full advantage of our great opportunities, we need a lot of sail and a lot of drive and a lot of yes's. We also need to know a lot of right answers to the important questions:

> Industry—yes.
> Character—yes.
> Spirituality—yes.
> Enthusiasm—yes.
> Great goals—yes.
> Hard work—yes.
> Accomplishment—yes.
> God—yes.
> Eternal life—yes.

"Yes" answers are not always easy answers. Many times our projected success gets its back up against the wall where the way out seems very uncertain, but the best way out is through. Then we get the "Yes Man's" answer of courage. The poet said:

> Do not be discouraged, brother,
> Though you have weary grown.
> Though no one comes to aid you
> And you seem to be alone.

> Though you have grown so weary,
> So foot-sore, tired, sad;
> The time will come, my brother,
> When you will be so glad.

> So glad you did not falter
> And lay your burdens down,
> So glad you made the effort
> To reach the higher ground.

> The higher ground from whence you see
> The world in different light,
> The hill above the valley
> Where all was dark as night.

So aim to reach the summit,
    Aim to do your very best,
Aim to do your nearest duty,
    Aim some other life to bless.

And you will be rewarded,
    For each effort be repaid,
For the help you've given others,
    For the sacrifice you've made.

Behind each successful business and inside of each individual who reaches his maximum, there is a "Yes Man" who stubbornly and persistently refuses to take "No" for an answer. We sometimes personify this trait of courage in the great explorer who discovered this continent. In spite of many reasons to quit, Christopher Columbus continuously refused to turn back; instead he said, "Sail on, sail on, sail on and on." Columbus was a "Yes Man," and when things get tough is when "Yes Men" really go to work.

Lincoln was a "Yes Man." He said, "I do the best I can, the very best I know how, and I mean to keep on doing so until the end." If we take a good look at some of the milestones in Lincoln's life, we know that he meant what he said. Lincoln's mother died when he was nine. On her death bed she had said, "Abe, go out there and amount to something." But—

in 1831 he failed in business.
In 1832 he was defeated for the legislature.
In 1833 he failed in business again.
In 1834 he was elected to the legislature.
In 1835 his sweetheart died.
In 1836 he had a nervous breakdown.
In 1838 he was defeated for Speaker.
In 1840 he was defeated for elector.
In 1843 he was defeated for Congress again.
In 1855 he was defeated for the Senate.
In 1856 he was defeated for Vice President.
In 1858 he was defeated for the Senate again.
And in 1860 he was elected President of the United States.

In spite of these twelve crushing defeats to two successes, Lincoln is today acknowledged as one of the greatest men who ever lived. He said "Yes" to freedom and "Yes" to honor.

The Prophet Job was a "Yes Man." For a time everything went

wrong for Job. He lost his wealth, he lost his health, and he lost his family. His friends turned against him, and even God seemed to forsaken him. In trying to make him into a "No Man," his friends said, "Curse God and die." They meant that he should give up and quit. But there was not enough difficulty to cause Job to run away. He said, "The Lord giveth, and the Lord taketh away. Blessed be the name of the Lord." (Job 1:21.) As he firmly maintained his faith in God, he said, "Though he slay me, yet will I trust in him," and we might shout, "God for Job!" He was not only a "Yes Man"; he was a great "Yes Man."

All the great prophets have been "Yes Men." Nephi, the renowned ancient American prophet, said, "I will go and do the things that the Lord has commanded, for I know that the Lord giveth no commandments unto the children of men, save he prepare a way for them, that they may accomplish the things that he hath commanded them." That is the spirit of saying "Yes" to life and "Yes" to God and "Yes" to opportunity.

There is a definite procedure for saying "Yes." One can say "No" blindly, but before one can intelligently say "Yes," he must sift and sort and screen and think. Then he sifts and sorts and screens and thinks some more. Someone has put it this way:

1. Get the facts.
2. Filter the facts.
3. Determine the cost.
4. Appraise the benefits.
5. Consider the alternatives.
6. And make the decision.

Then you plan, organize, motivate, and drive, and the project goes forward. Never tolerate any temptation to make you forget, or sidestep, or delay, or vacillate. Sometimes we may say "Yes" with our reason, but say "No" with our industry. There must be an expert performance in the pattern of a "Yes Man." His eleventh commandment is, "Thou must deliver the goods."

Many people are afflicted with a dread disease that someone has called "the doubting folly." That is the human trait that spoils your vacation by worrying you about whether or not you locked the front door or turned off the gas. Evil gremlins perch on people's shoulders, tormenting them with all kinds of doubts, fears, and worries, trying to paralyze their muscles and prevent their progress. Many people accept a job or get married or join the Church and then spend their lives suffering from "the doubting folly." The gremlins are "No" men; they advise waiting. They say, "Think it over. Sleep on it, why the hurry?"

Sometimes the worst single enemy of success is caution. It lives very close to cowardice. By the time a "No" man gets around to pulling the trigger, the game has gone. Determination loses its steam while waiting; ambition cools off quickly when it is idle. So often we say "No" by default. We say "No" by procrastination. We say "No" by indecision. We say "No" by ignorance. We say "No" by lethargy. We say "No" by intertia.

Think of how many excuses you can count for not doing things. However, one of the greatest secrets of success is not to procrastinate but to attach, and our time is already running out. Our success needs larger sails and more horsepower, with smaller anchors and fewer brakes dragging on our wheels. We need more positrons and fewer negatrons; more faith and less doubt; more steam and less ice water; more industry and less conversation. We need more righteousness and less sin. The Lord once said, "Behold, I say unto you, that were it not for the transgressions of my people, . . . they might have been redeemed even now." (D&C 105:2.) Building the kingdom requires yes's and it includes building chapels, building people, building ourselves. We are not called into the Lord's vineyard merely to eat the grapes. He also calls us to get busy and do a little of the hoeing. We are also expected to develop more "Yes's" to righteousness and more "Yes's" to God, and more "Yes's" to purpose. It is a lot of fun to be a "Yes Man." And it is also very profitable. A "Yes Man" is a great man, with a great philosophy that is able to say "Yes" to life, and therefore take a more important part in the religion of Jesus.

May God grant us some big "Yes's" to serve as answers to the big questions of life.

The Year of the Locust

SOME TIME AGO FRED J. GREVE DISCUSSED THE INTERESTING PHIL-
osophy of the very important role that human tragedy plays in
life. Life is a mixture of pleasure and pain, ease and hardship, success and failure. And there is usually some relationship or balance
between them. Whether we like it or not, every heart bears some
burden of sorrow, and each soul knows some disappointment, adversity, and suffering. There are many circumstances in every life over
which we are given little or no control. However, our attitude
about our adveristy and what we do as a consequence are often far
more important that what the event itself may be. And fortunately
for us, we do have full and complete authority over our own reactions.

Mr. Greve tells the helpful story about some South African
locusts. It seems that vast hordes of these insects visit certain parts
of South Africa in cycles. As the locusts would pour over the land,
the landowners would rush out and try to kill them or drive them
away. But once the locusts came, all of the people's efforts seemed
useless, and the land would soon be barren. Then the waving fields
that once gave a verdant expression of hope would be stripped of
their growing treasure. And the tangible promise of future sustenance would be one of devastation.

Such experiences have plagued mankind since time began. They
remind us of the statement made by the ancient Prophet Joel. He
said, "That which the palmerworm hath left, hath the locust eaten,
and that which the locust hath left, hath the cankerworm eaten, and
that which the cankerworm hath left, hath the caterpillar eaten."
It is a common experience for us to have periods of depression and
great suffering, and much want is known to us in one form or
another. Egypt had her seven years of famine. There have also been
wars and difficulties. The two once great nations of Israel and Judah
were carried away to serve in foreign slavery. But Mr. Greve gives
us the interesting information, that after the South African insects
had gorged themselves, they died and were piled up in windrows.
Then these broken-hearted and impoverished people would plow
these dead predators into the ground, and from the fertilizing
strength thus added to the soil by the bodies of these natural enemies

came the greatest crops that had ever been known. And throughout the rest of their lives these people kept this year of tragedy alive in their memories. They referred to it as the "Year of the Locust." Our years of personal tragedy may also be remembered in this way, as our heartbreak and trouble may also be followed by our most productive years.

The Lord spoke to a latter-day prophet about some problems that were almost unendurable and said, "Know this my son, that all of these things shall give thee experience and shall be for thy good." And at another time, speaking about some very severe difficulties, the Lord said, "And if thou shalt endure them well, God shall exalt thee on high." So frequently it is not the problem itself, but how we handle it that is important. It is a significant fact that our world is planned for good. This was indicated by the Apostle Paul, when he said to the Romans, "All things work together for the good of them that love God." That is, if we love God, if we think right, if we have the right attitude, then everything works for our good. Uphill is as important as downhill; labor is as necessary as ease. Disappointments can build our character quite as effectively as pleasant surprises if we have the right attitude about them. Even the crickets will leave us a benefit if we love God.

It always requires hard pounding to make good steel, and some-times the best thing that can happen to us is to get a good swift kick in the pants occasionally. It is our enemies that keep us alert and on our toes, whereas the opiate of the over-kind friend often puts us to sleep and invites disaster. The opposition in our lives often does for us what a good sparring partner can do for a prize-fighter. But a good prizefighter is required to *pay* an opponent to give him a good licking three times a week, whereas life often gives us a licking designed for our improvement and charges us nothing.

Many years ago I knew a young man who had a drunken, ne'er-do-well father. But this young man loved God. He thought straight, and nothing could have been a more potent teacher of righteousness than this close-up view of his father's bad example. Even Satan is permitted upon this earth for our benefit. That is, God could destroy Satan at any instant that he desired. "Then," we might ask, "why doesn't he?" He himself gave us the answer when he said, "And it must needs be that the devil should tempt the children of men, or they could not be agents unto themselves; for if they never should have bitter, they could not know the sweet." (D&C 29:39.)

We are the offspring of God, and a little pounding on his anvil can often make our lives better. If we love God a few visits from the crickets and a good boot in the pants now and then can make our lives superior to anything that can happen to us. Even sickness and death serve our eternal purposes quite as well as health and life.

Oscar Wilde once said that if God wished to punish us, all he would need to do would be to answer our prayers. That is, if all of our prayers were answered, then no one would ever get sick, and no one would ever die. We would always get our own way; we would have no difficulty, and there would be no strength. It is an important part of our existence that into every life some rain must fall. If all we knew was sunshine, then our entire earth would be a vast Sahara Desert. However, life sends us no problems that we can't solve if we love God and have the right attitude about them.

This is one of the most constructive philosophies ever known in the world. With the right attitude, everything comes out all right. Then we can plow under all of our difficulties and fertilize our success with even our worst problems.

It may have been that the Lord had this kind of situation in mind when he spoke to the Prophet Joel and said, "Be glad then, ye children of Zion, and rejoice in the Lord your God; for he hath given you the former rain moderately, and he will cause to come down for you . . . the former rain, and the latter rain, . . .

"And the floors shall be full of wheat, and the vats shall overflow with wine and oil.

"And I will restore to you the years that the locust hath eaten, the cankerworm, and the caterpillar, and the palmerworm, my great army which I sent among you.

"And ye shall eat in plenty, and be satisfied, and praise the name of the Lord your God, that hath dealt wondrously with you: and my people shall never be ashamed." (Joel 2:23-26.)

One of the biggest problems in our world of opposites is to learn how to deal with our problems. Because the good and the evil grow side by side in God's world of free agency, we sometimes select the evil; or sometimes we look with envy at our erring friends and talk ourselves into adopting their sins by saying to ourselves, "Everybody's doing it." A thing is not right or wrong depending on how many people are doing it or are not doing it. No righteous person could reasonably argue that to be drunken is good for us, or that immorality advances our best interests, or that lying helps us to be happy. Truth is not determined by what people may think about it.

An all-wise God determined what was right and what was wrong even before this earth was formed, and he has said, "If ye love me, keep my commandments." If we love him and if we effectively love ourselves and our own interests, we will always stay on the right side of that yellow line that separates the good from the evil. However, because we don't always do this, a visit from the locust is sometimes about the only other way that the Lord has of bringing us back to our senses.

Because we become arrogant and proud when the Lord sends us blessings, he is compelled to send the locust to eat up our substance so that we can get rid of our false pride and become a little more teachable. Only then are we able to get hold of the plow and make fertilizer for our land out of our problems. It is because of our unsolved problems that the scriptures foretell wars, pestilence, famine, and earthquakes that are to desolate the earth in the last days. Our present cold war and the hotter war in Viet Nam that is presently eating up such a large part of our substance are warnings for our sins. But by and large we are not repenting of our evil, either nationally or individually. Our crimes, drunkenness, nicotine, and delinquencies have brought on the palmerworm and the canker-worm and the locusts. But even though we are having an increase in nervous disease and our national debt is going up, yet we are not plowing under very many crickets to make the future years better. To stimulate our imagination, Professor Greve tells of some of those who have fertilized their lives with their problems.

William Wilberforce was a small, sickly English preacher. For twenty years he did not have a moment without pain, even though he was often under heavy sedation. But Wilberforce used this pain to develop sympathy for others. There is a purifying benefit that comes from suffering. And sheer misery represented his year of the locust. Later James Boswell wrote of him, "When I went to hear him preach, I saw a shrimp in the pulpit. But as I watched and listened, he became a man of great stature before my eyes." The agony of Wilberforce helped him grow in wisdom, and he so stirred up the conscience of England that she voluntarily freed her slaves.

Pearl S. Buck, the authoriess, grew up in a land literally dev-astated by the locust. Her parents were missionaries in China, where Pearl was born and where her parents now both lie buried. A great deal of tragedy came into this young girl's life, one of which was that her own daughter was retarded. But as best she could she plowed under her difficulties and has so fertilized her life that it has brought forth a number of best-selling books. Her *Good Earth* won for her the Pulitzer Prize for literature. Of her year of the locust she says, "There is an alchemy in suffering—one that gives inner growth and restoration."

Nathaniel Hawthorne saw some years of the locust. He spent twelve frustrating years of unemployment. Then for two years he had a job at the Boston custom house, but he lost this two years later when the administration changed. Then he became a surveyor until another change of administration left him stranded. As he was achieving success as a writer, Hawthorne was struck by another great tragedy. He saw his beloved wife, with her dress aflame, burn to death. He tried to beat out the flames with his hands but was unsuccessful, and after her death, he became lonesome and desolate. Nevertheless, he went on to translate Dante's *Divine Comedy* into English, and he turned out a great deal of the most creative literary work.

We try to avoid affliction, and yet sometimes it can prove to be our salvation. It has triggered some of the world's greatest accomplishments. And when the great lessons are plowed into the inner person, new insights are sometimes born, and new response patterns and new capabilities sometimes produce their most abundant crop in the shreds and shards of our broken lives. If we have enough DDT to stop the locust on the outskirts of town, we should certainly learn our lesson and do it.

Most of the locusts of life can be kept away from our crops if we would always do as we should. But if some get through and start eating our wheat, then we might remember that the Lord may be trying to get a message through to us. And if we will fertilize our lives with the lesson, he will, as Joel says, send the former rains and the latter rains, and our floors shall be full of wheat, and our vats will overflow with wine and oil. Then the Lord will repair the damage done by the locust and the caterpillar and the cankerworm. Then we will eat and be satisfied and praise the name of the Lord, who hath dealt so wondrously with us. May God give us many *good* years, but may he also help us to make the most of our "years of the locust."

Index

fall of, 88
honest, 53, 96
new, 52
of limited means, 201
old, 52
reverse minded, 206
self-made, 298
spirit of a great, 162
young, 71, 155, 261
Man, the Unknown, by Dr. A. Carroll, 231
"Man Without a Country, A," story by, E. E.
    Hale, 254
Management, 105
Manager, a sales, 215
Manhood, tragic waste of, 95
Manufacturers, automobile, 297
Mariner, the, 185
Mark Anthony, 11
Marriage, 105, 255, 285, 286
a good, 106
morganatic, 8
Mary, the mother of Jesus, 175, 178
Masterpiece, 298
God's greatest, 196
great religious, 159
McCaulley, T. J., 305
McCay, James T., 45
McKay, President David O., 31
Mealtime, 99
Meaning, interesting, 69
Meanings, 224
Mediocrity, v, 166
Memory, 100
Men, bad, 58
good, 58
two fine young, 184
wise, 22
yes, 303ff
Menace, serious, 75
Merit, gradations of, 248
indicators of, 167
system of recognizing, 169
Message, greatest, 127
the most important, 240
wrong, 260
Messages, effective, 236, 259
Messina, Strait of, 219
Mill, Sutter's, 33
Millennium, 4
after the, 92
Milton, John, 44
Mind, badlands of the, 34
celestial, 117
depraved, 117, 171
healthy, 131
human, 267
unbalanced, 262

Minds, 263
subconscious, 39
Minister, a prominent, 64
Ministry, mortal, 124
postmortal, 126
Miracle, 84
Miracles, one of the most significant, 292
Miser, 48
Misery, eternal, 77
worst, 199
Mission, divine, 23
the American, 25ff
Missionaries, religious, 15
Missionary, great Christian, 55
Missouri, Jackson County, 19
Mistake, a serious moral, 184
Misunderstanding, 76
Mixed up, 114
Models, hillbilly, 37
Moisture, precious, 137
Mole, 230, 253
Momentum, 205
Money, 74
Monster, 219
Moon, possession of the, 27
Moors, 32
Morale, 38, 191
"Morality, new," 65, 197
Moroni, 277
Mortality, 272, 273
Moses, 42, 94, 172, 242, 294
Mother, a young, 130
Mothers, Bible, 175
Motivated, properly, viii
Motivation, 190
negative, 253
positive, 253
Motive, 190
Motives, 63
Motto, a, 181ff
national, 15
Mount Ararat, 20
Mozart, 71
Mule, Aesop's, 82
Muscles, our, 259
Music, 181
Myths, ancient, 188

— N —

Name, a temporary, 173
Napoleon, 26, 120, 199
Narcotics, 129ff
Nation, Communist, 28
great, 13
greatest, 15
Jaredite, 21
Nations, wealth of, 2